C000256676

'Artie' – Bomber Command Legend

'ARTIE'
BOMBER
COMMAND
LEGEND

The remarkable story of
Wing Commander Artie Ashworth
DSO, DFC and Bar, AFC and Bar, MID

By Vincent A. Ashworth

Published in 2014 by Fighting High Ltd,
www.fightinghigh.com
New Zealand edition by Vincent A. Ashworth, 2012

British Library Cataloguing-in-Publication data. A CIP
record for this title is available from the British Library.

ISBN – 13: 978-0992620752

Designed and typeset in Adobe Minion 11/15pt
by Michael Lindley www.truthstudio.co.uk

Printed and bound in China by Toppan Leefung.
Front cover design by www.truthstudio.co.uk

**For the 55,573 Bomber Command aircrew who flew into hell
and never returned 1939-1945**

The moral tests to which the crew of a bomber were subjected reached the extreme limits of human valour and sacrifices. Here chance was carried to its most extreme and violent above all else. They never flinched or failed. It is to their devotion that in no small measure we owe our victory. Let us give them our salute.

Winston S. Churchill

The lethal skies over Germany in World War II were no place for the faint hearted. It took great courage to climb into fuel and bomb laden aircraft and fly from bases in Britain to the Ruhr Valley, Stuttgart, Berlin, Kiel and any one of the many targets, all strongly defended with searchlights, anti-aircraft guns and hordes of night fighters.

For six long years the RAF's Bomber Command carried the war to Nazi Germany. The bomber crews paid a heavy price – 55,000 dead – including 1,850 New Zealanders, one in every three who served in Bomber Command.

All gave the best years of their lives to their country and to the cause of freedom and justice. All were volunteers and all deserve to be remembered with pride and gratitude.

Max Lambert, *Night After Night*

Contents

Foreword

I am honoured to write a foreword for this book. It should be read by all young New Zealanders. It is a story of uncommon bravery and sacrifice made in an earlier time and which, who knows, they may one day be called upon to emulate.

The Second World War was a long time ago, but we who took part remember it well and are unlikely to forget it. It predated modern sophistication, television, the mass entertainment industry and social service industry. Life was more simple and direct; we made our own fun, were fiercely independent and adventurous. There was not much money, but it didn't seem to matter.

I recall walking down the main street of my home town, Taumarunui, as a fifteen-year-old, when Len Joyes, the father of a friend of mine, was outside his shop having his first cigarette of the day. 'Have you heard the news?' he asked. 'The King is dead.' (George V, 1936.) I was shocked and speechless. Kings were important then. The whole town was quiet. So when the call to arms came in 1939 we responded in droves.

I don't know that we were any more patriotic than the young of today, but we were always seeking adventure and the call was very strong.

The story of Bomber Command has been told many times. But rarely has it been painted as vividly as this accounting of Artie Ashworth's experiences, all listed as accurately as in his logbook.

Fate decreed that I was not to share in this experience; my war was in the Middle East.

But for Artie, the strain of flying over the most heavily defended cities in the world, night after night after night, for years, will be obvious to any reader. Also this was at a time when the development of aero-engines and aircraft was in its infancy and navigation was largely by clock and compass.

It is a tragedy that after-effects of malaria should cut short such a promising career as Artie's; a tragedy to himself, his family and, I suggest, to the Royal Air Force.

Charles Gibbs, Air Vice-Marshal RAF (Rtd), CMG, DFC and Bar
Taupo, New Zealand

Acknowledgements

Included in the narrative are many quotations that serve to illustrate the enormous risks faced by the aircrews of Bomber Command during the Second World War. In some cases they explain the background to various episodes and developments such as that of the famed Wellington and Lancaster bombers. Wherever possible, I have received permission to quote, sometimes at length, the work of these authors. These include Max Lambert's *Night After Night*, Colin Hanson's *By Such Deeds*, Errol Martyn's *For Our Tomorrow* (three volumes), the late Rex Daniell's *What Did You Do in the War, Poppa Rekka*, Christopher Coverdale's *Pathfinders 635 Squadron – A Definitive History*, Peter Wheeler's *Some Kiwis Do Fly*, and *Wednesday Bomber Boys*, and Ken Rees's *Lie in the Dark and Listen – The Remarkable Exploits of a WWII Bomber Pilot and Great Escaper*.

For those whose work I have quoted without having obtained permission and where copyrights may have been breached, I apologise. In all cases the work has been duly acknowledged. Moreover, I will not receive any pecuniary gain from the sale of the book. The proceeds will be given to a charitable education trust, which I was instrumental in having established some years ago. The charity is administered by the Alexandra Rotary Club as trustees and makes grants to disadvantaged children to assist with their education.

The comparatively late start on the necessary research for this book has meant that most of Artie's contemporaries had passed from this world by the time I realised what a valuable resource they would have been. It has, however, been a privilege to have met some of the few still alive who either knew Artie or served with him at some time in his career. These include the late Rex Daniell of Maroochydore, Australia, who trained with Artie at Wigram; Ted Edwards of Whangarei, New Zealand (NZ); Trevor Pearce of Auckland who flew with Artie in No. 17F Squadron in the Pacific; Nick Carter of Hamilton, NZ, a former Pathfinder and member of No. 75 (New Zealand) Squadron; Don Briggs of England, who shared his memories of Artie at the Empire Test Pilots' School; and Ken Calton who flew as flight engineer in Artie's Lancaster crew for thirteen operational sorties over Germany in 1945. Former RAF officers who served with Artie, including Hugh Westell of Scotland, No. 139 Squadron, Peter Masterman, Don Atlee and Tony Smythe, all of England, and who served in No. 59 Squadron when Artie was the CO, have kindly recorded their memories. Former RAAF officer Russ Law of Australia told me of his memory of Artie during the former's secondment to 'B' Squadron.

I am also grateful to the following people who shared historical material with me. These include Alan Ashworth of Hamilton, NZ; Val Crankshaw of Tallon, Australia; Paul Chunn of Te Awamutu, NZ; Martin Lucas of Canterbury; and Roger Sheldrake of England.

Frank Prebble of Auckland, who flew in No. 635 Squadron in 1944–45 and was on many of the same operational sorties in which Artie participated, shared with me his reminiscences of 635, of RAF Downham Market and its surrounds, and of some of the 'characters' in the Pathfinder Squadron, who included Artie Ashworth. I am eternally grateful to him for allowing me to read and quote from his valuable handwritten manuscript.

My thanks also to the many who provided assistance, guidance and in some cases important information. These include Max Lambert, Errol Martyn, Mathew O'Sullivan, RNZAF Museum, for permission to use museum photos, Peter Wheeler for permission to reproduce photos from his collection and Stewart Boys, among others whose names escape me and for which I apologise. Special thanks to author Steve Brooking of England, who researched No. 75 Squadron records on my behalf and who offered valuable guidance on where to locate various documents.

Former flight engineer of Artie's No. 635 Squadron crew, Ken Calton of England, assisted considerably with his memories of Artie and of their wartime experiences. To have talked with a member of Artie's Lancaster crew was a great thrill for which I shall be always grateful.

I have deeply appreciated the help of Artie's daughter-in-law, Maria Ashworth, who kindly obtained copies of Artie's RAF service records, provided copies of photos and helped answer what must have seemed endless questions about Artie, whom she greatly admired and loved.

I will be forever in debt to Artie's widow Kay, who kindly gave me his logbooks and his original medals for safe keeping. These are indeed precious. Without recourse to the logbooks, the story would have had many gaps and probably inaccuracies. Kay also shared Artie's photos and various papers as well as helping to date many photos. Her remarkable memory has proved a valuable resource. She still lives in the house she and Artie shared in Bournemouth.

My grateful appreciation also to Alison and Stuart Macfarlane of Auckland for their meticulous editing of the final draft. And for their useful comments on the overall presentation. Thanks to my daughter-in-law Ruth Hungerford for reviewing the story and for that final editing. Also thanks to James Read of Huntly, NZ, for his comments on an early draft. And to Larry Hill who kindly reviewed the draft manuscript and made helpful comments on the structure. My gratitude also to Kristy Hill and to my niece Kimberlee Spiers for the first draft of their cover ideas.

I am particularly honoured that Air Vice-Marshal (RAF Rtd) Charles Gibbs of Taupo, generously agreed to write the foreword to this story.

Finally, I have to thank my wife, May, for her tolerance of my inattention to matters domestic as I engrossed myself in writing and seemingly endless reading. She also assisted with editing and made pertinent comments on the many drafts, all of which resulted in an improved product.

And for those who have assisted in one way or another and whose help I have not acknowledged, please accept my apology and my deep appreciation.

Introduction

With four brothers ultimately being on His Majesty's Service, the war was something very big in my early life. It helped shape many of the values and beliefs that I have held to throughout my life – duty to one's country and community, patriotism, faith in the monarchy, and belief in the causes of freedom and justice and of the weak and underprivileged against the strong. My brother Arthur (Artie) had already volunteered to join the air force prior to the outbreak of war. He was soon followed by his close friend and younger brother, Corran, who would be killed in action in 1944. Then in August 1942, my eldest brother, Archie, volunteered and was to spend two and a half years as an air bomber in England and Italy. Then in early 1945 my brother Donald was conscripted into the air force but was discharged when the war ended in 1945.

It had never occurred to me that one day I would write the story of my personal hero, my brother Artie. The catalyst for writing the story of my fighter pilot brother, Corran, who was killed in Normandy in August 1944, was the discovery of the place where his blazing aircraft crashed into the River Seine and the unveiling of a beautiful memorial on the banks of the river opposite where he died.

Having written Corran's story, I then knew I needed to record the life of a very special man, Artie Ashworth, who became a living legend. I've always felt he never received the recognition in New Zealand, or for that matter in the RAF, that he deserved. As the narrative will show, his distinguished career speaks for itself.

I can't say I knew my brother that well. It is one of my deep regrets. He left home when I was only seven. Apart from brief visits home on annual leave and then two short visits after he joined the air force in 1939, my knowledge of him was through his quite frequent letters to my mother. I saw something of him during his fairly long RAF leaves in 1943 and again in 1949. And I kept in touch with him through irregular letters.

The next time we met was in 1971 when, along with my family, we stayed a week with Artie and his wife Kay in Bournemouth on our way home from an assignment in Afghanistan. Then in 1976 I was appointed to the permanent staff of the World Bank and we moved to live in Washington DC. My work involved frequent travel, which invariably meant a stopover in London. Whenever possible, I would visit Artie in Bournemouth, where he spent most of his retirement years.

It was during those visits that I came to know him better. Sadly, we never talked about the war or about his subsequent RAF career, something I deeply regret.

During the 1971 visit he showed my children his medals, of which he was deservedly immensely proud. He also loved children. He greatly enjoyed my four and I suspect it was a disappointment that he had only one child of his own, a son he called Corran after his close friend and brother.

Artie was a very proud RAF officer, but for all that he remained an 'ordinary bloke'. He had a great sense of humour and an engaging, somewhat mischievous smile and, despite his long absence, he remained very much a New Zealander. His accent, although somewhat modified, could still be detected.

I have drawn on three main sources of information for this story. The first is a brief, but valuable personal memoir outlining his career that Artie wrote, probably sometime in the 1970s or later. It is a rather matter-of-fact record. Except for one experience when he admitted to being scared, it lacks any emotion. One is left wondering just how he really felt about things.

The second source is his remarkable logbooks, some pages of which are presented in this book. The third source is the considerable literature compiled by military historians and by former aircrew who served, especially in Bomber Command, during the Second World War, which is listed in the Bibliography.

Thus, the story is wider than just the career of Artie Ashworth. I have tried, even if briefly, to present something of the setting in which his wartime career in particular took place. I hope younger generations who read this story will understand just what these men had to experience in order to preserve the freedom and way of life we know and treasure. And regretfully, all too often, take for granted.

The story also includes brief descriptions of the wartime careers of some of those with whom Artie first trained in New Zealand, as well as some fellow New Zealanders who either flew with him or with whom he was close friends. Too many did not survive to tell their stories.

Although the focus is on Artie, the first chapters, 'His Early Life', include much family history and is essentially a repeat of that presented in my book about my fighter pilot brother Corran, *For Our Tomorrow He Gave His Today – A Fighter Pilot's Story*. The chapters do, however, reveal the beginning of that daredevil but brave and honourable man, who emerged to serve his country with distinction and honour.

PART 1:
THE BEGINNING

Haywards, Hutt Valley, c.1925. Standing from left: Edna, Mum, Margaret, and Iris. Corran and Arthur on the chair.

Chapter 1

His Early Life, 1921–28

Arthur Ashworth was born at Gisborne, New Zealand, on 3 May 1920. He was the seventh born of Edna Mary and Arthur John Ashworth, my parents. He was the third son. His older brothers were Stanley John and Frank Archibald. Stanley John was the twin brother of our eldest sister, Margaret Ivy. He died at Gisborne in April 1916. Arthur had four older sisters; Margaret Ivy, Phyllis Henrietta, Edna Alice and Catherine Iris.

Artie, as he will be called throughout this narrative, was named after his father. Some believe my father was called after his father, John Ashworth, our grandfather. Some researchers have suggested that my grandfather's full name was John Arthur Ashworth but this has never been adequately proven.

My mother was a descendant of one of New Zealand's pioneering families. Her great-grandparents, Pascoe and Frances Perry, landed at New Plymouth from Cornwall on 5 September 1841, after a five-month voyage in the sailing ship *Amelia Thompson*. The family included eight children, one of whom was born during the long voyage. Pascoe Perry, having been involved in the tin industry in Cornwall, England, was the first person in New Zealand to try smelting iron from the west coast iron sands.

My father, Arthur John Ashworth, was the youngest son of John and Margaret Ashworth. John came to New Zealand in 1862. Margaret, along with her sister Agnes, arrived in 1863. Arthur and Margaret were married in Cromwell in 1866. They first lived at Kawarau Gorge, which at that time was a thriving gold-mining centre and where John was one of the mining pioneers. In the early 1870s they moved to what became known as Ashworth's Flat, which is situated on the Upper Shotover, upriver from Skippers, near the remote Branches sheep station.

At the time of Artie's birth, my father was a stock drover at Matawhero near Gisborne. The family moved back to Rongomai near Eketahuna soon after Artie was born.

By all accounts, both parents were strict disciplinarians and had decided views on what children did and did not do. Doing the family chores was obligatory and there was never any doubt that education was a must. I never knew my father as he died when I was but a babe-in-arms. Despite the great difficulties she faced following my father's death, my mother ensured that this tradition continued. She showed much determination and great courage, characteristics that Artie inherited to the full.

In 1923, when Artie was aged three, the family moved to Haywards, in the Hutt Valley. My father was the manager of Manor Park Estate, a farm owned by a Mr W.W. George.

My sister Edna (born on 16 January 1916) recalls:

Mum milked the cows and helped around the farm. She was a very hard-working person, and very strict. She was, however, fair when it came to punishment. We were seldom smacked, but would be deprived of special outings instead. She used to convene fabulous Guy Fawkes parties. If anyone was in trouble or was sick, Mum was there. She was the unofficial district nurse. She had no training, of course, but had the experience of bringing up a large family and living in remote areas with no ready access to medical help. There was a notice on the dining room wall: 'Speak when you are spoken to'. Both parents were very strict on manners and behaviour. At meals we ate what was put in front of us. Dad made all the pickles and jams while Mum made the soups. Arthur, Corran, Iris and I would catch huge eels in the nearby stream. We'd put them in kerosene tins until Dad had time to kill them. He used the skins to make shoelaces while the carcases were boiled up and fed to the hens, which Mum kept for the eggs. She always had hens, even in her later widowed life. I recall we were virtually self-sufficient with the egg supply. During the peak laying season my mother used to preserve the surplus eggs with a brine solution in a four-gallon kerosene tin, which seemed to be plentiful in those days.

Iris, Edna and Arthur went to school at Silverstream, Lower Hutt. They travelled to school by train, which Edna says was great fun. She remembers the time the school was closed because of an outbreak of what was then called infantile paralysis (poliomyelitis). Lessons were published in the *Dominion*, which newspaper was delivered by the train driver, who threw it out as they went past. She recalls how they wished the paper would get lost or the driver would forget it.

Edna continues: 'Saturdays were chore days. The boys would be outside and the girls got the inside chores. I remember having to clean all the shoes. Another job was cutting the tobacco blocks for father's pipe. When we lived at Stokes Valley, Dad had some sheep of his own. He had to cross the Hutt River to check on them. He crossed the river using a flying fox, which were quite common in those days. We were not allowed to use it, but one day when the river was in flood, Corran and I attempted to cross. We got stuck halfway. Dad had to saddle his horse and swim out to rescue us. He nearly drowned. Boy, did we get into trouble!'

The year 1926 saw dramatic changes. Artie was a little over six years old when the family left Haywards. Silverstream school attendance records show he was enrolled in 1926. This would have been just prior to the family moving to Queenstown before leaving for the Falkland Islands, a group of British islands in the South Atlantic.

In 1926, my father was selected to be the manager of an experimental sheep farm, which the colonial government at the time wished to establish in the Falkland Islands. It was quite an honour. He was selected from among 498 applicants by the then British-owned stock and station firm of Dalgety & Co. When announcing the selection the company commented: 'Mr Ashworth has been known to us for many years as a capable and thoroughly trustworthy man. He has an excellent knowledge of sheep and cattle and also is an expert agricultural man.'

My father sailed for the Falklands in 1926, leaving my mother and the family resident in Queenstown where Artie went to school. Dad was accompanied by his deputy, Mr Tex Faithful from Invercargill. My eldest brother, Archie (mostly known as Tex), at that time aged fifteen, sailed with my father in a ship called *Kia Ora*. They travelled with a cargo of Corriedale sheep. According to sister Edna, the ship caught fire during the voyage and much of the sheep feed, mainly hay, had to be abandoned (I also recollect my mother talking about the ship being on fire[1]). They arrived at Port Stanley in November 1926. The Falkland Islands archives recorded that 164 head of sheep were imported.

Some six months after the departure of my father, my mother, Edna, Iris, Arthur, Corran and baby Donald, who had been born in 1926, left for the Falklands.

Sister Edna recalls there being a great panic in Wellington while they were waiting to board the ship. Arthur had disappeared! Despite assistance from the police, he could not be found until he was reported to have gone on his own and boarded the waiting ship. Not a good start to a great adventure, but perhaps a sign of the daredevil who was to emerge later on.

The Falklands farm, known as 'Anson', was situated at Port Louis some distance from Port Stanley. The family sailed from Stanley to Port Louis in a 'cutter' and then on horseback to the farm. Their arrival was anything but promising for a mother with five children including a babe-in-arms.[2] My father reported to the colonial secretary:

> On July 6, 1927, I brought my wife and family to 'Anson' by J. Davis's cutter, although the house was by no means ready for occupation on account of none of the drainage being completed, but temporary drains have since been put in, but I hope that the drainage will be completed as soon as the pipes arrive as all around the house is in a very bad state on account of there being so many open drains and heaps of earth. The hot water system has proved a failure, the water never being any more than luke-warm and even by stoking up with coal and making the stove red hot it will not get hot. Another thing is that the range, apart from the hot water system, will never be of any use for burning peat on account of the fire box being too small, which does not allow sufficient peat to be put in to heat up enough to cook with.

Edna recalls: 'We went to the farm on horseback. Mum had Donald up front on her horse and Arthur and Corran doubled. Iris and I had a horse each.'

Despite this inauspicious beginning described by my father in his report to the colonial secretary, Edna remembers a very fine house:

The house as I recall was beautiful. The 'flashest' house I've ever lived in. It had a huge lounge, dining room and a kitchen with huge peat ranges. I remember the piles of peat stacked up outside. Iris and I had a yellow bedroom with a washstand and two chamber pots. Baby Donald had his own room.

Iris, Corran, Arthur and I would often saddle the horses and go down to the beach where we would pinch the penguin eggs. Sea lions, sea elephants, seals and penguins were in abundance. Mum used to make meringues out of the penguin eggs. They were always pink. We used to love chasing the wild geese and got into lots of trouble for our efforts! I remember one day Corran and Arthur blew up the shed and nearly killed themselves. They were trying to make funnels for boats out of detonators. The blast killed a sheep! Dad had to take them to Stanley on horseback to the hospital.

My mother never liked the Falklands. She said the weather was terrible! The sorry state of the house on her arrival certainly wouldn't have warmed her to the area, as well as the comparative isolation. Another factor was the birth and death of a son. The records show that Eric Ashworth was born on 4 May 1928, and died a day later. She would have had little time to recover from the emotional upset of the birth and death of her son before they left the islands for New Zealand. So, apart from my father's contribution to the establishment of the sheep farming industry in the Falklands, a little bit of Ashworth remains there forever.

The experimental farm was successfully established but, on the instructions of a new governor my father received notice in March 1928 that the farm was to be closed and his employment terminated. Apparently, the new governor knew nothing about farming and agriculture, but the fact that the establishment of the farm had been recommended by a New Zealand consultant, did not go down well with him. He believed the matter had not been sufficiently researched and asked: 'How could a New Zealander know anything about farming in the Falklands?'

On completion of his service my father received the following letter from the colonial secretary: 'I certify that Mr. A.J. Ashworth has been in the employment of the Government of the Falkland islands since the 24th October, 1926, in the appointment of Manager of the Government

Experimental Farm, and that the sole reason for his leaving such employment is the decision taken by the Government through no fault of his
own, to close down the Experimental Farm. During his service in the
Colony Mr. Ashworth has shown himself to be thoroughly trustworthy,
hardworking, and efficient and he can be confidently recommended as
an experienced stockman and general farmer.'

So the family returned to New Zealand after what was a brief stay in
the Falklands. We now turn to the next phase of Artie's early life.

Chapter 2

His Early Life, 1928–39

The family sailed from the Falklands on 22 May 1928, having been resident in the islands for around one year. They arrived in Wellington on 8 August of that year, having visited Valparaíso (Chile), Balboa (Panama) and the Pitcairn Islands en route.

On their return from the Falklands, they went first to Queenstown where my father's eldest sister, Aunt Maria Davies, arranged rented accommodation. There they were reunited with my sisters, Margaret and Phyllis, who had remained in Queenstown while the family were in the Falklands.

It was the beginning of what eventually became the Great Depression and work was not easy to find. Dad found a job with the Public Works Department, working on the construction of the Kingston–Frankton highway, which was a major undertaking at that time. George Thomas, the husband of Margaret Ashworth, one of my father's elder sisters, was also employed on the road construction. It is also likely that this was where he first met Harry Koberstein, who was to marry my eldest sister Margaret in 1932. All of the children went to school in Queenstown.

Queenstown is the family ancestral home in New Zealand. Our grandparents, John and Margaret Ashworth, were gold miners and moved to the Upper Shotover from Kawarau Gorge around 1870. They lived at the 'Sandhills', which is upriver from Skippers on the Branches road. Around 1880 they moved to live at Millers Flat near Arrowtown, where my grandfather had bought land. My father was born in Queenstown in 1882.[3] Most of the family went to school at Millers Flat, Arthur's Point or Queenstown. My father's eldest sister, Aunt Maria, owned Golden Terrace, which was the premier guesthouse in Queenstown for the early part of the twentieth century. She was also a part owner of Laurel Bank, also in its day a prestigious guesthouse in Queenstown. My grandparents and four of their siblings are buried in the Queenstown cemetery. Maria Davies and her husband James, as well as Margaret and George Thomas, are also buried there. Maria was the eldest and Margaret the fourth daughter of John and Margaret Ashworth.

There is a photo taken on the lake front at Queenstown. It looks across Lake Wakatipu towards the Queenstown Gardens with the Remarkables mountain range in the background. I believe it was taken some time in 1928 or early 1929 after the family had returned from the Falklands. Uncle Archie and Aunt Mary were obviously visiting Queenstown in the old car, probably a Ford Model T (note the solid rubber tyres). The children are in their Sunday best, probably dressed for church. My uncle was a long time elder of the Presbyterian Church. Moreover, in those times, being well dressed would have been expected when the male head of the family, Archie, came to visit.

In 1929, my father was appointed manager of a Department of Agriculture experimental dairy farm situated at Galloway near Alexandra. The farm was a part of the Galloway irrigation scheme. The 'experimentation' was with the use of border dykes, which were a new irrigation technology at that time. Corran, Arthur, Edna and Iris all went to school at Galloway, which was a very small but close-knit farming community. The family much enjoyed Galloway. My mother always spoke fondly of the many friends she made in the district.

In 1931, the Department of Agriculture decided to sell the Galloway farm. My father then obtained a position as an agricultural instructor based in Alexandra, where the family went to live. Given that he had no formal education, this was no mean achievement and reflected the fine reputation he enjoyed in farming circles. He was held in high regard by members of the farming community.

So the family moved to Alexandra. Artie, along with Corran, Edna, Iris and Donald, went to the Alexandra District High School, which included both primary and secondary schools. At that time Alexandra was a very small rural town with a population of around 500 or 600. It was a closely united community where everyone seemed to know everyone. The school was not large but the secondary department catered for students over a quite large rural area, which was dotted with small country schools.

By all accounts Artie was a solid student. He was a very good rugby player and played a useful game of tennis. There is no record of him taking part in cricket, at which game Corran excelled. I suspect it was not the sort of game that would appeal to an action-oriented personality like Artie. However, he said he played a few games when at Bassingbourn, shortly after arriving in England. He admitted 'to not being very good at it!'

We all inherited a love of gardening from our parents. Artie and Corran were no exceptions as the following report in the *Alexandra Herald*, as it was called in 1932, confirms: 'The Alexandra District High School won quite a number of honours at the Dunedin Winter Show. Corran Ashworth (Form One) won the second prize for three red intermediate carrots (16 entries) and second for his essay on "Agricultural Weeds" (four entries). In this class, his brother Arthur worthily supported him by securing third prize. All these pupils are members of the School Boys and Girls Agricultural Club.'

Artie was an active member of the Alexandra Boy Scout Troop. Along with Corran, Donald and myself, we all benefited from our Scouting days. There were regular annual camps at the Manorburn Dam and in the Waikeria Valley. The latter camp always involved a climb to the summit of what is known locally as the Old Woman range (around 2,000 metres), the correct name being the Dunstan range. In the mid-1940s, I participated in one of these expeditions. In a cave of the Old Woman Rock, a very large tor[4] at the summit, I found an old tin in which were recorded the names of those who had climbed the mountain in 1936. There was inscribed the name Corran Ashworth.

My mother was made a life member of the Alexandra Scout Troop in recognition of her long service and support to the Scouts. In 1945–46 she presented a cup to the troop to be awarded to the Scout who excelled in first aid. It was known as the C.P. Ashworth Memorial Cup.

Arthur Gladstone was a contemporary of Arthur and Corran at primary school. He has fond memories of growing up in Alexandra and of the adventures he shared with my brothers:

> My earliest memories of the Ashworth family date back to the early
> 1930s when they arrived at the Galloway experimental farm. For
> leisure pursuits, we were blessed with the freedom of a wonderful
> area, sculpted by nature to contain everything that a boy could desire
> for his education and maturing along the path to manhood. It was
> definitely a boys' own territory. Girls were not included in the scheme
> of things until we were old enough to go to the 'henhouse' dances at
> St Aidan's hall or began to play mixed doubles on the tennis court.[5]
> Our favourite weekend past time was playing 'kicks' at the goalposts
> at the 'Rec'.[6] We seldom had actual games of rugby but occasionally
> the older among us would participate in the multiple seven-a-side
> tournaments, which were popular at that time.
>
> As we grew older we used to go shooting. Artie and Corran were
> my constant companions in this pursuit. Our favourite stomping
> ground was on the 'Knobbies' about three ridges back from the old
> water reservoir above the town, where an enormous rabbit warren
> existed. We would position ourselves on top of the ridge and shoot
> up to 24 rabbits, which we skinned on the spot. Artie and Corran
> took all the skins. I had first choice of the carcasses and was allowed
> a minimum of six for which my father paid me three shillings. That
> was very good pocket money in those days and kept me in ammu-
> nition and a visit to the flicks (local movies which were shown on a
> Saturday). It cost sixpence ($5.45 in 2011 New Zealand dollars
> (NZ$)) a ticket. There were many times when we were together at
> the local swimming pool, or in the Manuherikia river or up at the
> Ngapara pools.[7]

Arthur continues: 'Somewhere in my memorabilia is an old fashioned
school ruler marked in inches and tenths along one side and metric along
the other. On the face are the signatures of Form V, ADHS, 1936. Amongst
the signatures are those of A. Ashworth, C.P. Ashworth as well as other
members of local families, J.D. Lunn, R.G. Smith, J. Nightingale,
E. Nightingale and K. Taylor-Cannon.'

Arthur served in the army during the war. He participated in the battle for Casino among other actions of the New Zealand Division in Italy. Along with Corran, Jack Lunn and Keith Taylor-Cannon were RNZAF pilots killed in action during the Second World War.

The Gardner family lived near to our house in Alexandra. Brian was a contemporary at school with Arthur and Corran. Brian recalled that the two boys were very good at helping their mother. She made their many friends welcome and the house always seemed to be full of raucous young boys. Something I vividly remember.

Later, my own friends like Dennis Cronin, Ian Duncan, Peter Robertson, Doug Grant and Dave Gunn, among others, received the same warm welcome from my mother.

Dave Simpson, 'Mousey' as he was nicknamed, was a contemporary of my brothers. They were in the same class at high school and played rugby together. Dave was the son of the postmaster, the latter being an important person in the community in those days. Dave said:

> Artie became a very well known and respected personality in Bomber Command. He was certainly a dare-devil. As kids we used to go swimming in the Ngapara pools, which were very deep dredge holes up the 'flat'. Artie was always the one to jump or dive off the highest branch. He would have become a very high-ranking Air Force Officer but unfortunately he developed an eye problem and was prematurely retired. His brother Corran was a much more subdued nature but still had that Ashworth trait of determination and courage, just like their mother. Mrs Ashworth did a tremendous job in bringing up the family on her own. She was a great battler, a wonderful person who stood no nonsense. She was held in very high respect by us kids who used to go up to their home in Station Street frequently both before and after the war.

Dave Simpson flew bombers during the war. He finished with the rank of flight lieutenant and in 1944 he was awarded the Distinguished Flying Cross. Dave died in Timaru in 2000.[8]

Dave Simpson, DFC Citation

'Flight Lieutenant Simpson is a skilful pilot, and courageous leader who, throughout his operational career, has displayed a fine fighting spirit and great devotion to duty. He has shared in the destruction of three enemy supply ships, and an "R" boat and a 1,500-gallon fuel dump on an Aegean Island. On one occasion when flying with another Beaufighter aircraft, he shared in the destruction of two enemy aircraft and severely damaged a third. In June 1944, this officer led a formation of eight aircraft in an attack against a large escort vessel, which was an outstanding success, the vessel being sunk. Following his return to the UK in late 1944, Flt Lt Simpson joined 143 Squadron RAF (Mosquito) and flew rocket-firing, anti-shipping strikes along the Norwegian coast until April 1945.' (Hanson)

St Enoch's Presbyterian Church, Alexandra is rich in the history of the Ashworth family. Almost all of our family, including Artie, worshipped here. The funeral services for my father (1932) and mother (1970) were held here, as was that of my sister Iris in 2006. The marriage of my eldest sister Margaret was celebrated in this church in 1932 shortly before my father was killed. Our uncle, Archibald Ashworth, was an elder of the church for some twenty-five years. Both Artie and Corran were presented with pocket bibles by the parish at their farewell functions. Both carried them throughout their careers.

The family had hardly settled to living in Alexandra when tragedy struck. In November 1932, my father was killed when the car he was driving overturned on the Roxburgh Road at Gorge Creek. He was aged fifty. Our mother was left in dire financial circumstances, with six dependent children: Edna (sixteen), Iris (fifteen), Arthur (twelve), Corran (eleven), Donald (six) and myself, an eleven-month-old babe-in-arms.[9]

It was the time of the Great Depression. There was no generous state welfare at that time. Left with no income apart from a very small government employee pension, the family relied entirely on the support of relatives, local charitable organisations and the generosity of friends. We were forced to move from the comfortable rented house in which we lived. Our uncle, Archibald Ashworth, my father's elder and only brother, provided a small house in Station Street, Alexandra. This would be the family home for over thirty years until the mid-1960s when my wife and I were able to accommodate my mother in a more spacious and comfortable home in Chapel Street.

The family quickly became self-sufficient in vegetables. I recall the ground freezing solid during the winter. Vegetables like carrots, parsnips and potatoes had to be dug and sorted before the winter frosts set in. They were stored in an earth pit that was lined with straw. I also recall walking close by the railway line and picking up pieces of coal, which had fallen off the tender of the engines. I suspect sympathetic engine drivers would deliberately toss quite large lumps out for us to recover. My sister Iris recalled that from time to time Mum used to borrow Uncle Archie's horse and dray and, along with children helpers, would gather firewood on the Manuherikia riverbed. Having spent most of her life on farms she was very competent with horses.

The old Station Street house that became Artie's home was very basic. It was corrugated-iron clad, comprised two small bedrooms, a small kitchen/living room, a lounge, which served as a third bedroom, and a bathroom. The toilet was outside. Sewerage was not available until the late 1930s. It was bitterly cold in the winter but our mother did her best to keep it warm and cosy in the living area. In winter the only warm room was the kitchen/living room where the coal range was situated. Just how my mother fitted six children into the house has always intrigued me. I suspect there were many arguments about who slept where, but my no-nonsense mother would have soon dealt with that sort of thing! Those who persisted would have felt the full force of her discipline. Do what I say or take the consequences, which I can testify from experience were not worth suffering.

The heating in the old house consisted of a coal range. Later, a chimney and open fire were installed in the lounge. It was very inefficient and seldom used. I remember the roof leaked in places in the kitchen area. Thankfully the rainfall in Alexandra is one of the lowest in the country, so the leaks were not a huge problem, although irritating when it did rain.

Coming on top of the death of my father, moving into this house with six dependent children must have been a traumatic experience for my mother. It's hard to imagine how she managed, but somehow she did.

Our mother always kept a few chickens and, when they became too old for laying, they provided a welcome variety for meals. From time to time meat was generously donated by the local butcher, the Carline family. Wild rabbits, shot by Arthur and Corran, and later Donald and myself, were frequently on the menu. The two girls still at home, Edna and Iris, had to find work. First Edna, and later Iris. The boys stayed at school.

Mother was a truly remarkable person who somehow managed the incredibly difficult circumstances in which she found herself in 1932. Artie appreciated this and always spoke very respectfully of her. She in turn was immensely proud of her famous son.

Public service employment was highly prized during the 1930s and 1940s. The Great Depression saw much hardship with many thousands of men and women from all walks of life out of work and income except, that is, for a very meagre unemployment benefit. The spectre of economic depression deeply affected the psyche of New Zealanders. For many years the ambition of the majority was to obtain secure employment in the public services. The 'slump mentality' as it was called, dominated political and social thinking and policy until well into the 1960s.

Before being eligible for permanent employment in the civil service, recruits had to first pass what was known as the Public Service Examination. Both Arthur and Corran had successfully passed this exam in the mid-1930s.

Artie completed part of his matriculation (university entrance) in 1937 and 1938. He joined the Public Works Department in Wellington as a cadet clerk. His starting salary was £80 (about NZ$7, 900 in 2012). In 1938 he became a cadet draughtsman with a salary of £115 (NZ$11,100 in 2011). Interestingly, his position in the department was not officially terminated until 1949.

In March 1938, Artie was joined by his brother Corran, who was employed in the Post Office head office in Wellington. The brothers took lodgings together. Family legend has it that at one stage they were so poor they shared one pair of socks between them. Both brothers continued their active involvement in sport. Artie played rugby for the Public Works team. He was also a member of the Wellington Rowing Club, where he rowed with Ted McSherry who was later to be the navigator in a Wellington bomber crew captained by Artie. As navigator, Ted flew twenty operations with Artie. He was later killed in action.

Artie and Corran spent Christmas 1938 at home in Alexandra where, among other things, they spent time with old school friends. This was Artie's last visit home as a civilian. Christmas 1939 saw him in Alexandra as Acting Pilot Officer Ashworth on leave from RNZAF Taieri, before transferring to RNZAF Wigram.

Despite the many family shifts and the death of my father, Artie grew into a mature young man. He was popular with his peers. He had grown up in a large family environment where real values prevailed, and with all the advantages of rural life. After the death of my father in 1932, life was not easy, especially for our mother, who had to cope with the stress of financial stringency and rearing a large family on her own. That she succeeded is a tribute to her determination and tenacity, characteristics that Artie inherited. Like Corran, the brother to whom he was close, Artie did what he could to help ease the burden on my mother. He had already shown the firmness of purpose and daredevil traits that were to characterise his air force career. The mischievous smile was ever present. He was always prepared to 'have a go' at things.

The next step in Artie's life was about to begin. In 1939 he volunteered for the air force. He was just eighteen years old. Since he was under twenty-one when the time came for him to serve overseas, he would have first required my mother to give her consent. The horrors and carnage of the First World War were still a vivid memory and I suspect she would have given her permission with some reluctance.

PART 2:
ON HIS MAJESTY'S SERVICE, 1939–40

YEAR: 1939		AIRCRAFT.		PILOT, OR 1ST PILOT.	2ND PILOT, PUPIL, OR PASSENGER.	DUTY (INCLUDING RESULTS AND REMARKS).
MONTH.	DATE.	Type.	No.			
—	—	—	—	—	—	—— TOTALS BROUGHT FORWARD
October	21	Tiger Moth	3639	P/O Mackenzie	Self	Air Experience
October	23	Tiger Moth	3671	F/O Adams	Self	Straight & level, Stalling, climbing, gliding
October	23	Tiger Moth	3671	F/O Adams	Self	Straight & level, Stalling, climbing, glidin
October	24	Tiger Moth	3671	F/O Adams	Self	turns.
October	25	Tiger Moth	3671	F/O Burbidge	Self	Take offs, circuits & landings
October	26	Tiger Moth	3671	F/O Adams	Self	Take offs, circuits & landin
October	26	Tiger Moth	3671	F/O Adams	Self	Take offs, circuits & landin
October	27	Tiger Moth	3936	F/O Lambert	Self	Take offs, circuits & landin
October	28	Tiger Moth	3936	F/O Lambert	Self	Take offs, circuits & landin
October	31	Tiger Moth	3638	F/O Lambert	Self	Take offs, circuits & landin
Summary for October 1939						Tiger Moth – 4:50
Unit : No.1 E.F.T.S. Taieri					Aircraft	2
Date : 31st October 1939					Types	3
Signature : *all. Burbidge. F/O*						4
C.F.I.						
November	3	Tiger Moth	3638	P/O Page	Self	Take offs, circuits & landin
November	4	Tiger Moth	82231	F/Lt Lett	Self	Take offs, circuits & landin
November	4	Tiger Moth	3638	P/O Page	Self	Take offs, circuits & landin
November	6	Tiger Moth	3638	P/O Page	Self	Take offs, circuits & landin
November	6	Tiger Moth	3638	P/O Page	Self	Take offs, circuits & landin
November	7	Tiger Moth	3638	P/O Page	Self	Turns & spins.
November	7	Tiger Moth	3638	P/O Page	Self	Take offs, circuits & landin

GRAND TOTAL [Cols. (1) to (10)].

9 Hrs. 15 Mins.

TOTALS CARRIED FORWARD

SINGLE-ENGINE AIRCRAFT.				MULTI-ENGINE AIRCRAFT.						PASSEN-GER.	INSTR/CLOUD FLYING (Incl. in Cols. (1) to (10).)	
DAY.		NIGHT.		DAY.			NIGHT.					
DUAL.	PILOT.	DUAL.	PILOT.	DUAL.	1ST PILOT.	2ND PILOT.	DUAL.	1ST PILOT.	2ND PILOT.		DUAL.	PILOT.
(1)	(2)	(3)	(4)	(5)	(6)	(7)	(8)	(9)	(10)	(11)	(12)	(13)
:15												
:25												
:25												
:20												
:45												
:35												
:20												
:30												
:35												
:40												
:45												
:35												
:40												
:35												
:35												
:35												
:40												
9:15												
(1)	(2)	(3)	(4)	(5)	(6)	(7)	(8)	(9)	(10)	(11)	(12)	(13)

TIGER MOTH (GIPSY III).

Chapter 3

His Legendary Logbooks and Summary of Air Force Service

The story of Artie Ashworth's air force career would not be complete without drawing attention to his remarkable logbooks. They are unique and an integral part of the legend. All those who have had the privilege of viewing them are astonished at their precision. As Air Vice-Marshal Hogan, RAF, wrote in his letter of January 1958, in all his twenty-eight years of service he had never seen one so perfectly kept.

Flight Lieutenant Don Briggs, RAF (Rtd), DFC, who worked with Artie at the Empire Test Pilots' School and later served in No. 635 Pathfinder Squadron, asked me if I had access to his logbooks. Don said: 'Artie's logbook was a masterpiece. Every entry written in copperplate script. Every crew member who ever flew with him entered in his immaculate handwriting.'

As is presented in this book, from the first entry on 21 October 1939, until the last on 28 March 1961, the perfect presentation never varied. They are indeed a masterpiece. The meticulous, flawless recording is all the more remarkable when considering the strain Artie would have been experiencing at critical times throughout the war. There would have been periods when he must have been under almost unbearable stress, especially in RAF Bomber Command in 1941 and 1942, when the danger of flying to distant, heavily defended targets in the dead of night was at its peak, and aircrew losses were high.

All aircrew considered their logbooks special. And so they were. The logbook was their precious and valuable record of a period in their lives of which they were all very proud. All were thankful that they had survived an experience they wouldn't have missed but which they had no wish to repeat.

The final entry recording his last flight on 28 March 1961, was also in an Anson, which, interestingly, was also the first type of twin-engined aircraft he ever flew. The logbook records the total flying time over twenty-two years at 3,904 hours and 5 minutes, of which 3,628 hours was as captain of aircraft.

On completion of his training in New Zealand and arrival in England in June 1940, Artie completed No. 12 OTU (Operational Training Unit) at Benson and then No. 11 OTU at Bassingbourn before being posted to No. 75 Squadron at Feltwell in January 1941. He completed his first operational tour with No. 75 Squadron on 29 August 1941.

His second operational tour was with Nos 38 and 216 Squadrons, first in Malta, and then Egypt. Starting in early July 1942, his third tour was again with No. 75 Squadron at Feltwell and then Mildenhall. This he finished at the end of August when he was posted to the headquarters of the Pathfinder Force at Wyton.

From May to September 1943, on loan to the RNZAF in New Zealand, he attended the Army Staff College at Palmerston North before being posted as a staff officer to the RNZAF Headquarters No. 1 (Islands) Group at Espiritu Santo and then Guadalcanal.

He returned to New Zealand in May 1944 where he began training as a fighter pilot. He began his fighter pilot operational tour at the beginning of August 1944, serving with No. 17F RNZAF Squadron at Espiritu Santo, Guadalcanal and Bougainville before returning to New Zealand on 1 November 1944.

Artie travelled back to England at the end of 1944, and after completing a course at the Pathfinder Navigation and Training Unit, he began his fifth operational tour with No. 635 Pathfinder Squadron at Downham Market.

With the end of the war in August 1945, he was posted in September to No. 35 Squadron at Graveley. Then followed a posting as an instructor at the Officers' Advanced Training School in Amman, Jordan. After some eight months he went to the Middle East School of Administration in late September 1946.

In July 1947 he took command of the Iraq and Persia Communications Flight stationed at Habbaniya, Iraq. He left the flight in February 1948 when he was selected to attend the Empire Test Pilots' School at

Farnborough. He finished the ETPS in December 1948, after which he went on leave to New Zealand.

On his return to England he was posted to the Photographic Flight of the Royal Aircraft Establishment at Farnborough. He served there from June 1949 to December 1951. He was then appointed to the headquarters of No. 1 Bomber Command Group at Bawtry.

Artie remained at Bawtry until July 1953 when, after a short course on the Canberra Operational Training Unit, he took command of No. 139 (Jamaica) Squadron based at Hemswell.

His tour with No. 139 Squadron ended on 23 October 1955 when he took up the position of Deputy Director of Operations at the Air Ministry in London.

From 6 January to 15 June 1956, he completed a course at the Royal Air Force Flying College at Manby. After Manby he was sent to Gütersloh, Germany, to form a new Canberra squadron, No. 59, from the remnants of four former Bomber Command squadrons. The squadron transferred to Geilenkirchen near the Belgian border in November 1957.

His last flying appointment came in May 1958 when he took command of 'B' Squadron of the Aeroplane and Armament Evaluation Establishment at Boscombe Down. At the beginning of April 1961 he left Boscombe Down to become the Deputy Director, Flight Safety, at the Air Ministry.

This appointment ended on 6 July 1964 when he was transferred to the NATO base at Laarbruch in Germany as the wing commander in charge of administration. Increasing blindness forced him to leave Laarbruch and enter the RAF hospital at Halton, England. From there, in 1967, he became a civilian. So ended the air force career of Artie Ashworth.

During his twenty-two-year flying career, his flying time totalled 3,904 hours of which 3,628 hours was as captain of aircraft. He had flown 94 different types of aircraft (Appendix 2), most of which as first pilot, and used 251 airfields or landing grounds in 51 different countries (Appendix 3).

The logbook details the type of aircraft flown during his career. The list includes the makes of the respective engines. Later he produced a revised and more detailed list of aircraft flown, which is shown in Appendix 2.

Chapter 4

The Road to War: Training in New Zealand

Throughout the 1930s the Royal Air Force had offered a limited number of Short Service Commissions to applicants from the Empire, as it was known in those days. War was looming in 1938. Artie had a secure job in the Public Works Department but his adventurous spirit ensured he wanted to be in the action. He was the first person from Alexandra to volunteer for the air force in 1939.

After the war he was asked why he volunteered in 1939. He answered: 'With the war coming up I decided I preferred not to walk. I also saw it as an escape from the humdrum existence in a drawing office of the Aerodrome Services of the Public Works Department in Wellington. There were secondary considerations: the hope for adventure, patriotism, envy of some companions who had already joined the RAF, and a desire to learn to fly.'

In early 1939 he applied for a Short Service Commission in the Royal Air Force and was accepted. Together with others, he was due to sail to England in early 1940, but when war was declared in September 1939 they were asked to accept instruction in New Zealand instead. So they trained at the RNZAF stations at Rongotai, Taieri and Wigram. Half of them flew Tiger Moths, Vildebeests and Gordons. The other half were taught in Tiger Moths and Oxfords. Artie said that when this half reached England they were posted to fly Blenheims and very few survived for long.[10]

Rex Daniells from Masterton was a member of the group that reported to Rongotai in September 1939. In his epic book *What Did You Do in the War, Poppa Rekka?*, he recorded that the first month at Rongotai was one of intense study and physical training. Within the first week they were wearing the uniform of pilot officers, having taken the King's commission on oath. In the official records they figured under what he considered was the depressing heading of 'Acting Pilot Officers on Probation (paid)'.[11]

During their time at Rongotai, Rex said that others he got to know at that time were Arthur Ashworth, Jack Cave and Charlie Stewart, a pipe major, who was everybody's friend. Their stay at Rongotai was a happy one. After four weeks the group set sail for Taieri near Dunedin. Rex recorded the trip as being a jolly one with Charlie Stewart's pipes leading their exuberant spirits.[12]

When the group arrived at Taieri many of the buildings were still under construction, but they were housed in a new barrack block with each officer having a quite comfortable room.

Artie made his first flight on 21 October 1939 in a Tiger Moth DH86 and his first solo on 23 November. Apart from periodic check flights with his instructor, Pilot Officer Page, he continued training solo in Tiger Moths until 16 December 1939.

In late December the group was transferred to RNZAF Wigram. Rex Daniell considered their time at Taieri had not been wasted and they were sorry to say goodbye to the hard-working instructors, who would probably have had to ply their exacting trade for the rest of the war.

Before shifting to Wigram, Artie spent Christmas with his mother in Alexandra, which town in those days was a day's train journey from Dunedin.

Flying training at Wigram began with the Vildebeests and continued until mid-January 1940 when they switched to Fairey Gordons. Artie flew solo in the Gordon for the first time on 13 January after only one dual flight with his instructor, P/O de Lange. In April he started training on the twin-engined Avro Anson.

An assessment by the officer commanding (OC) of No. 1 Flying Training School made at Wigram in April 1940 of Artie's ability on Gordons, read as follows: 'Pilot: average; pilot-navigator: average; bombing: below average; air gunnery: above average.' By this time he had completed 132 hours' flying time. He was not considered one of the top pilots at Taieri and, together with this Wigram assessment, nothing suggested he was to become a highly skilled and renowned bomber and test pilot.

Robert (Bob) Spurdle was one of the trainee officers at Wigram. He remarked that most of them wanted to be fighter pilots but to their consternation they were told their fate was to be on light bombers. Bob said the days at Wigram included swotting, hours of flying in an open cockpit in oily biplanes, bombing, navigation and aircraft recognition, Morse code, ground signals, air-to-air and air-to-ground firing, drill and ceremonial, the stripping of Lewis and Browning machine guns, and so on.

In their lighter moments Bob recalled they relaxed, with escapades as wild and irresponsible as those of university students! One pilot passed out at a party and was carried, bed and all, to the middle of the airfield. He awoke in broad daylight with planes trundling around and a furious chief flying instructor (CFI) bearing down on him.

Bob said while fooling with a Very pistol, Artie Ashworth accidentally fired it inside the control tower. The blazing magnesium projectile rocketed from wall to wall and finished up on a book entitled *Heat, Hell and Humour*.

Training was completed at the end of March 1940. Those who qualified were presented with their flying badge, the coveted 'wings'. A special passing-out parade was held, at which the officers were congratulated by the Group Captain Commanding, W.I. Saunders.

Charlie Stewart was absent, sick, at the time the formal 'wings' photo was taken. Of the seventeen who gained their wings at Wigram in March 1940, only six survived the war. Their fate is described in the next chapter.

The last Wigram entry in Artie's logbook was on 4 April 1940 when he recorded flying a Fairey Gordon to Taieri and back. The first pilot on the outward flight was Bob Spurdle, destined to be one of New Zealand's fighter aces. The positions were reversed on the return flight with Artie being first pilot. The next entry on 19 June was at Kemble in England.

Following the successful completion of the Wigram training, the formal commissioning was confirmed. Artie's commission as a pilot officer was dated 20 June 1940.

Sadly, the original document was severely water damaged and has been partly restored. The King's titles shown on the commission will seem pompous to many of the current and future generations, but in 1940 the British Empire and the monarchy were still important in the world.

Passing-out festivities were followed by final leave before embarking for England. Artie went to Alexandra, visiting family and close friends.

Throughout the war the Alexandra community always held a public farewell to servicemen departing for overseas. These farewells were an opportunity for the community to display its patriotic fervour. They were always well attended. The old town hall would be decorated with red, white and blue bunting and the Union Jack would be greatly in evidence. Patriotic songs of the day, *There'll Always Be An England* and *Rule Britannia* would be sung with great gusto, as would the national anthem of the time, *God Save the King*.

Much speechifying by the local dignitaries usually took place. The mayor, local MP, president of the RSA and others, including local clergy, would invariably speak. It seems that in Artie's case no such celebration was held during his final leave, which is strange indeed. However, at a farewell function in June 1940 my mother was presented with a gift for Artie on behalf of the community. The official newspaper report stated that each serviceman was presented with an inscribed watch. On behalf of the Presbyterian parish, my mother was also given a pocket bible for Artie. Religion was not a big part of his life but he carried this bible with him throughout the war. In his memoir he mentioned regularly attending, with a fellow pilot, a local church near one of the stations, Downham Market, where he was posted in 1945.

On 26 April 1940, along with those with whom he had trained at Wigram, Artie embarked on the *Rangitiki* for England. He didn't record anything of the voyage but kept a photo inscribed 'somewhere in the Tropics'.

The following account of the voyage is adapted from Rex Daniell's, *What Did You Do in the War, Poppa Rekka*:

Somewhere about midnight on the NZ Shipping Co's vessel *Rangitiki*, we pulled out into the stream with only the desultory cries of dockworkers to bid us 'bon voyage'. There was no cheerfulness as the lights of Auckland faded from view. Each man was concerned with his own thoughts. Well we knew that for many of us it would be the last view of the homeland.

There were some eighty Air Force fellows on the passenger list, all recently trained aircrew. These along with about 20 civilians made up the total passengers on a ship with peacetime accommodation facilities for 600 persons so there was plenty of room.

After three weeks, on one showery day we arrived at the Panama Canal Zone and were able to step on dry land once more. Panama City was my first view of a foreign town. During our time ashore, we dressed in civies[13] [sic]. It was novel to be driven on the right hand side of the road by a big black West Indian. We visited the American Air Force Station at Old Panama where Morgan the pirate had waged his famous campaigns. We also visited the slum area, which appalled us with its squalor and vice. The locals seemed to know we were flying men. They made rude signs about Hitler and wished us God-speed.

The journey through the canal of 56 miles and seven locks took 7.5 hours. In the Caribbean we passed our sister ship the *Rangitata* homeward bound. After 2–3 days we called at Bermuda but were not permitted to go ashore. There were some 30 ships awaiting our arrival before heading out into the Atlantic with a single armed merchantman as our escort. Of this we took a dim view. About a week later we were joined by about 30 ships from Canada and from there on proceeded at the speed of the slowest ship, about 7–8 knots.

Some 300–400 miles off Land's End while I was on submarine watch in low cloud and rain, I was concerned to spot a thundering great four-engine aircraft approaching dead ahead. A report to the Skipper caused no concern as he recognised it as a Sunderland Flying Boat of RAF Coastal Command. Thus we had reached Britain's air protection for the remainder of our voyage. Soon the convoy split up and we sped up the English Channel independently and at speed. We passed the White Cliffs of Dover to finally dock at Tilbury on 8 June 1940.

The final dinner on *Rangitiki* took place on the evening of 5 June 1940. Those who signed the menu were guests of the captain, Commander H. Barnett. The signatories on the back of the menu, from the top, were: Harry Morgan, Beresford Smith, Don MacKenzie, Chas de V. Halkett,

Jack Cave, Nelson Mansfield, Winton Shand, Bob Raymond, Lloyd Parry, Artie Ashworth, Rex Daniell, C.E. Langdon, Arthur Fisher, Eddie Topp and Bill Gasquoine. Along with Bob Spurdle and Charlie Stewart, whose departure was delayed, these are the seventeen who trained together and successfully graduated from Wigram.

The menu suggests that at least as far as dining at sea was concerned, the New Zealand Shipping Line was not yet in wartime mode.

Sergeant Frank Chunn,[14] RNZAF, who was later to fly seven operations over Germany in Artie's crew as the rear gunner, recorded the following incident in his diary as the convoy in which he sailed neared England:[15]

I had done my morning underwater watch from four to seven and then went back to bed. Shortly after 7 o'clock we heard an explosion and the alarm bells ringing. We tore into our life-jackets and raced up on deck to our lifeboat stations. One of our convoy was torpedoed, a ship carrying wood pulp and timber, the *Humber Arm*. She sank in 50 minutes and her crew were in the lifeboats. The destroyers raced to the scene quite close to our ship and started dropping depth charges. These rocked our ship, which crammed on full speed and raced ahead. Everyone was very excited but there was no panic, mostly just curiosity as we watched the ship slowly sink. The destroyers claimed to have sunk two submarines. All day they kept up the depth charging and sleep was impossible. We were told to pack our trunks as we were docking tomorrow. England at last! We saw an outbound convoy at around 10pm and then retired to bed.

Chapter 5

The Fate of the Wigram Course 11 Pilots

Of the sixteen in the wings group photo, plus Bob Spurdle and Charles Stewart, a total of eighteen, only six survived the war. According to Bob Spurdle, two of these six saw very little action, being relegated to ground duties due to what he described as 'personality weaknesses'.[16] Of the fifteen who sailed in the *Rangitiki* on 26 April 1940, ten were to be killed either in action or as a result of an accident during training. Those who survived were: A. Ashworth, R. Daniell, W. Gasquoine, and A.B. Smith.[17] R. Spurdle and C. Stewart were not in the official photo, both being away sick at the time. Both embarked on a later sailing. The fate of L. Parry is unknown.

A brief outline of the fate of those for whom I have been able to find records is presented below. That of Charles Stewart, the piper, and Bob Spurdle, are also included. According to Errol Martyn (*For Your Tomorrow*, vol. 3, p. 454), Charles Stewart did not fly between 21 November 1939 and 17 January 1940, due to sickness. He received his pilot's badge on 6 April 1940, and embarked for the UK on 6 June of that year.

Pilot Officer A.V. Fisher came from Kerepehi on the Hauraki Plains. He was killed as a result of an aircraft accident on 6 August 1940. He was stationed at Benson, Oxfordshire, with No. 12 OTU. Shortly after take-off at 2315 hours at around 1,000 feet, his aircraft swung to starboard and then port before crashing to the ground and bursting into flames. He was aged twenty-three and is buried at Benson.[18]

Edward Topp, RAFVR, from Hamilton, was serving with No. 150 Squadron, RAF, at Snaith in Yorkshire. He was captain of a Wellington bomber, which was shot down over Germany on the night of 16–17 July 1941. Only one of the six crew survived. Edward Topp had flown sixteen operations and was aged twenty-four. He is buried at Ohlsdorf near Hamburg in Germany.[19]

Charles Langdon, RAF, from Hawera, was serving with No. 261 Squadron in Malta. On 26 February 1941, flying a Hurricane fighter, he took off at about 1300 hours to intercept an incoming raid of 90–100 enemy aircraft. He was one of three who failed to return. The Hurricanes climbed to 28,000 feet before diving on bombers below, flying at 10,000 feet, but were followed down in turn by enemy fighters. He was credited with having destroyed one enemy aircraft. Charles Langdon was twenty-two. He is commemorated on the Malta memorial.[20]

Squadron Leader Cuthbert Raymond, RAF, DFC, was captain of a Stirling bomber of No. 218 Squadron, RAF, which took off at 0315 hours for a raid on Flensburg, Germany, on the night of 23 September 1942. The Stirling was shot down by a night fighter off the West Frisian Islands and crashed into the North Sea. All seven crew died and are commemorated on the Runnymede memorial. Squadron Leader Raymond was on his fifty-first operation. He was twenty-five.

Squadron Leader Raymond, Citation for Distinguished Flying Cross

'One night in May 1941, Flight Lieutenant Raymond and Sergeant Bushell were captain and rear gunner respectively in an aircraft which carried out an attack against Berlin. After spending considerable time over the target area waiting for a break in the clouds to permit accurate bombing, a steady run was made over the target and, despite heavy and accurate anti-aircraft fire, a well-aimed stick of bombs was finally released over the objective. The aircraft was then hit by shell-fire. After flying a short distance it caught fire and began to lose height. After the fire had been put out the aircraft was subjected to a determined attack by an enemy night-fighter but Sergeant Bushell coolly engaged the enemy and enabled his captain to manoeuvre his aircraft and finally evade the attacker. In the face of many difficulties

THE LOGBOOK

SINGLE-ENGINE AIRCRAFT.				MULTI-ENGINE AIRCRAFT.						PASSENGER.	INSTR/CLOUD FLYING [Incl. in Cols. (1) to (10)].	
DAY.		NIGHT.		DAY.			NIGHT.					
DUAL.	PILOT.	DUAL.	PILOT.	DUAL.	1ST PILOT.	2ND PILOT.	DUAL.	1ST PILOT.	2ND PILOT.		DUAL.	PILOT
(1)	(2)	(3)	(4)	(5)	(6)	(7)	(8)	(9)	(10)	(11)	(12)	(13)

Aircraft Flown

Aircraft	Engine	Aircraft	Engine	Aircraft	Engine
Tiger Moth	Gypsy Major	Harvard II, IIA	Pratt & Whitney	Olympia	Nil Rolls-Royce
Vickers Vildebeeste	Bristol Pegasus	Corsair F4U X,VII,	Pratt & Whitney Rolls-Royce	Mosquito 35	Merlin 113 Bristol
Avro 626	Armstrong Siddeley Cheetah V	Lancaster III	Merlin XXXVIII Rolls-Royce	Tempest II VII,VIII,NF31,	Centaurus V Rolls-Royce
Fairey Gordon	Armstrong Siddeley Panther IIA	Lancaster I Consul	Merlin XXIV Leonides	Meteor IV	Derwent V
Avro Anson	Armstrong Siddeley Cheetah IX	Oxford III	Cheetah X Warner	F. Junior Viking	Walter Mikron Bristol
Fairey Battle IA,ID,IC	Rolls-Royce Merlin II	F. Argus X,XXI	Super Scarab	V. Valetta	Hercules 230 D.H.
Vickers Wellington	Bristol Pegasus XVIII Rolls-Royce	Anson XII	Cheetah XV	D.H. Devon XVI,	Gipsy Queen 71 Rolls-Royce
Vickers Wellington II	Merlin X	Anson XIX	Cheetah XV	Spitfire	Merlin Pratt & Whitney
D.H. 86	Gypsy Six Bristol	Proctor III	Gypsy Queen	Dakota Youngman Baynes	Twin Wasp
Bristol Bombay	Pegasus XXII Rolls-Royce	Lodestar I,IA	Twin Wasp	Gipsy Queen	Rolls-Royce
Hawker Hart	Kestrel X Bristol	Ventura V	Double Wasp	S. Sturgeon	Merlin 140
Vickers Wellington III	Hercules XI	Lodestar II	Wright Cyclone Rolls-Royce	F. Storch	Argus AS10-C/3 Rolls-Royce
Whitney Straight	Gypsy Major	Lincoln I	Merlin 68 Rolls-Royce	A. Athena	Merlin XXXV
Miles Mentor	Gypsy Six Bristol	Seafire 47 NF10,	Griffon 87	Kranich	Nil
Westland Lysander	Perseus XII Rolls-Royce	Vampire I	D.H. Goblin II	S. Tutor	Nil
Mosquito IV	Merlin XXI	Auster V	Lycoming Rolls-Royce	B. Grunau	Nil
Hornet Moth	Gypsy Major	Firefly I	Griffon XII	S. T21B	Nil Wright Cyclone 1820/97
D.H. Moth Minor	Gypsy Minor	Dominie III	Gypsy Queen Rolls-Royce	Fortress B17 PR3,B2,I4,B6,IU,	Rolls-Royce
Searwin 40E,K,M,N	Le Blond	Mosquito III	Merlin XXV Bristol	Canberra B/U8 PR7,B(I)12,PR9,T13,	Avon RA 2 RA3 109
Kittyhawk	Allison	Sea Fury	Centaurus XVIII Rolls-Royce	Prentice	D.H. Gipsy Queen Rolls-Royce
Liberator PB4Y	Pratt & Whitney	Meteor III	Derwent I	Gloster E1/44	Nene

| (1) | (2) | (3) | (4) | (5) | (6) | (7) | (8) | (9) | (10) | (11) | (12) | (13) |

Year: 1939		Aircraft.		Pilot, or 1st Pilot.	2nd Pilot, Pupil, or Passenger.	Duty (Including Results and Remarks
Month.	Date.	Type.	No.			
—	—	—	—	—	—	— Totals Brought Forward
November	8	Tiger Moth	3638	P/O Page	Self	Take offs, circuits & landing
November	8	Tiger Moth	3638	P/O Page	Self	Take offs, circuits & landing
November	9	Tiger Moth	3638	P/O Page	Self	Take offs, circuits & landing
November	13	Tiger Moth	3638	P/O Page	Self	Take offs, circuits & landing
November	14	Tiger Moth	3638	P/O Page	Self	Take offs, circuits & landing
November	14	Tiger Moth	3638	P/O Page	Self	Take offs, circuits & landing
November	15	Tiger Moth	3643	P/O Page	Self	Take offs, circuits & landing
November	15	Tiger Moth	82231	F/Lt Lett	Self	Check
November	17	Tiger Moth	3638	P/O Page	Self	Take offs, circuits & landing
November	17	Tiger Moth	3638	P/O Page	Self	Take offs, circuits & landing
November	18	Tiger Moth	3638	P/O Page	Self	Take offs, circuits & landing
November	18	Tiger Moth	3638	P/O Page	Self	Take offs, circuits & landing
November	20	Tiger Moth	3638	P/O Page	Self	Take offs, circuits & land
November	20	Tiger Moth	3638	P/O Page	Self	Take offs, circuits & land
November	21	Tiger Moth	3638	P/O Page	Self	Take offs, circuits & land
November	21	Tiger Moth	3638	P/O Page	Self	Take offs, circuits & land
November	22	Tiger Moth	3638	P/O Page	Self	Take offs, circuits & lan
November	22	Tiger Moth	3638	P/O Page	Self	Take offs, circuits & lan
November	23	Tiger Moth	3638	P/O Page	Self	Take offs, circuits & lan
November	23	Tiger Moth	3638	F/O Burbidge	Self	Test for Solo
November	23	Tiger Moth	3638	Self	Solo	Solo
November	24	Tiger Moth	3638	P/O Page	Self	Check
November	24	Tiger Moth	3638	Self	Solo	Take offs, circuits & landi

GRAND TOTAL [Cols. (1) to (10)].

20 Hrs. 50 Mins.

Totals Carried Forwa

SINGLE-ENGINE AIRCRAFT.				MULTI-ENGINE AIRCRAFT.						PASSEN-GER.	INSTR/CLOUD FLYING [Incl. in Cols. (1) to (10).]	
DAY.		NIGHT.		DAY.			NIGHT.					
DUAL.	PILOT.	DUAL.	PILOT.	DUAL.	1ST PILOT.	2ND PILOT.	DUAL.	1ST PILOT.	2ND PILOT.		DUAL.	PILOT.
(1)	(2)	(3)	(4)	(5)	(6)	(7)	(8)	(9)	(10)	(11)	(12)	(13)
9:15												
:05												
:20												
:35												
:30												
:40												
:25												
:35												
:50												
:35												
:25												
:25												
:35												
:35												
:40												
:55												
:40												
:40												
:20												
:35												
:25												
	:10											
:10												
	:25											
20:15	:35											
(1)	(2)	(3)	(4)	(5)	(6)	(7)	(8)	(9)	(10)	(11)	(12)	(13)

YEAR: 1941		AIRCRAFT.		PILOT, OR 1ST PILOT.	2ND PILOT, PUPIL, OR PASSENGER.	DUTY (INCLUDING RESULTS AND REMA...
MONTH.	DATE.	Type.	No.			
—	—	—	—	—	—	— TOTALS BROUGHT FORW...
January	25	V.Wellington	T3218	F/Lt.Morton	Self	Methwold to Feltwell
February	4	V.Wellington	T3218	F/Lt.Morton	Self	Dual instruction
February	14	V.Wellington	T3218	F/O.Collins	Self	Dual instruction
February	17	V.Wellington	T3218	Self Sgt.Minikin		Circuits & bumps
February	18	V.Wellington	R3166	Sgt.White Self	Sgt.Harrison Sgt.Kelly Sgt.East Sgt.Campbell	N.F.T.
February	21	V.Wellington	R1177	Sgt.White	Self	Aerodrome test
February	21	V.Wellington	R3166	Sgt.White Self	Sgt.Harrison Sgt.Kelly Sgt.East Sgt.Campbell	War ops. Wilhelmshaven Lan... at Wittering.
February	22	V.Wellington	R3166	Sgt.White Self	Sgt.Harrison Sgt.Kelly Sgt.East Sgt.Campbell	Return to base
February	23	V.Wellington	R3166	Sgt.White Self	Sgt.Kelly Sgt.East Sgt.Campbell	N.F.T.
February	24	V.Wellington	R3166	Self		to Methwold
February	25	V.Wellington	R3171	F/O.Collins Self	Sgt.Coll Sgt.Miller Sgt.Gilmore	Instrument test
February	26	V.Wellington	R3166	Sgt.White Self	Sgt.Harrison Sgt.East Sgt.Campbell	N.F.T.
February	26	V.Wellington	R3166	Sgt.White Self	Sgt.Harrison Sgt.Kelly Sgt.East Sgt.Campbell	Blitz on Cologne. Landed at ... Load: (5)500 (1)250 (2) S.B.C.

GRAND TOTAL [Cols. (1) to (10)].

392 Hrs. 25 Mins.

TOTALS CARRIED FORW...

—	—	—	—	—	—	TOTALS BROUGHT FORWARD
April	9	V. Wellington	R3166	Sgt. Faulkner Self	Sgt. Wheelan / Sgt. Webb / Sgt. Davis / Sgt. Watkins	Attack on Berlin. Very accurate searchlights & heavy A.A. fire. Load: (4) 500 (1) 250. fighters encountered ⑦
April	11	V. Wellington	L7848	Self		from Methwold
April	12	V. Wellington	R1163	Self	Sgt. Wheelan / Sgt. Davis / Sgt. Dawson / Sgt. Watkins / Lt. Holm (R.N.R.) / A.C. Morgan	Petrol consumption test
April	13	V. Wellington	R3169	Sgt. Faulkner Self	Sgt. Wheelan / Sgt. Webb / Sgt. Dawson / Sgt. Watkins	Petrol consumption test
April	16	V. Wellington	R1458	P/O. Simich * Self	Sgt. Hardy / Sgt. Blundell / Sgt. Cotton / Sgt. Abbott	Raid on Bremen. Bombs (7) 500, seen to burst in target area ⑧
April	17	V. Wellington	R1458	P/O. Simich Self	Sgt. Hardy / Sgt. Blundell / Sgt. Cotton / Sgt. Abbott	Attack on Berlin. Accurate search-lights & heavy A.A. fire. Load (1) 500 (6) Landed at Ternhill. Aircraft damage flarepath downwind.
April	18	V. Wellington	R1177	P/O. Simich Sgt. Reid * Self	Sgt. Hardy / Sgt. Blundell / Sgt. Cotton / Sgt. Abbott / Sgt. Nation * / Sgt. Haycock *	return to base
April	19	V. Wellington	R1409	Self	P/O. Key / P/O. Barnett D.F.M. / Sgt. Blundell	testing lorenz instruments
April	20	V. Wellington	R1648	Self	A.C. Ettle / A.C. Holt / A.C. Magan	N.F.T.
April	20	V. Wellington	R1648	Self	Sgt. Hardy / Sgt. Blundell	practice for ground gunners.

* Killed in Action.
Ø P.o/W. (o.k.)
Killed in flying accident
□ Awarded D.F.C.
Awarded D.F.M.

GRAND TOTAL [Cols. (1) to (10)].
459 Hrs. 00 Mins.

TOTALS CARRIED FORWARD

YEAR: 1941		AIRCRAFT		PILOT, OR 1ST PILOT	2ND PILOT, PUPIL, OR PASSENGER	DUTY (INCLUDING RESULTS AND REMARKS)
MONTH	DATE	Type	No.			
						TOTALS BROUGHT FORWARD
April	21	V.Wellington	R3166	Self	Sgt. Cotton / Sgt. Abbott	N.F.T. & Lorenz test
April	22	V.Wellington	R3166	Self		N.F.T.
April	23	V.Wellington	R1409	P/O. Simich / Self	Sgt. Blundell / Sgt. Cotton / Sgt. Abbott	Lorenz test
April	24	V.Wellington	R1409	P/O. Simich / Self	Sgt. Hardy / Sgt. Blundell / Sgt. Cotton / Sgt. Abbott	War ops. to Kiel. Intense & a... A.A. fire. Load: (6) S.B.C. (1) 500... Homed on Marham beam.
April	26	V.Wellington	R3218	Self	Cpl. Norris	Drogue towing test.
April	27	V.Wellington	T2835	P/O. Hamlin / Self	Sgt. Rigden / Sgt. Jenkins / Sgt. Birchell / Sgt. Twisleton	N.F.T. & Lorenz test.
April	29	V.Wellington	R1409	P/O. Simich / Self	Sgt. Hardy / Sgt. Blundell / Sgt. Cotton / Sgt. Abbott	N.F.T.
April	29	V.Wellington	R1409	P/O. Simich / Self	Sgt. Hardy / Sgt. Blundell / Sgt. Cotton / Sgt. Abbott	Blitz on Mannheim. Bombs dropped in target area. Loa... (6) S.B.C. (3) 500. Very intense a... acc. heavy flak in target are...
May	8	V.Wellington	T2747	Self / P/O. Wilson	Sgt. McSherry / Sgt. Welby / Sgt. Broad / Sgt. Palmer	Attack on submarine shipbu... yards at Hamburg. Bombs ((6) (2) 500) hit target, starting first... Badly beaten up by heavy f...
May	8	V.Wellington	T2747	Self	Sgt. Harrison	N.F.T.
May	9	V.Wellington	T2747	Self / P/O. Wilson	Sgt. McSherry / Sgt. Welby / Sgt. Broad / Sgt. Palmer	Blitz on Mannheim. Bombs i... target area. Load (6) S.B.C. (3) 500...

* Awarded D.F.C. killed himself at W...
§ Missing on 8/0...

GRAND TOTAL [Cols. (1) to (10)]. **490** Hrs. **40** Mins.

TOTALS CARRIED FORWA...

| SINGLE-ENGINE AIRCRAFT. | | | | MULTI-ENGINE AIRCRAFT. | | | | | | PASSEN-GER. | INSTR/CLOUD FLYING [Incl. in Cols. (1) to (10).] | |
| DAY. | | NIGHT. | | DAY. | | | NIGHT. | | | | | |
DUAL. (1)	PILOT. (2)	DUAL. (3)	PILOT. (4)	DUAL. (5)	1ST PILOT. (6)	2ND PILOT. (7)	DUAL. (8)	1ST PILOT. (9)	2ND PILOT. (10)	(11)	DUAL. (12)	PILOT. (13)
4:15	123:45	3:00	6:55	13:45	177:45	9:25	6:05	9:45	55:20	57:35	11:35	11:00
					1:00							
					:30							
						:45						
								7:30				
					:30							
						:45						
					1:00							
								6:30				
								6:25				
								5:35				

DUAL. (1)	PILOT. (2)	DUAL. (3)	PILOT. (4)	DUAL. (5)	1ST PILOT. (6)	2ND PILOT. (7)	DUAL. (8)	1ST PILOT. (9)	2ND PILOT. (10)	(11)	DUAL. (12)	PILOT. (13)
4:15	123:45	3:00	6:55	13:45	179:45	11:55	6:05	21:45	69:20	57:35	11:35	11:00

YEAR: 1941		AIRCRAFT.		PILOT, OR 1ST PILOT.	2ND PILOT, PUPIL, OR PASSENGER.		DUTY (INCLUDING RESULTS AND REMARKS)
MONTH.	DATE.	Type.	No.				
—	—	—	—	—	—		— TOTALS BROUGHT FORWARD
August	29	V.Wellington	Z8347	Self / Sgt.Cook	Sgt. Smalley / F/Sgt. Brown / Sgt. Jenkins / Sgt. Holford / L/Cdr. Burdett		Hampstead Norris to North End (Gibraltar)
August	30	V.Wellington	Z8347	Self / Sgt.Cook	Sgt. Smalley / F/Sgt. Brown / Sgt. Jenkins / Sgt. Holford		North End (Gibraltar) to Luqa (Malta)
September	1	V.Wellington	T2330	Self / Sgt.Cook	Sgt. Smalley / F/Sgt. Brown / Sgt. Jenkins / Sgt. Holford		Power House at Tripoli (15) 250 Bombs failed to go.
September	4	V.Wellington	T2330	Self / Sgt Cook	Sgt. Smalley / F/Sgt. Brown / Sgt. Jenkins / Sgt. Holford		M.T.Yard at Tripoli. (5) 500 (5) 2 (W.S.B.C. 1st stick of 500's at 7.00 2nd stick at 300' direct hit. Hit by flak.
September	9	V.Wellington	R1182	Self / Sgt.Cook	P/O. Ferguson / F/Sgt. Brown / Sgt. Jenkins / Sgt. Holford		Shipping at Palermo. (8) 500. Accurate light flak. Burst on wheel on landing.
September	18	V.Wellington	Z8729	Self	P/O. Ball / Sgt. Smalley / F/Sgt. Brown* / L.A.C. O'Conner		Consumption test.
September	19	V.Wellington	Z8729	Self / P/O.Knowles†	P/O. Ball / F/Sgt. Brown / Sgt. Jenkins / Sgt. Holford		Shipping at Tripoli. (16) 250
September	23	V.Wellington	W5648	Self / P/O. Knowles	P/O. Ball / Sgt. Watson / Sgt. Jenkins / Sgt. Holford		Stores at Tripoli. (8) 500
September	25	V.Wellington	Z8797	Self / P/O.Knowles	P/O. Ball / P/O. Stones D.F.C. / Sgt. Watson / Sgt. Holford		M.T.Yard at Tripoli (16) 250
					GRAND TOTAL [Cols. (1) to (10)]. 679 Hrs. 25 Mins.		TOTALS CARRIED FORWARD

* Killed in Action
Awarded B.M. to RN for Defence of Malta

© Killed in Action. D.F.C.

Single-Engine Aircraft				Multi-Engine Aircraft						Passenger	Instr/Cloud Flying [Incl. in Cols. (1) to (10).]	
Day		Night		Day			Night					
Dual	Pilot	Dual	Pilot	Dual	1st Pilot	2nd Pilot	Dual	1st Pilot	2nd Pilot		Dual	Pilot
(1)	(2)	(3)	(4)	(5)	(6)	(7)	(8)	(9)	(10)	(11)	(12)	(13)
4:15	125:05	3:00	6:55	13:45	255:55	11:15	6:05	107:10	69:25	60:10	11:35	13:00
					9:00							
					7:30							
								3:35				
								3:45				
								3:00				
					1:05							
								3:35				
								4:00				
								4:05				
04:15	125:05	3:00	6:55	13:45	263:30	11:15	3:05	129:10	69:25	60:10	11:35	13:00
(1)	(2)	(3)	(4)	(5)	(6)	(7)	(8)	(9)	(10)	(11)	(12)	(12)

YEAR: 1942		AIRCRAFT.		PILOT, OR 1ST PILOT.	2ND PILOT, PUPIL, OR PASSENGER.	DUTY (INCLUDING RESULTS AND REMARKS
MONTH.	DATE.	Type.	No.			
—	—	—	—	—	—	— TOTALS BROUGHT FORWARD
July	16	Tiger Moth	T6316	Self	S/L Denton DFC.	to Hendon
July	17	Tiger Moth	T6316	Self		return
July	20	V. Wellington	BJ584	Self	F/Sgt Chambers P/O. Thistle P/O. Chunn	N.F.T.
July	21	V. Wellington	BJ584	Self	F/Sgt Chambers P/O. Thistle P/O. Chunn	N.F.T.
July	21	V. Wellington	BJ584	Self	P/O. Taylor F/Sgt Chambers P/O. Thistle P/O. Chunn	Ops. Duisburg. 9 x S.B.C.
July	23	V. Wellington	BJ584	Self	F/Sgt Chambers P/O. Thistle P/O. Chunn	N.F.T.
July	23	V. Wellington	BJ584	Self	P/O. Taylor F/Sgt Chambers P/O. Thistle P/O. Chunn	Ops. Duisburg. 36 x Flar 7 x 500
July	24	V. Wellington	BJ584	Sgt. Melbourne / Self	F/Sgt Chambers P/O. Thistle P/O. Chunn	N.F.T.
July	25	V. Wellington	BJ584	Self	F/Sgt Chambers P/O. Chunn	N.F.T.
July	25	V. Wellington	BJ584	Self	P/O. Taylor F/Sgt Chambers P/O. Girvan P/O. Chunn	Ops. Duisburg. 9 x S.B.C.
July	26	V. Wellington	BJ584	Self	F/Sgt Chambers P/O. Girvan P/O. Chunn P/O. Harkness	N.F.T.
July	26	V. Wellington	BJ584	Self	P/O. Taylor F/Sgt Chambers P/O. Girvan P/O. Harkness	Ops. Hamburg. 9 x S.B.C.
July	28	V. Wellington	BJ584	Self	F/Sgt Chambers P/O. Girvan P/O. Chunn	N.F.T.

○ MISSING
✶ Awarded DFC.
☐ DFC on Mohne Dam.

GRAND TOTAL {Cols. (1) to (10)}.

961 Hrs. **25** Mins.

TOTALS CARRIED FORWARD

SINGLE-ENGINE AIRCRAFT.				MULTI-ENGINE AIRCRAFT.						PASSEN-GER.	INSTR/CLOUD FLYING [Incl. in Cols. (1) to (10).]	
DAY.		NIGHT.		DAY.			NIGHT.					
DUAL.	PILOT.	DUAL.	PILOT.	DUAL.	1ST PILOT.	2ND PILOT.	DUAL.	1ST PILOT.	2ND PILOT.		DUAL.	PILOT.
(1)	(2)	(3)	(4)	(5)	(6)	(7)	(8)	(9)	(10)	(11)	(12)	(13)
4:45	132:00	3:00	6:55	15:55	423:15	26:40	3:05	203:55	69:25	86:20	11:35	13:00
	1:20											
	1:15											
					:20							
					:25							
								3:45				
					:20							
								4:10				
					:20							
					:20							
								4:10				
					:20							
								5:25				
					:20							
04:45	134:35	3:00	6:55	15:55	425:40	26:40	3:05	221:25	69:25	86:20	11:35	13:00
(1)	(2)	(3)	(4)	(5)	(6)	(7)	(8)	(9)	(10)	(11)	(12)	(13)

WELLINGTON

YEAR: 1945		AIRCRAFT.		PILOT, OR 1ST PILOT.	2ND PILOT, PUPIL, OR PASSENGER.	DUTY (INCLUDING RESULTS AND REMARKS)
MONTH.	DATE.	Type.	No.			
						TOTALS BROUGHT FORWARD
March	12	Lancaster	PB926	Self	Crew	Ops. - Dortmund 1×4,000, 6×1,000, 3×500 18×500 68
March	13	Lancaster	PB926	Self	Crew F/O. Eyre	Ops. - Wuppertal 40×Flares, 4×1000 69
March	14	Lancaster	PB926	Self	Crew	Ops. - Zweibrücken 40×Flares, 3×1,000 70
March	16	Lancaster	PB926	Self	Crew	Ops. - Nuremburg 71
March	19	Lancaster	PB958	Self	Crew	to Gransden Lodge
March	19	Lancaster	PB917	F/L. Jarvis	Crew Self & Crew S/L. Hawes, D.F.C.	return
March	21	Lancaster	PB926	Self	Crew F/O. Eyre	Ops. - Bremen 4×T.I., 6×1,000 72
March	22	Lancaster	PB949	Self	Crew A.C. Woodward	Local
March	23	Lancaster	PB916	Self	Crew F/O. Eyre	Training
March	24	Lancaster	PB926	Self	Crew S/L. Hawes	Ops. - Bottrop 6×500 T.I., 4×1,000, 1×4,000. 73
March	25	Lancaster	PB926	Self	Crew F/L. Prebble	Ops. - Osnabrück 6×1,000 T.I., 4×500 74
March	27	Lancaster	PB926	Self	Crew F/L. Bresslof	Training
March	28	Lancaster	PB928	Self	Crew	× Country
March	30	Lancaster	PB926	Self	Crew	Training
March	31	Lancaster	PB926	Self	F/Lt. Macmillan & Crew F/O. Wilson, D.F.C.	to Woodbridge, Wyton & return

Summary for: March 1945
Unit: № 635 Squadron
Date: 1st April 1945
Signature: P R Meller

1. Oxford
2. Lancaster I & III

S/Ldr., D.F.C.

O.C. "A" Flight

Afterwards D.F.C.
DSV

GRAND TOTAL [Cols. (1) to (10)].
1415 Hrs. **45** Mins.

TOTALS CARRIED FORWARD

SINGLE-ENGINE AIRCRAFT.				MULTI-ENGINE AIRCRAFT.							PASSEN- GER.	INSTR/CLOUD FLYING [Incl. in Cols. (1) to (10).]	
DAY.		NIGHT.		DAY.			NIGHT.						
DUAL.	PILOT.	DUAL.	PILOT.	DUAL.	1ST PILOT.	2ND PILOT.	DUAL.	1ST PILOT.	2ND PILOT.			DUAL.	PILOT.
(1)	(2)	(3)	(4)	(5)	(6)	(7)	(8)	(9)	(10)		(11)	(12)	(13)
5:25	413:40	3:50	16:45	18:20	467:50	26:40	3:35	281:00	69:25		306:50	15:40	13:40
					4:50								

65:25	413:40	3:50	16:45	18:20	503:20	26:40	3:35	294:45	69:25	308:40	15:40	13:40
(1)	(2)	(3)	(4)	(5)	(6)	(7)	(8)	(9)	(10)	(11)	(12)	(13)

YEAR: 1948		AIRCRAFT.		PILOT, OR 1ST PILOT.	2ND PILOT, PUPIL, OR PASSENGER.	DUTY (INCLUDING RESULTS AND REMA
MONTH.	DATE.	Type.	No.			
		—	—	—		TOTALS BROUGHT FOR
March	25	Meteor	EE397	Self		first solo.
March	30	Vampire	TG386	Self		familiarization.
March	31	Anson	VP509	Self	F.L. Mulkern F.O. Sykes F.O. Briggs Mr. Briggs MissNewman	Local.
				Summary for March 1948		1. Mosquito III
				Unit: E.T.P.S. Farnborough		2. Lincoln
				Date: 1st April 1948		3. Dominie
				Signature: {ʃHamsʃf S.L.		4. Meteor
				O.C. Flying, E.T.P.S.		5. Anson
						6. Seafire
						7. Vampire
						8. Auster
						9. Firefly
						10. Harvard
						11. Sea Fury
April	1	Mosquito III	VP342	Self		Partial climb.
April	2	Mosquito III	VP342	Self		Determination of F.T.H.
April	5	Lincoln	RF535	S.L. Parrott F.L. Saxelby, D.F.C. Self	F.L. Glanville F.O. Bradley-Feary	Partial climbs.
April	6	Harvard	FX281	S.L. Brown, A.F.C.	Self	Practice partial climb.
April	8	Vampire	TG388	Self		Oscillation assessment.

4,000 bks/5/44—1588] JUN 61

* Afterwards A.F.C & Bar, O.B[...]

GRAND TOTAL [Cols. (1) to (10)].

1955 Hrs. 50 Mins.

TOTALS CARRIED F

YEAR:	AIRCRAFT.		PILOT, OR 1ST PILOT.	2ND PILOT, PUPIL, OR PASSENGER.	DUTY (INCLUDING RESULTS AND REMARKS).
MONTH. DATE.	Type.	No.			
— —	—	—	—	—	—— TOTALS BROUGHT FORWARD
	Total Flying as at 1st January 1951:~				
	Tiger Moth				
	Vildebeeste				
	Avro 626				
	Gordon				
	Battle		Total Experimental Flying as at 1st January 1951 :~		
	Lysander				
	Hart				
	Whitney Str.				
	Mentor		Day :	169 Hrs. 00 Mins.	
	Hornet Moth				
	Harvard		Night:	33 Hrs. 50 Mins.	
	Rearwin				
	Moth Minor		Total :	202 Hrs. 50 Mins.	
	P40				
	F4U				
	Argus				
	Proctor				
	Auster				
	Tempest				
	Spitfire				
	Youngman-Baynes				
	Seafire				
	Vampire				
	Firefly				
	Sea Fury				
	F. Junior				
	Storch				
	Athena				
	Vega Gull				
	Hudson				
	Anson				
	Wellington				
	Oxford				
	Bombay				
	D.H.86				
	Dakota				
	Mosquito				
	Liberator				
	Ventura				
	Dominie				
	Lodestar				
	Lancaster				
	Valetta				
	Devon				
	Viking				
	Lincoln				

GRAND TOTAL [Cols. (1) to (10)].

_____ Hrs. _____ Mins.

TOTALS CARRIED FORWARD

RECORD OF SERVICE.

UNIT.	DATES.		UNIT.	DATES.	
	FROM	TO		FROM	TO
G.T.S. Rongotai Wellington.	Sep 20. 1939	Oct. 18. 1939	Path Finder Force H.Q. Wyton.	Aug. 30. 1942	Feb. 10. 19
E.F.T.S. Taieri Dunedin	Oct. 20. 1939	Dec. 18. 1939	Staff College, Palmerston North	May. 24. 1943	Sep. 4. 19
I.F.T.S. Wigram Christchurch	Dec. 19. 1939	Feb. 10. 1940	Nº 1 (Islands) Group H.Q. Espiritu Santo	Sep. 14. 1943	Jan. 6. 19
A.F.T.S. Wigram Christchurch	Feb. 11. 1940	Mar. 6. 1940	Nº 1 (Islands) Group H.Q. Guadalcanal	Jan. 7. 1944	Apr. 15. 19
Nº 1 R.A.F. Depot Uxbridge	Jun 8. 1940	Jun 17. 1940	C.F.S. Tauranga	May 1. 1944	May 15. 19
Nº 4 (C) Ferry Pilots Pool, Kemble	Jun 17. 1940	Jun 30. 1940	A.T.S. Woodbourne	May 16. 1944	May 28. 19
Nº 12 O.T.U. Benson	Jun 30. 1940	Dec. 6. 1940	Nº 2 O.T.U. Ohakea	May 30. 1944	July 8. 19
Nº 11 O.T.U. Bassingbourn	Dec. 7. 1940	Jan 24. 1941	Nº 17 Squadron, Ardmore	July 9. 1944	Aug. 4. 19
Nº 75 (N.Z.) Sqdn. Feltwell	Jan. 25. 1941	Aug 12. 1941	Nº 17 Squadron, Espiritu Santo	Aug. 8. 1944	Aug 30. 19
Nº 3 B.A.T.F. Mildenhall (att.)	Mar. 17. 1941	Mar. 23. 1941	Nº 17 Squadron, Guadalcanal	Aug. 31. 1944	Sep. 20. 19
Nº 15 O.T.U. Harwell	Aug 13. 1941	Aug 28. 1941	Nº 17 Squadron, Bougainville	Sep. 21. 1944	Nov. 1. 19
R.A.F. Gibraltar	Aug 29. 1941	Aug 30. 1941	Nº 1 O.A.T.S. Cranwell	Jan. 3. 1945	Jan. 24. 19
Nº 38 Sqdn. Luqa, Malta.	Aug 31. 1941	Oct. 25. 1941	P.N.T.U. Warboys	Jan. 31. 1945	Feb. 21. 19
Nº 38 Sqdn. Shallufa, Egypt.	Oct. 26. 1941	Dec. 11. 1941	Nº 635 Sqdn. Downham Market	Feb. 22. 1945	Sep. 3. 19
Nº 216 Sqdn. Khanka, Egypt.	Dec. 11. 1941	Apr. 75. 1942	Nº 35 Sqdn., Graveley	Sep. 4. 1945	Jan. 8. 19
U.S. Military Mission, Iraq. (att.)	Jan. 21. 1942	Jan. 29. 1942	Nº 5 P.D.C., Blackpool	Jan. 2. 1946	Jan. 14. 19
R.A.F. Station, Habbaniya, Iraq. (att)	Jan. 30. 1942	Feb. 13. 1942	Nº 2 O.A.T.S., Amman	Feb. 5. 1946	Sep. 21. 19
R.A.F. Transit Camp, Almaza	Apr. 25. 1942	Apr. 29. 1942	Nº 2 (M.E.) School of Admin, Amman	Sep. 22. 1946	Jul. 20. 19
R.A.F. Transit Camp, Apapa.	May 1. 1942	May 4. 1942	A.H.Q. Iraq Comm. Flt., Habb.	Jul. 22. 1947	Feb. 4. 1
R.A.F. Station, Takoradi	May 4. 1942	May 6. 1942	E.T.P.S., Farnborough.	Mar. 1. 1948	Dec. 17. 1
R.A.F. Transit Camp, Kissy	May 6. 1942	May 14. 1942	M.O.S. (Supy), Dept. 9 (b). (Leave)	Dec. 18. 1948	Jun. 7. 1
R.A.F. Transit Camp, Waterloo	May 14. 1942	Jun. 3. 1942	E.F.D., R.A.E., Farnborough.	Jun. 8. 1949	Dec. 28. 1
Nº 75 (N.Z.) Sqdn. Feltwell	Jul. 5. 1942	Aug 15. 1942	H.C., G.I.S., Detling	Jul. 1. 1951	Jul. 7. 1
Nº 75 (N.Z.) Sqdn. Mildenhall	Aug 15. 1942	Aug 29. 1942	H.Q., Nº 1 Group, Bawtry	Dec. 29. 1951	Jul. 5. 19

Flight Lieutenant Raymond and Sergeant Bushell both displayed the greatest courage and determination throughout. (Sergeant Bushell was awarded the Distinguished Flying Medal for his conduct during this operation).'[21]

Pilot Officer Charles Stewart, RAF (the piper), was flying Spitfires with No. 485 New Zealand Squadron when they were attacked by enemy fighters at 23,000 feet. Stewart's aircraft was lost without trace over the Straits of Dover on 11 July 1941. His body was never recovered. He was aged twenty-four and was on his 138th operation as a fighter pilot. Previously he had had a rather exciting career. On 4 August 1940, while flying with No. 54 Squadron, RAF, he was slightly injured when he was shot down by friendly anti-aircraft fire. He baled out and was picked up by air-sea rescue some sixty minutes later. He next flew with No. 222 Squadron, RAF, when on 1 October 1940 he crashed while on night patrol but was uninjured. Then on 15 November he came down while on a training flight, again being unhurt. On 12 March 1941, he collided with another aircraft of No. 485 Squadron while on operation, once more lucky to escape injury.[22]

Pilot Officer Harry Wright Morgan, RAF, was on his ninth operation when his Whitley bomber of No. 78 Squadron, RAF, was shot down over the Netherlands by a night fighter on the night of 1–2 October 1940. All five crew perished and are buried at Hummelo near Arnhem. A sheep farmer from Ashburton, he was twenty-seven years old.[23]

Pilot Officer Winton Shann, RAF, while serving in No. 107 Squadron, RAF, flying Blenheims, was shot down and killed on a raid on Calais on the night of 24–25 October 1940. It was his sixth operation. Along with other members of his crew he is buried at Guemps. He was twenty-three.[24]

Pilot Officer Jack Cave, RAF, from Whakatane, was on his seventeenth operation, a patrol over Belgium and Holland, when his Blenheim bomber crashed in poor visibility near Coleby in Lincolnshire. He was aged twenty-one. All three of the crew are buried at Waddington. His brother, Flight Lieutenant Verner Cave, RNZAF, was killed on 31 March 1945 while flying with No. 37 Squadron, RAF, on an operation over Yugoslavia. According to his younger brother, Gary, this was to be Vern's last operation before returning home to New Zealand.[25]

Charles de Vic Halkett, RAF, died on 9 September 1940 while flying a Blenheim bomber of No. 107 Squadron, RAF, on a raid over France. It is believed his aircraft was shot down after bombing the target. All three crew members are buried at Wambercourt in France. Charles was twenty-four.[26]

Squadron Leader Don MacKenzie, RAF, DFC, died on 12 June 1943 while flying a Lancaster bomber over Germany with No. 467 Squadron, RAAF. He had previously flown twenty-three ops as a Hurricane fighter pilot with No. 56 Squadron, RAF. Don served for a short time as a test pilot at Hucknall, where he flew various types of aircraft including jet propulsion testing. He was on his thirtieth operation with No. 467 Squadron and is buried in the Rheinburg war cemetery. He was twenty-two. Don MacKenzie's brother Angus, a bomber pilot, was killed on 9 June 1942 while on a bombing raid over Germany.[27]

Squadron Leader Alan Beresford Smith from Alfredton near Masterton was on a delivery flight from the UK to the Middle East. When flying from Gibraltar to Malta the aircraft was shot down by a Vichy French fighter off Sidi Ahmed, Tunisia, on 29 November 1940. One of the crew of three was killed and the others were interned in Tunisia and, later, Laghouat in southern Algeria. Beresford Smith arrived back in the UK around 13 November 1942. It appears he was on instructional and/or air-sea rescue duties for the rest of the war. He died in 1972.

Squadron Leader William Gasquoine, RAF, received the King's Commendation for Brave Conduct on 1 January 1943. The letter of commendation from the Secretary of State for Air, Sir Archibald Sinclair, stated that Sir Archibald was charged to record His Majesty's high appreciation of the service rendered. In December 2001 Squadron Leader Gasquoine recalled that one day in March or April 1942, while serving at RAF Cleave on the Cornwall coast, he was standing near the cliff edge watching Henley aircraft tow a banner for a live anti-aircraft shoot. The aircraft was hit by ground fire and crashed into the sea some 200 yards offshore. He saw the pilot and winchman manage to get out of the aircraft but the pilot was not a very good swimmer. Squadron Leader Gasquoine then slid down the cliff face, clambered over the rocks, swam out to the pilot and towed him back to the rocks where they were met by the crash fire crew who then took over.[28]

Wing Commander Nelson Mansfield, RAF, DFC. Nelson Mansfield came from Christchurch. After his arrival in the UK in June 1940, he completed operational training on Blenheims and later Wellington bombers. On 29 June 1940 he was posted to No. 218 Squadron flying Blenheims. From August 1941 until July 1942 he was an instructor with No. 23 OTU. He then joined No. 97 Squadron and soon after No. 156 Squadron, both squadrons flying Lancasters. Nelson was killed on 14 January 1944 while carrying out a raid on the German city of Brunswick. He was thirty-one. A total of thirty-eight bombers were lost on this particular raid. All seven crew members are buried in the Bergen-op-Zoom war cemetery in Holland. Sixty-three years later the Dutch authorities erected a monument on the site of the crash to commemorate the bravery of the Lancaster crew.

Wing Commander Mansfield, Citation for Distinguished Flying Cross

'This officer has undertaken a large number of sorties during which many well defended and far distant targets have been attacked with success. His efforts have been featured by outstanding determination while on more than one occasion his great skill has been responsible for the safe return of his aircraft in the face of difficulties. Squadron Leader Mansfield has at all times displayed great devotion to duty.'

Squadron Leader Robert Spurdle, DFC and Bar, MID. Bob Spurdle served in the RAF from July 1940 until July 1945. He was on loan to the RNZAF from December 1942 until November 1943. After the war he rejoined the RNZAF until April 1946. He was a Second World War fighter ace, having been credited with the destruction of ten enemy aircraft (eight German, two Japanese), two and a half probables, and at least nine damaged, while serving with Nos 74 and 91 Squadrons in England, No. 16 Squadron in the Solomons and No. 80 Squadron in Europe. During the Battle of Britain, he flew with No. 74 Squadron. He was a member of the 'Caterpillar Club', having baled out over England on 22 October 1940. He completed five tours of duty involving 564 fighter sorties. He also served with the Merchant Ship Fighter Unit, in which Hurricanes were catapulted from specially fitted merchant ships to give convoy protection against German reconnaissance bombers. Once launched the pilot had the option of flying to the nearest coast, ditching into the sea or baling out.

After a year with the RNZAF in New Zealand and the Pacific in 1943, Robert returned to the UK where he served briefly with No. 130 Squadron, RAF (Spitfires). He then became commanding officer (CO) of No. 80 Squadron (July 1944–January 1945), and afterwards was a ground/air controller for the direction of 'cab-rank' fighter/ground-attack aircraft in direct support of the British Army's crossing of the Rhine. He was attached to the 6th Airborne Division and on 24 March 1945 he took part in the airborne assault on the Rhine defences, carrying out his 565th sortie in a Horsa glider containing his three operational teams and mobile ground radio equipment, etc. He recorded his wartime experiences in his book *Blue Arena*. Bob died in Whitianga in 1994.

Squadron Leader R. Spurdle, Citation for Distinguished Flying Cross

'This Officer is a keen and determined pilot. He has destroyed five, possibly destroyed four and damaged several more enemy aircraft. His devotion to duty has set a praiseworthy example.'

Citation for Bar to DFC

'26 January 1945: Since the award of the DFC this officer has taken part in a large number of operational sorties. He has destroyed at least four enemy aircraft and damaged a further six. Squadron Leader Spurdle has served on both the Pacific and Western Fronts. An outstanding and courageous leader, he has, throughout, displayed a fine fighting spirit and great determination.'

Citation Mention in Despatches

'For distinguished service with the 6th Airborne Division as ground/air controller.'[29]

Squadron Leader Rex Daniell, RAF, DFC, AFC, Flying Cross (Neth.). Rex Daniell had a remarkable war career spanning three theatres: Europe, Middle East and India. On arrival in the UK in June 1940, he first went to RAF Uxbridge and then to RAF Kemble for navigation training. He was then transferred to the Operational Training Unit at RAF Bicester, where the chief flying instructor was New Zealander Sam Elworthy. Lord Elworthy, as he was later known, attained the rank of Marshal of the Royal Air Force, the highest possible RAF rank and the only New Zealander ever to achieve this distinction.

After completing his OTU training, Rex was posted first to No. 82 Blenheim Squadron, where he undertook his first operation – a daylight raid on the strategically important Dortmund–Ems canal in Germany. Due to there being no cloud cover over the target area the raid was abandoned. He spent four weeks training with paratroopers who were heading to capture aquaducts in Italy. After several ops flying Blenheims, Rex, along with his crew, volunteered to serve on the same aircraft in the Middle East. After much delay he finally found himself ferrying a Bristol Bombay transport aircraft to the Middle East via Gibraltar and supposedly Malta. In the end they proceeded to Egypt via Gibraltar and Tobruk and ultimately to Heliopolis, Cairo, where he joined No. 216 Squadron but was almost immediately transferred to Khartoum to the newly formed No. 117 Squadron.

Then followed a long period ferrying aircraft, supplies and personnel to and from Takoradi in West Africa and throughout the Middle East, including Iran and Malta. Following the defeat of the German Afrika Korps in Tunisia in May 1943, he was based in Tripoli where he participated in delivering supplies, mainly to Malta, with evacuees on return flights. In September 1943, No. 117 Squadron moved to Catania in Sicily where they continued army support ops, which included the US Army landing at Salerno.

In November 1943, the squadron moved to Rawalpindi, then in north-west British India (now Pakistan). The 'Pindi' operations saw many weeks of training some 6,000 Gurkha and Sikh paratroopers for action in Burma. Until March 1944 the squadron was involved in supply operations to the 14th Army facing the Japanese in Arakan and Burma. March 1944 saw Rex with his crew posted back to England and to No. 48 Squadron, which squadron was focused on training paratroopers in Horsa gliders (towing) in preparation for the coming invasion of Europe. Rex wrote: 'D-Day, 6 June 1944, arrived and I led 25 Tugs and gliders joining forces with hundreds of other combinations heading for Normandy. The escorting fighters were most reassuring and made us feel proud of the enormous military operation that was unfolding. As we approached the coast we dropped down to our "dropping" height of 2,500 feet and marvelled at the sight of the British and Canadian forces battling it out on the beaches.'[30]

These paratroopers were in support of the 6th Airborne Division that was the first to land in France shortly after midnight on D-Day. The paratroopers' objective that night was to capture the now-famous Pegasus Bridge over the River Orne, the attainment of which was vital to the success of the Allied campaign. Displaying incredible courage, the gliders landed close to the bridge and took the German defenders completely by surprise. They succeeded in securing the bridge and, against all odds, managed to repulse the German counter-attack until they were relieved by the glider-borne paratroopers (with jeeps and light artillery) towed in by Rex's squadron.

Following D-Day, the squadron made regular trips to Normandy to evacuate the wounded. In late July they carried out a mass take-off of eighteen Dakotas within sixty seconds, which had become a 'speciality' of Rex's. The head of the RAF, Marshal of the Royal Air Force, Lord Trenchard, who was visiting the station and to whom Rex was later introduced, was suitably impressed.

The next major operation was towing Horsa gliders and paratroopers to the ill-fated Arnhem landing in Holland. Rex was later awarded the Netherlands Flying Cross for this action. He also participated in flying paratroopers for the crossing of the River Rhine, another major and successful operation. During the latter part of the war, in 1945, he was busily engaged with flying supplies and evacuating wounded servicemen and

POWs from German camps. His last flight with the RAF took place on 27 July 1945, after which he returned to New Zealand. In July 1945, His Majesty King George VI invested Rex with the DFC and the AFC.

After the war Rex served briefly with the then National Airways but resigned in 1960. Along with co-founder Robert Anderson, he established South Pacific Airlines of New Zealand (SPANZ), the first commercial airline of its type in post-war New Zealand.[31] SPANZ provided a much-needed service to – at that point – neglected provincial towns such as Alexandra, Hokitika, Taupo and so on. For the first time, the monopoly of the state-owned NAC was challenged. SPANZ ceased operating in 1966 and in 1967 Rex joined Ansett Airline in Melbourne. He retired in 1983 and died in Maroochydore, Queensland, in October 2010, a few days short of his 90th birthday.[32]

Squadron Leader R. Daniell, Citation for Distinguished Flying Cross (1945)

'Acting Squadron Leader Daniell is a highly efficient flight commander, whose great keenness for air operations, coupled with fine qualities of courage and resolution, has set a worthy example. He has participated in a very large number of sorties, including Arnhem and the Rhine crossing airborne operations. The skill with which he executed his allotted task in these operations was an important factor in the success achieved.'

Citation for Air Force Cross (1944)

'This officer has been employed as a pilot on transport work in the Middle East command. During the Western Desert and North African campaigns he has completed numerous flights, transporting vital supplies to the battle area and evacuating casualties. By his keenness and devotion to duty he has been an excellent and inspiring example to his Flight.'

Citation for Netherlands Flying Cross (1945)

'As Flight Commander, Squadron Leader Daniell towed a glider aircraft on the first day of the airborne invasion of Holland. Later, he was engaged in dropping supplies in the Arnhem area. Despite intense enemy opposition, Squadron Leader Daniell displayed high courage and fortitude and set an excellent example.'[33]

PART 3:
MAKING OF THE LEGEND, 1940–41

YEAR: 1941		AIRCRAFT.		PILOT, OR 1ST PILOT.	2ND PILOT, PUPIL, OR PASSENGER.	DUTY (INCLUDING RESULTS AND REMARKS).
MONTH.	DATE.	Type.	No.			
—	—	—	—	—	—	TOTALS BROUGHT FORWARD
June	12	V.Wellington	T2747	Self P/O.Wilson	Sgt. McSherry Sgt. Welby Sgt. Broad Sgt. Palmer	War ops. to Hamm. Load:(6) S.B. (3) 500 (1) 250 (18)
June	16	V.Wellington	T2747	Self	Sgt. McSherry Sgt. Welby Sgt. Hume Sgt. Palmer	N.F.T.
June	16	V.Wellington	T2747	Self P/O.Williams	Sgt. McSherry Sgt. Welby Sgt. Hume Sgt. Palmer Sgt. McSherry	War ops. Dusseldorf. Acc. Heavy flak. Load:(6) S.B.C. (3) 500 (1) 250 (19)
June	18	V.Wellington	T2747	Self		N.F.T. & Blind Approach.
June	18	V.Wellington	T2747	Self	F/Sgt. McLauchlin Sgt. McSherry Sgt. Welby Sgt. Hume Sgt. Palmer	Attack on Scharnhorst at Brest. Lost on way home & came through Balloon barrages. Load: (7) 500 (1) 250 (20)
June	20	V.Wellington	W5621	Self	Sgt. McSherry Sgt. Welby Sgt. Hume Sgt. Palmer Sgt. McSherry	Formation flying & fighter co-operation at Colley Weston (3 seperate flights)
June	21	V.Wellington	T2747	Self	Sgt. Welby Sgt. Hume Sgt. Palmer Sgt. McSherry	N.F.T.
June	21	V.Wellington	T2747	Self Sgt Matetich	Sgt. Welby Sgt. Hume Sgt. Palmer	Blitz on Köln. Load:(6) S.B.C. (3) 500 (1) 250. Intense, acc. heavy flak. (21) Hit by flak. Bust geodetic & petrol pump
June	23	V.Wellington	T2747	Self P/O.Wilson	Sgt. McSherry Sgt. Welby Sgt. Palmer	N.F.T.
June	24	V.Wellington	T2747	Self P/O. Wilson	Sgt. McSherry Sgt. Welby Sgt. Hume Sgt. Palmer	War ops. Kiel. Load:(6) 500. Forced to jettison when held in searchlights over target. Intense & acc. heavy & light flak. (22)
					GRAND TOTAL [Cols. (1) to (10)]. 555 Hrs. 05 Mins	TOTALS CARRIED FORWARD

Chapter 6

RAF Bomber Command – Part 1
The Structure and Commander

This chapter gives a general overview of the environment into which Artie was about to enter. The structure of RAF Bomber Command in 1940, the bombing strategy and the controversy that surrounded it, is summarily outlined. Also included is a brief picture of the resolute man who commanded Bomber Command for most of the war and his admiration for the achievements and courage of the men who flew the bombers.

In 1940 Bomber Command was made up of five groups, each commanded by an air vice-marshal. No. 1 Group was sent to France and became part of the Advanced Air Striking Force. The number of groups was later increased to seven with the addition of No. 6 Group (RCAF) and No. 8 Group, the elite Pathfinder Force.[34] The number of squadrons in each group differed, but in 1940 they were usually made up of six squadrons. By 1945, when Bomber Command was at its powerful peak, the total in each group had greatly increased. The types of aircraft flown by each varied from light, medium to heavy bombers such as the Wellington. Later the heavy Stirling, Halifax and Lancaster bombers were introduced.

A bomber station could include several squadrons and was normally commanded by a group captain. A wing commander was in control of each squadron while a squadron leader would be in charge of each of the two or three flights, which usually made up a squadron.

At the outbreak of war in 1939 Britain had about 170 military airfields. By the end of the war in 1945 there were 670, of which 135 were operated by Bomber Command.[35] Pre-war RAF stations like Feltwell, Mepal and Mildenhall, where No. 75 Squadron was stationed, were comparatively comfortable, but the new ones could be anything but. The sleeping and

mess quarters were very often cold, uninviting Nissen huts built of corrugated iron. Other facilities could be equally primitive and 'temporary'.
Initially, many of the runways were just grass strips.

All RAF aircrew were volunteers. More than any other British service, the
RAF represented the British Empire at war. The Commander-in-Chief,
from February 1942, Air Marshal Sir Arthur Harris, was an Englishman
who had spent his youth in Rhodesia and throughout the war English-
men, Canadians, New Zealanders and Australians commanded the force's
groups.

According to Patrick Bishop's *Bomber Boys – Fighting Back 1940–1945*,
a total of 130,000 men, almost 40 per cent of airmen in the RAF, were from
the Dominions. One in four Bomber Command aircrews were from overseas and 15,661 lost their lives, including 9,881 Canadians and 1,850 New
Zealanders. New Zealand suffered disproportionately: of the 6,000 New
Zealanders who served in Bomber Command, nearly one in three perished.

The intermingling of men from the Dominions went right down to the
level of individual bomber crews, there being at least two nationalities
in every crew. Later in the war the Australian government insisted that
'their' squadrons should be staffed with Australians only, a move which
some Australian aircrew felt was not in the best interests of the squadrons
concerned. Overall, Australians and New Zealanders provided about one
in ten of bomber crews. According to author Martin Middlebrook,
both New Zealanders and Australians made particularly reliable bomber
pilots and many went on from the main force squadrons to distinguish
themselves in the Pathfinder Force.[36]

Patrick Bishop commented that those who served in Bomber Command
'were rich, middling and poor, and they came from every corner of Britain
and the Empire. They were the best of their generation and they were
heading for one of the worst tasks of the war.'

While not on duty, the 'colonial' aircrews paid little heed to rank.[37]
Although there were separate mess facilities for officers and non-
commissioned personnel, for the most part Empire aircrew went on leave
together, drank together and played together irrespective of rank. This
easy-going approach was not the case with most RAF personnel, where
the class and rank divisions were strictly maintained even when not on

duty.

A 'tour' for bomber crews normally comprised thirty operations. Aircrew were then assigned to 'rest' usually as instructors at an Operational Training Unit. Second tours were generally shorter, being twenty to twenty-five ops, depending on how the individual was able to bear the strain. As the war advanced second and third tours were comparatively common. This stage, however, coincided with the strengthening of the German defences and the progressive effectiveness of their night-fighter skills. As a consequence aircraft losses were at their peak during 1942 and 1943. A bomber crew had about a 35 per cent chance of surviving their first tour. It was during this period that Artie Ashworth gained legendary status.

Bomber Command's contribution to the defeat of Germany was significant, despite the debate about its overall effectiveness and the controversy about its tactics. It was the only way that Britain could strike at Germany and military targets in the occupied territories during the early part of the war. It was also important in Britain's relations with Russia after that country was invaded by the Germans. Hard pressed as they were, the Russians demanded the Allies should open a second front in the West so as to divert German forces from the Eastern Front. In his exchanges with the Russian leader Joseph Stalin, Britain's Prime Minister, Winston Churchill, was able to argue that the RAF bombing campaign was indeed a 'second front'.

In the early stages, the bombing campaign had comparatively little effect on German war production. As the intensity and accuracy of the bombing steadily increased, however, the Germans were forced to divert over 1 million men and 55,000 artillery guns to anti-aircraft defence within Germany. Professor Richard Overy, who made a study of the bombing campaign, made the point that it was not so much a question of what the bombing did to Germany but what Germany would have achieved had there been no bombing or had it been less effective. Professor Overy considered that Bomber Command made a larger contribution to victory in Europe than any other element of Britain's armed services.

Air officer commanding, RAF Bomber Command, Air Marshal Sir Arthur

'Bomber' Harris, determined that the way to shorten the war was to bomb German cities into wastelands. This, he believed, would break the morale of the German people, thereby undermining the effectiveness of their formidable war machine. Others considered that the priority should be military targets like industrial plants, aircraft factories, railway marshalling yards, submarine bases, strategic communication centres, the Romanian oilfields – which supplied the bulk of the fuel for the German armed services – and so on. In the end, until 1944 when operations were focused on preparing for the great D-Day invasion of Europe, Harris's view largely prevailed, but the controversy continues to this day.

The Harris strategy saw enormous devastation in many German cities and heavy loss of civilian lives. Cities such as Hamburg, Essen and later Dresden, were largely reduced to little more than rubble.

Commonly known as 'Bomber' Harris by the press, and often within the RAF as 'Butch' Harris, he was Air Officer Commanding-in-Chief (AOC-in-C) of RAF Bomber Command (from early 1943 holding the rank of Air Chief Marshal) from February 1942 until the end of the war in 1945. In 1942 the Cabinet agreed to the 'area bombing' of German cities. Harris was tasked with implementing Churchill's policy and supported the development of tactics and technology to perform the task more effectively. Harris assisted British Chief-of Air Staff, Marshal of the Royal Air Force, Charles Portal, in carrying out the United Kingdom's most devastating attacks against the German infrastructure.

Harris's preference for area bombing over precision targeting in the last year of the war remains controversial, partly because by this time many senior Allied air commanders thought it less effective and partly for the large number of civilian casualties and destruction this strategy caused in continental Europe. The Butt Report[38] correctly noted that in 1941, 'of those aircraft recorded as attacking their target, only one in three got within five miles'. By 1944, however, many technical and training improvements, not the least being H2S radar technology and the Pathfinder Force, combined to improve the effectiveness of the bombing campaign.

Harris gave high praise to the courage of those who flew the bombers during the war:

There are no words with which I can do justice to the aircrew who fought under my command. There is no parallel in warfare to such courage and determination in the face of danger over so prolonged a period: of danger which at times was so great that scarcely one man in three could expect to survive his tour of 30 operations.

It was a clear and highly conscious courage, by which the risk was taken with calm forethought, for the aircrew were all highly skilled men, much above the average in education, who had to understand every aspect and detail of their task. It was, further-more, the courage of the small hours, of men virtually alone, for at his battle station the airman was virtually alone. It was the courage of men with long drawn apprehensions of daily 'going over the top'. They were without exception volunteers, for no man was trained for aircrew with the RAF who did not volunteer. Such devotion must never be forgotten. It is unforgettable by anyone whose con-tacts gave them knowledge and understanding of what these young men experienced and faced.[39]

At the end of the war Harris attempted to have a special medal issued to all who had served in Bomber Command during the hostilities.[40] He fought a hard battle with the British authorities responsible for such matters, but in the end was unsuccessful. He was very bitter about this decision and in response refused to accept any honours offered to him. Following his retirement to South Africa, however, he was persuaded by Churchill to accept a baronetcy. He did succeed, though, in having a special emblem awarded to those aircrew who completed a tour of Pathfinder duty. The Pathfinder badge is proudly worn by all those to whom it was awarded. The badge was among Artie's most precious possessions.

Chapter 7

RAF Bomber Command – Part 2

Flying into Hell

Bomber Command paid a heavy price in men's lives. The casualty rates were the highest among Britain's armed forces. According to Max Lambert's *Night After Night*, of the 125,000 who served in Bomber Command almost 60 per cent – 75,000 – were aircrew casualties. Their average age was twenty-two. Around 10,000 became prisoners of war and 4,000 returned wounded from raids. Author Mel Rolfe described bombing sorties as 'Looking into Hell'.[41] Another unnamed observer suggested that the life expectancy of Bomber Command aircrew was probably less than that of an infantry subaltern[42] on the Western Front in the First World War. Max Lambert considered each operation was akin to 'going over the top' in the First World War.[43] Casualty rates reached appalling levels at times; in some squadrons they were so bad that hardly anyone finished a tour. In many cases those who did were mental wrecks and no longer fit for active service, condemned all too often to a life of alcohol addiction, nightmares and distress.

The impact of these losses was widely felt among the respective communities. Behind every casualty were grieving families – mothers, fathers, brothers, wives, children and girlfriends – given the news that no one wished to hear. My own family experienced the grief. The knock on the door to find the postmaster bearing the telegram advising that my fighter pilot brother was missing, believed killed, came as a terrible shock. This was followed by the official condolence letter from the Minister of Defence on behalf of the government. Later, the letter of sympathy from the unit's commanding officer arrived with the unwelcome news that there was no possibility of my brother having survived. Still later, the message of sympathy and thanks for a life so nobly given from His Majesty the King. All very correct and sympathetic but nothing could compensate for the loss. Artie learned the fate of his brother five days after Corran was reported missing, believed killed, via a telegram from RNZAF Headquarters in London. He was at that time (August 1944) serving with No. 17F RNZAF Fighter Squadron in the Pacific. While he never really talked about it, those near to him knew that he mourned the loss of his close friend and brother for the rest of his life.

For the families of those reported 'missing in action', the anxiety could extend over many months. Unless finally reported as being a prisoner of war, 'missing in action' casualties were later deemed as 'presumed killed', which was the case with my brother Corran. His body was never recovered from the River Seine in Normandy into which his fighter plunged in flames.

As Max Lambert wrote, it took great courage to climb into fuel-and bomb-laden aircraft night after night. He vividly described the terror of each operation:

> Every moment in the air they were at risk of sudden and violent death; of an unseen enemy night fighter unleashing a torrent of shell into their aircraft; of flak spitting up from radar-controlled gun batteries on the ground to smash great holes in the wings and fuselage or knock out engines; of collision with other bombers flying overhead; of engine failure that could start a fire. They were in danger from the instant they took off coaxing a fully laden aircraft into the air until they touched down at base at the end of the homeward journey. Enemy intruders lurking over England at night hunting unwary prey meant unflagging vigilance was necessary from the moment of take-off to the moment of landing. When flames licked at wings or fuselage an aircraft could explode in an instant with an enormous blast of fire that left nothing but torn bodies and twisted wreckage plunging to earth.

Bomber crews faced the possibility of particularly violent, sometimes gruesome, and sudden ends. Some fatally damaged aircraft continued

Wing Commander A. (Artie) Ashworth RAF, DSO, DFC and Bar, AFC and Bar, MID, Pathfinder.
(*Ashworth Family*)

A family picnic at Rongomai, c 1923. Corran would be nearly two and Arthur nearly four. From left: Iris, Phyllis, Mum, Edna, Dad, Arthur with Corran in front. (*Ashworth Family*)

Family group at Queenstown c1928-29. From left: Arthur (sitting on the mudguard) aged 8-9, Corran in front aged about 7-8, Mother, baby Donald aged 2-3, Edna and Iris in the front with the sunhats, Phyllis standing behind, with possibly cousin Marjory Ashworth at the back to the left of Phyllis. The adult at the back is Aunt Mary, wife of Archibald Ashworth standing on the far right. Aunt Margaret Thomas, sister of my father, is sitting. (*Ashworth Family*)

Falklands 1927: From left: Iris, Artie, Corran, Edna. Mother at back with baby Donald. (*Ashworth Family*)

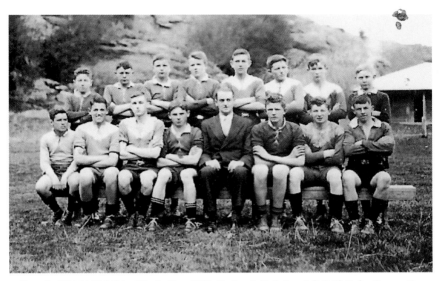

Alexandra District High School Rugby Team 1936 – Roxburgh. Back: from left: Keith Taylor-Cannon, Guy Mooney, Kevin Holden, Peter Campbell, Jack Lunn, Peter Weaver, Dan Butler, Lex Brown. Front: Corran Ashworth, Brian Gardner, John Nightingale, Jack Lindup, Rudolf McLay (Coach & Head Teacher), Ron Smith, Ivan McPherson, Arthur Ashworth. (*Lex Brown*)

The brothers in Wellington 1938. (*Ashworth Family*)

Acting Pilot Officer Artie Ashworth RNZAF Taieri 1939. (*Ashworth Family*)

Right: Acting Pilot Officer Artie Ashworth RNZAF Taieri 1939. (*Ashworth Family*)

Pupil Officers No. 1 Elementary Flying Training School RNZAF Station Taieri 1939. Back Row from left: W. S. Shann, A. V. Fisher, D. C. MacKenzie, C. E. Langdon. O. P. Davies, R. W. Filmer, N.R. Mansfield, C. de V. Halket. Middle Row: J.Watters, A.J.W Parker, C. Raymond, R. D. Daniell, H. Wright Morgan, J. M, Cave, A. B. Smith, J.V.M Kean. Front Row: W.H. Phelan, E.B. Topp, D. Rockel, A. Ashworth, L.E.F Parry, C. Stewart, R.L Spurdle. (*Ashworth Family*)

In front of Tiger Moth with fellow trainee Acting-Pupil Officers, Taieri 1939. From Left: Don Mackenzie, Eddie Topp, unknown, Artie, Bob Spurdle. (A. *Ashworth*)

Right: 'Passing out' festivities. Artie second from left. Jack Cave front second from left. Charlie Stewart the piper. (*Ashworth Family*)

Below: Official 1940 portrait. (A. *Ashworth*)

With girlfriend Joan, Wellington, April 1940. (A. *Ashworth*)

Wedding of Sgt Jimmy Blundell, Southport 3 May, 1941. Air crew from left: Sgt Abbott, P/O Ron Simich, Sgt Jimmy Blundell, Sgt Hardy, P/O Artie Ashworth. (A. *Ashworth*)

The crew Artie 'inherited' from Sqdn Ldr Southwell for his first Op as first pilot. From left: Sgt Ted McSherry RNZAF, P/O A. Ashworth, P/O Wilson , Sgt Broad. (A. *Ashworth*)

Artie, far right, with two crew members standing next to Wellington R1458. On 5 and 7 March 1941 Artie flew night tests in this Wellington and later flew as second pilot to Ron Simich in this aircraft for attacks on Bremen and Berlin. (A. *Ashworth*)

Above: Somewhere in the Western Desert 1941. Artie far right. (A. *Ashworth*)
Below left: Squadron Leader Artie Ashworth, Alexandra. Below right: Queenstown 1943. (A. *Ashworth*)

Artie, last on right, with pilots of his section. Bougainville 1944. (A. *Ashworth*)

Panorama of RNZAF Camp Guadalcanal 1943. (A. *Ashworth*)

RNZAF 20 Squadron Corsairs arriving at Guadalcanal from Espiritu Santos 1944. (A. *Ashworth*)

The 'Odds & Sods' Lancaster Crew 635 Squadron 1945. Back From Left: F/O D.J. Parry; F/Lt A.G. Jarry; F/O J.K. Calton; Artie; F/Lt H.L. Morgan; F/Sgt W. Snowden; Front: F/Sgt J. Hailey; Flt Sgt G. Sindle. (A. *Ashworth*)

Photo taken from Artie's Lancaster of attack on
Mathias Stinnese oil plant. (A. *Ashworth*)

Bombs falling from Artie's aircraft on
Berchtesgaden. (A. *Ashworth*)

Above left: Artie at Downham Market at the end of
the war. (*Ashworth Family*)

Above: Pathfinder, Squadron Leader A. 'Artie'
Ashworth DSO, DFC and Bar, AFC and Bar, MID.
The photo from Artie's collection (c1945) was used
by Thorne Lancaster at War. Thorne described
Artie as a 'New Zealand born leading member of
No. 635 Squadron'. (*Ashworth Family*)

Left: The Distinguished RAF Officer in Tropical
Uniform 1946. (*Ashworth Family*)

Test pilots at Farnborough 1948. Artie in the front row 7th from the left. (*A. Ashworth*)

Above: Wedding Day 22 December, 1950.
(*A. Ashworth*)

Right inset: Outside Buckingham Palace before
being invested with the AFC by His Majesty King
George VI c1952. (*A. Ashworth*)

Squadron Leader Ashworth about to board his Canberra. (*A. Ashworth*)

Above left: The CO's moustache was a big attraction for this Canadian Air Force lady. (*A. Ashworth*)
Above right: Artie is introduced to the Mayor of Kingston by the Governor, Sir Hugh Foote. (*A. Ashworth*)

Above: B Squadron with Commanding Officer Artie seated in the middle of the front row. Russ Law is seated third from the left in the front row. (*A. Ashworth*)

Above: Artie with nephew Stanley Koberstein, Stonehenge, c1960. (*A. Ashworth*)

Right: Artie Ashworth's ribbons and Pathfinder badge. (*Ashworth Family*)

Right: The Distinguished Poppy Seller.
(*A. Ashworth*)

The mischievous Artie Ashworth. (*A. Ashworth*)

A Legend in his Time. Wing Commander Artie Ashworth RAF, DSO, DFC and Bar, AFC and Bar, MID, Pathfinder. (*A. Ashworth*)

to fly more or less normally for a time, allowing crews to take to their parachutes. Some pilots even crash-landed successfully. But it wasn't usually like that. A damaged plane spinning earthwards created centrifugal force that pinned the crew down, making it almost impossible for them to move, to grab a parachute, or to reach an escape hatch. A steep, straight, high-speed dive had the same effect. Even getting out of a crippled plane flying more or less level was tricky. Bulky flying suits hindered the movements of crew fighting their way in the dark along the narrow fuselage littered with sharp obstructions toward an escape hatch that might be damaged or jammed. Men trapped in blazing, falling aircraft had little chance of surviving and knew they were about to die. The final seconds of roaring engines, a flash, an awful explosion made even worse if the payload was still aboard and detonated on impact. Few aircrew were pulled alive from crashed planes.

In short-of-fuel or combat-damaged aircraft trying to reach the safety of England – their crew tossing out anything moveable in a desperate attempt to lessen the weight and maintain height – they faced their own Armageddon: the terrifying North Sea, graveyard of thousands of aircraft reported as 'lost without trace'. Even if they escaped from the ditched plane, men struggled to stay alive in a tossing rubber dinghy. Swimming, even wearing a Mae West, meant almost certain death. Despite the bravery of air-sea rescue, the chances of being saved after ditching were slim, especially at night or in winter.[44]

Flight Lieutenant Nick Carter, DFC, a wireless operator/air gunner, flew a tour with No. 75 Squadron, where he knew Artie. Nick was later to join the Pathfinders in No. 156 Squadron, completing sixty operations and two tours over enemy territory. Nick has said that the scene when approaching the target looked quite spectacular, even attractive, as shells exploded and searchlights scanned the skies: 'The reality hit when you realised you had to fly through that cauldron and somehow survive.' He remembers those harrowing nights, the dangerous penetration deep into Germany, the heavy defences, the mass of searchlights and colours below, and remarks that once caught in a searchlight cone you were lucky to survive. It was like being a fly in a web. He vividly recalls the relief every time they made it home. 'And then those empty places at the breakfast tables. It wasn't a time to have friends.' They relied on the close bonds between crew members, knowing that they depended on each other for their survival.

Author Max Lambert described just what bomber crews experienced night after night:

> Aircrews climbed into a bomber every three or four nights, frequently more often, and laid their lives on the line attacking targets in Germany or occupied Europe. They took off after the sun went down and flew for hours, often seven or eight, sometimes nine or ten, their bomb-laden aircraft droning through the blackness toward distant dots on a navigator's chart. For however long they flew they were assailed by the roar of engines, four of them on big bombers. Noise was a constant fatiguing presence. They operated in all weather the year round. They flew through snow, rainstorms and belts of lightning on cold winter nights when it was minus 50 degrees centigrade outside, often battling the astonishingly quick build-up of ice on the wings and fuselage that could mean disaster.

Dr Stafford-Clark, for four years a medical officer on a bomber station, wrote in 1949 that in his experience bomber crews were men with the quality of high courage. In the *Journal of Mental Science* he stated that aircrews of Bomber Command were not 'dauntless dare-devils, thirsting for action' and they resented what seemed occasionally to be a tacit assumption that they were so effortlessly gallant and irresponsibly 'devil-may-care' as to be insensitive to all but the immediate present and indifferent to their own ultimate fate.

He said the morale fluctuated and was highest at the start of a tour of operation. It began to fall after five sorties and reached its lowest point at twelve to fifteen sorties. Thereafter it rose again, but fell once more before the final sortie. Generally speaking morale among crews was maintained at an 'extraordinarily high level' and the incidence of mental breakdown over the whole period of the war in Bomber Command did not exceed 5 per cent, though the casualty rate for killed and missing was about 48 per cent and for killed, missing, wounded and injured about 61 per cent.

Stafford-Clark described bombing operations as like nothing else in the world. The aircrew flew in darkness – relieved only by the dim orange glow of a lamp over the navigator's table and the faintly green luminosity of the pilot's instruments – three or four miles high, through bitter cold over hundreds of miles of sea and hostile land with the thunderous roaring of engines shutting out all other sounds except when the crackling metallic voice of one member of the crew echoed in the others' earphones. For each man there was a constant awareness of danger – from the enemy; from suffering blinding convergence of searchlights accompanied by heavy accurate and torrential flak; from packs of night fighters unceasingly seeking to find and penetrate the bomber stream; from danger of collision; from ice in the cloud; from becoming lost or isolated; from a chance hit in a petrol tank leading to loss of fuel and a forced descent into the sea on the way back if nothing worse.

There was no single moment of security from take-off to touchdown, often highlighted by the sight of other aircraft hit by flak and exploding in the air or plummeting down, blazing, to strike the ground, an incandescent wreck.

The chances of any particular individual surviving his thirty trips alive, unwounded and without having been taken prisoner, or forced down over enemy territory, were generally accepted by the aircrew themselves as being about one in five.

Everyone looked forward to the completion of his tour, but so strong was the crew spirit that it was not uncommon for a man to volunteer for as many as ten extra trips so that he and his crew could finish together, if he had joined them with more operations to his credit than they had.

There was, however, a definite nervous toll on a man. His first two or three sorties were so full of novelty and amazement that unless he was fundamentally unsuited to operational flying, he would not suffer from actual fear to a great extent. But by the time he completed five to eight sorties he discovered the magnitude of the task he had undertaken. The extreme novelty of operations had gone, succeeded by a growing recognition of the cost. By the twelfth or fifteenth sortie he had reached the full realisation of the danger and unpleasantness of the job and the long stretch of sorties still before him. As his tour continued, morale rose, until by the twenty-fifth trip the cumulative stress and fatigue began to tell and morale fell during the last sorties.

An aircrew's attitude to losses and the death of friends was particularly striking. It was one of supreme realism, of matter-of-fact acceptance of what every one knew perfectly well was inevitable. They did not lunge into outspoken expression of their feelings nor did they display any compromise with conventional reticence about the fact of violent death. They said 'Too bad … sorry about old so-and-so … rotten luck.' Their regret was deep and sincere but not much displayed or long endured. They were apt and able to talk of the dead and missing friends before mentioning their fate, just as they talked of anyone else or of themselves. It took the loss of particular friends or leaders, flight commanders or squadron commanders, to produce marked reactions among a squadron. Then they might feel collectively distressed, have a few drinks because of that and go to a party and feel better.

But they made no effort to escape the reality of the situation nor was there any of the drinking to forget referred to in accounts of dying in the last war. They were young; they were resilient; they lived until they died.

They were never completely unconcerned about their fate, though, even if some were quite unemotional about the possibility that they might not last until the end of the war. A mushroom growth of superstition was noted and personal mascots, ranging from hare's feet to girl's stockings, were taken very seriously. One captain forbade his crew to take out a WAAF who had lost two men friends in quick succession. She was known as the 'chop blonde'. There was no point in adding to the risks, he said. Artie had his own superstitions. He said he would not walk under the extension that held the open hangar doors. And until it flew out the window, he always wore a peaked cap on top of his helmet. 'I always carried a penny with a hole in it which had been so afflicted in the Boer War.'

The cumulative stress of continued operational flying often produced in some men a reversal of their usual habits. The noisy, exuberant, extraverted type of fellow became silent, morose and solitary. The naturally shy or secretive individual assumed a false jocularity, often accompanied by alcoholic indulgence and unusual verbosity.

The effect of operations being scrubbed or cancelled is also commented upon. At any stage of the preliminaries to an operation – the operation meal, the main briefing, driving out to or standing by the aircraft – an order for alteration, cancellation, or delay, might come through. No one who saw the mask of age, which mantled the faces of these young men after a period of continued standing-by punctuated by inevitable false alarms, is likely to forget it. Their pallor, the hollows in their cheeks and beneath their eyes, and the utter fatigue with which they lolled listlessly in chairs about their mess, were eloquent of the exhaustion and frustration that they felt. In ten hours they seemed to have aged as many years.

Perhaps because the public were assumed to want their heroics simplified, propaganda about the RAF tended to misunderstand and underrate the quality of the courage of aircrews. The core of this quality is now more widely recognised. Its most terrible and unforgettable characteristic was the subordination of the instinct of self-preservation to an endeavour to fulfil a very high standard of war service; and a determination to see the job through despite the greater love for wife or child or for life itself.

It was flying into this cauldron that Artie found himself posted in January 1941. He was destined to survive with a distinguished record with No. 75 (New Zealand) Squadron, which became one of the premier squadrons in RAF Bomber Command during the Second World War.

Chapter 8

The Men Who Flew into Hell

This chapter records the feelings and experiences of some individual aircrew, including a brief outline of what, for many, was life as a prisoner of war (POW).[45]

Greg Gregon. British bombers were not heated. Often the crews had to deal with severe cold. Greg Gregon, a Bomber Command wireless operator/air gunner said it was freezing:

> The aircraft used to ice up. We had leaflets to drop and if you cut the pack and touched the knife to your skin it would stick. You tried to put as much clothing on as you could because you couldn't get a lot of movement in the aircraft such as jumping up and down to keep warm. One of the things I remember about the winter of 1939–40, for example, was the absolute cold. If I could get a pair of silk stockings I'd wear those, then woollen socks and then flying boots, which were fur-lined, then an inner jacket like a teddy bear with a canvas coating, then a leather jacket with fur, three pairs of gloves – a silk pair, wool, and then the leather gauntlets. Sheer cold is one of the worst things. You just had to sit there and think cold.

Wing Commander Rod Rodley, DSO, DFC, AE. Rod Rodley said he never spent much time wondering what was going on down below:

> I eased my conscience by feeling that the Germans must do what we'd been doing, which was to evacuate non-participants. I'd done my duty, which was to take a load of high explosive to an aiming

point laid down by those in authority above me whom I trusted. If I'd been an imaginative character I might have wondered exactly what happened when those bombs hit but I merely hoped I was hitting a factory or machine tools or something of that ilk. The only way I could have got a picture of the effect of a bomb attack on people was to go to the East End of London.

I was not troubled about the devastation and loss of life. We were fighting a very ruthless enemy. We all knew this. Our families were home behind us and we were rather like a crusader with his sword in front of them. My thoughts at the time were that I have a family, a bigger family – the public – and I was going to do my damnedest to stop the Germans coming across.

Wing Commander Guy Gibson, VC, DSO and Bar, DFC and Bar. In the early part of the war, when Bomber Command was flying daylight raids and using Hampden bombers, Guy Gibson wrote about what he regarded as a massacre. 'The Germans were flying in Messerschmitt 110 fighters, which had one gun that could fire sideways. Their mode of attack was to fly in formation with the Hampdens perhaps 50 yards out and slightly in front, and then pick off the outside aircraft with their one gun, aiming with a no-deflection shot at the pilot. The bomber boys could do nothing about it: they just had to sit there and wait to be shot down. If they broke away they were immediately pounced on by three Messerschmitt 109s waiting in the background. One by one they were hacked down from the wing man inwards. It was a terrible sight to see them bursting into flames at about twenty feet and then cart wheeling on one wing into the cold sea.'

Flight Lieutenant Harry Le Marchant. Harry was a Bomber Command observer. He said he prayed a lot:

I always prayed before I went on operations. We had our talisman. We took all the WAAF parachute packers out for a pie and a pint and a little WAAF very kindly got out her purse and gave me a Victorian bun penny, one of the very old coins with Queen Victoria when she was young with the bun of hair at the back. It had a hole in it. She said 'Here take this as a lucky charm for the future', which I did, and I always flew with it. My uncle gave me a silver cigarette case and I never flew without that too.

I had many friends who had girlfriends' stockings too. When we flew we had a white pullover but we were not allowed to wear a collar and tie because the collars in those days were detachable, and if you went into water the clothing might shrink and suffocate you. So everybody had gay coloured scarves or girlfriends' stockings around their necks. There were also lots of teddy bears, even ones in flying kit, and other things made by wives or girlfriends.

Lord Mackie, CBE, DSO, DFC. Lord Mackie was an aircrew observer:

There was always tension when going into Berlin. I always tried to get in early. I tried to get in with the Pathfinders when I could because I fancied I was as good as any Pathfinder. When you went in all hell let loose. The Pathfinders had extraordinary devices that exploded with a tremendous bang and it lit up the whole sky. The Pathfinders were remarkably good. Next thing 600 bombers were all around you. The risk of collision was very great. Looking down you gradually saw the city explode with bombs dropping. Looking back you saw Berlin burning. This was the turning point at which extreme caution had to be exercised. If everyone did not turn at the same time the risk of collision was high.

On one particular night two Lancasters collided in front of us and one of them exploded and went straight down. The other did two upward rolls with all four engines burning and exploded right in front of us, a hundred yards away. The pilot shouted to the gunners to turn away so that their night vision would not be impaired. One gunner asked why and when he was told his knees shook.

We accepted the fact that civilian deaths were a necessary part of the war. It occurred in Britain, it occurred in Germany. One got used to the fact that civilians were suffering and they were suffering all over the Eastern front and the Jews in Eastern Germany. Everyone accepted that this was total war. We were doing the job we were asked to do and we thought it was essential under the circumstances.

The whole attitude of Bomber Command was that we were the point of the spear and we had a job to do. It was highly dangerous. We had to accept that in modern war civilians were killed. In our eyes we were in a desperate situation and we knew it. The trials of the German nation did not worry us an awful lot.

Alex Kerr. Bomber pilot Alex Kerr's aircraft was coned by the searchlights. He described what happened:

We'd been briefed to attack an aircraft works at Hamburg. We bombed from about 9,000 feet and were on our way back when some flak hit the rear turret. The rear gunner was trying to extinguish the fire but couldn't put it out. The flames became obvious from the ground and we were caught in a cone of searchlights. About 20 lights homed in on us and it was like daylight. Though we got the turret fire out a night-fighter had come in and lined himself up. He polished us off and some of the bullets he fired set off flares inside the aircraft and set it on fire. I'd been hit several times, as had my navigator, and we were both lying on the floor.

We were lucky. The fire had put out the hydraulics on the rear turret and when the order was given to bale out the rear gunner was not able to go sideways as he normally would but had to crawl back inside the aircraft to get out of a hatch. He saw me lying on the floor and picked me up, sat me on the edge of the hatch, put my parachute on, put my hand on the rip-cord and said 'For God's sake pull it.' Then he chucked me out. I came to consciousness enough to pull the cord. I came down by parachute and I was taken to the nearest POW hospital, which was staffed by French prisoners. No one could speak English but there was a Professor of Surgery there from the University of Strasbourg, one of the few surgeons in Europe who was skilled enough to save my life.

The navigator was left inside the aircraft. He came to, looked around him, saw no one was there, got up to clip on his parachute, had a dizzy spell and dropped it through the hatch. He was in an aircraft that was on fire with no parachute! He walked up front, saw that there was no pilot there either and so got into the pilot's seat.

He decided to end it quickly and dive straight into the ground, but then he had second thoughts. He ended up bringing the aircraft down and landing it in a field in Germany about 1 o'clock in the pitch black morning with great skill. He ended up in the same hospital as I did a month later. He was badly wounded.

Wilkie Wanless. Wilkie's aircraft was part of a raid on Kassel in Germany when they were shot down by a German fighter. He described the event:

We were doing the diversion.[46] We flew past Kassel and then turned back. After the turn and coming back we got hit by a fighter. Nobody saw him. He came up underneath us with his upward firing cannons. He hit the starboard wing and he must have hit the fuselage too because he killed the mid-upper gunner. We were a ball of fire. Everyone got out except the mid-upper gunner and the pilot. Why the pilot didn't get out I don't know. I spoke to him from the rear turret: 'This is the rear-gunner. I'm going out, everyone else has gone.'

I pulled my chute in, buckled it on and flipped out backward. I was always very apprehensive about getting run into by another aircraft in the stream so I did a delayed drop, landed in a potato patch, undid my chute, buried it under some potato tops and took off my sheepskin trousers. I'd taken off my helmet in the aircraft otherwise you could break your neck if you baled out with it on. It was about 9 o'clock at night, 3 October 1943. I walked out to what I thought had been a river, but it was an autobahn. I walked along the highway and trundled along until I became utterly exhausted, when nervous reaction set in. I crawled into some brush and went to sleep.

I thought I'd get to Switzerland. We had escape kits and I had a beautiful silk map so I knew where I was. I was a mess. I'd fallen into a few ditches. The second night I hid and the third day I was in a ditch by a farmer's field. He came to look at his hay crop and saw me. I pretended I was French with my schoolboy language. He just shrugged and walked away.

Within a short time three men arrived and arrested me and marched me to the town hall. The Gestapo called me in and an old man who had been in England in the First World War acted as interpreter. They phoned Berlin. They locked me up in the city jail. During the night a couple of Luftwaffe guys arrived in a black maria and took me to the air base. They assigned me an armed guard and he took me by train to Frankfurt and the interrogation centre.

An elderly German went by and saw 'Canada' on my shoulder. He looked terribly disturbed and started screaming. It was a mob scene in seconds and my escort had to get his Luger out. He grabbed me by the arm and said 'run'. We ran down the platform as the train was coming in. You couldn't hold it against anyone. The RAF had been there a night or two before and the Americans had been there a day or two before as well. You could feel for them.

John Gee. Describing the after-effects of a raid, John Gee said:

Most people lit a cigarette. You waited for the crew bus to come and take you to the interrogation and debriefing session. The CO of the station and everyone else was there asking questions, making out the report on the effectiveness or otherwise of the raid. What the defences were like, etc? Your main feeling was to get that part over and then have a meal and get to bed. Having got to bed you couldn't sleep because you could still hear the engines and you were really wound up. I never slept after an operation, by which time it was daylight anyway. You couldn't sleep in the daytime, you were so highly strung. You tried to calm down but you really had to let steam off to do that. Possibly the next day you would not be flying. You would have a number of beers and get yourself into the state where you could sleep. That was how you got over it. You were just glad to have got back and survived.

Flight Lieutenant Chan Chandler, DFC and Bar, SMV. Chandler was thankful it was all over when he made his last entry in his logbook on 22 June 1945. The war had ended. He no longer had to go out in the middle of a cold night riding his luck through German flak, nor peer into the inky blackness for the first sign of an approaching night fighter. A veteran of 106 operations, 96 of them as a wireless operator/rear gunner in bombers, the rest as a cameraman with an RAF film unit, he had good cause to rejoice. Aged only eighteen when he joined the RAF in 1939, he had lived through hell a thousand times by the time he was twenty-four. Wounded five times, Chandler had flown in six bombers that were shot down or had crash-landed. He had returned eleven times from ops in badly damaged aircraft. His luck was phenomenal. He had flown with thirty pilots, over half of them being killed.

On 30 June 1941, on a bombing raid to Düsseldorf, the Hampden bomber was damaged by flak and crash-landed into the North Sea. Despite letting off flares and signalling to passing aircraft and boats, they drifted for nine days. Their meagre supplies were exhausted. The water had run out and they had begun drinking sea water. At dawn on the ninth day they huddled lethargically together in a dinghy. At first they ignored a single Hampden that roared out of the sun a mile away. It was high in the sky on a mission that would not involve looking down for a speck of yellow and four dying men. As the bomber drew nearer they struggled to hold the skipper upright as he flashed 'SOS' with a mirror.

To their disbelief and delight the bomber circled while its wireless operator got a fix. The four airmen, almost resigned to death, were now close to tears as the Hampden circled above them and exchanged thumbs-up with the crew. 'We thought we wouldn't survive another day. We were at the end of our tether. It was that close,' said Chandler. When rescued they were told that they were in the middle of a minefield.[47]

Many of of those who baled out over enemy territory did not survive the ordeal. Those who did faced uncertain life in dreary prisoner of war camps. For the most part, food was poor and inadequate. Periodic Red Cross parcels relieved the monotony and sustained many prisoners. The food and special treats like cigarettes were particularly welcome. Aircrew who survived but were severely wounded in the process received variable treatment. Most German doctors acted professionally, but a minority didn't and prolonged the suffering. A repatriation process handled by the Red Cross saw many severely wounded prisoners exchanged for Germans in a similar state. Allied servicemen were repatriated to England.

Those who landed in the towns and cities that had experienced heavy bombing were often subject to ill-treatment by civilians, angry at the horror, the destruction of their homes and the loss of life. They were usually saved by the arrival of police or soldiers, but even these were known to ill-treat the unfortunate airmen on occasions.

Groups of prisoners were transported to the prison camps crowded into cattle trucks with little or no food and water for days on end. Occasionally the train would stop to allow men to alight and attend to the calls of nature. As one who experienced such a journey said: 'We just squatted in the open where we alighted, watched over by armed guards. No such luxury as toilet paper or anything else for that matter. It was very degrading.'

Conditions in the camps during the European winter were severe, with little effective heating in the dormitories. Prisoners became expert scroungers of firewood and, in some cases, stealing coal. One of the biggest challenges for prisoners, however, was boredom. Most survived the ordeal but a few didn't and suffered mentally for the rest of their lives. Those captured in 1940 and 1941 were destined to spend four and five long, dreary years living with these conditions.

Many of the camps were situated in present-day Poland. As the Russian armies advanced into Europe in 1945, Hitler ordered the prisoners to be shifted west, ultimately into Germany. The huge majority were made to walk in extreme winter temperatures, frequently in snow. About 30,000 Allied POWs were force-marched westward across Poland and Germany in appalling winter conditions from January to April 1945.

The daily distances were long and the ordeal continued for weeks. Circumstances were brutal. Food was almost non-existent. Sleeping was in barns or outside in the freezing cold. Most suffered from dysentery at some stage of the journey. In one case, the prisoners were evacuated at 3.30 a.m. It was 19 January 1945. About 1,500 men were given two and a half days' rations and left the camp in a raging blizzard. They were told that for every man who fell five more would be shot! In three weeks they trekked 240 kilometres through deep snow, sleeping in cowsheds, surviving on starvation rations. After marching for seventeen days they were crammed into cattle trucks without water and taken to a place called Luckenwalde. They disembarked as tottering skeletons, suffering frostbite, dysentery and malnutrition. The new camp was grossly overcrowded and food was scarce. They were finally liberated by the Russians after some seventy-four days living in hell.[48]

With so little food they had been reduced to scavenging to survive, some eating dogs and cats and even rats and grass – anything they could lay their hands on. Those too ill to continue had fallen by the wayside and were mostly left to die or were shot dead on the spot. Because of the unsanitary conditions and a near starvation diet, hundreds of POWs had died along the way from exhaustion, as well as pneumonia, diphtheria, pellagra and other diseases. It was one of the most brutal acts of the war, never to be forgotten by those forced to participate.

Flight Lieutenant John Needham, RNZAF. John Needham of Morrinsville, New Zealand, was imprisoned at Stalag Luft III, a camp for Allied aircrew. He was the navigator in a Stirling bomber that was hit by flak during a raid on Wuppertal in the Ruhr Valley on the night of 24/25 June 1943. John was the only survivor of a crew of seven. He said that he was the first to bale out and, as he went, the plane blew up, killing all the remaining crew. After he landed, John buried his parachute and managed to hide from searching Germans for four days. He moved by night, hoping to reach the French border. On the fourth day he was captured and taken to an interrogation camp, from where he was sent to Stalag Luft III.

Stalag Luft III was the scene of the famous 'Great Escape', brilliantly described by Paul Brickhill in his epic book of that name. After secretly building several tunnels from the barracks to outside the camp perimeter wire, seventy-six men managed to escape on the night of 24-25 March 1944. Of these, only three finally made it to freedom. John recalled that for several days those in the compounds waited with hope and suspense only to learn that nearly all their mates had been recaptured in small groups. He said it was several weeks before they learned that fifty of those caught had been shot. It was one of the many merciless crimes committed during the war.

John was among the prisoners who were forced into what became known as the 'Death March'. When the advancing Russian armies crossed the River Oder the Germans suddenly announced, at nine o'clock on the evening of 27 January 1945, that all prisoners should be ready to leave on foot in one hour's time. They eventually moved out of the camp at around 4 a.m. dragging their belongings behind them on rapidly constructed sledges. John said: 'We marched 100 kilometres in five days under extremely cold conditions. I thought I was going to freeze to death.' They were then herded into cattle trucks, forty men per truck, for a two-day journey to a place near Bremen. In early April, as the British Army advanced from the west they were moved again, this time to Lubeck. John remarked that this journey was not so bad and although they slept out in the open the weather was perfect. 'The only real problem we had was the constant fear of being strafed by marauding Allied Air Force fighter-bombers who mistook the columns for German troop concentrations. Our column was strafed once and two prisoners were killed. Another column reportedly had 40 killed. We eventually reached the outskirts of Lubeck where we found that POW camps were filled to overflowing. On 23 April, our Senior British Officer managed to persuade the German Commandant to leave us in some barns until the end of the war or when we were overtaken by the advancing Allies. Liberation finally came on 2 May 1945, when a small British armoured car came across the encamped prisoners. The car was rapturously received. Freedom at last.'[49]

Chapter 9

Making of the Legend – Part 1
His First Tour, 1941

On arrival in England in June 1940, Artie went first to Uxbridge near London, then to Kemble near Cirencester. Rex Daniell said that they were unexpected at both places and there was much confusion before they were actually accepted at the respective stations. At Kemble, Artie flew his first RAF aircraft, a twin-engined Anson. He later commented that by a strange coincidence the Anson was also the last RAF aircraft he flew before retiring twenty-seven years later.

From Kemble, those of his group who had been trained to fly single-engined aircraft were sent to Benson, not far from Oxford, where they completed an Operational Training Unit (OTU) course. They were supposed to fly Fairey Battles, which aircraft had fared badly in France. The 'Battles', as they were known, were three-seater light bombers. When fully laden they proved no match for the much faster and better armed German fighters.

The expected training on Battles actually came to nothing and Artie found himself as a screened pilot flying the twin-engined Ansons on wireless operator training. His logbook shows that he was on Ansons for all of June 1940 and it was not until July and August that he found himself flying Fairey Battles. September saw him once more with Ansons, and this training continued until mid-January 1941.

Then came the move to Bassingbourn near Cambridge, again flying Ansons, but this time training navigators, mostly at night. This was part of 11 OTU. Instruction on Ansons continued until 12 January 1941. While with 11 OTU his logbook recorded a red endorsement: 'Taxying accident due to carelessness 1.10.40.' It would not be the last time an endorsement showed in his logbook.

Completion of his training on the Ansons was followed by the big and fateful move. Artie commented that having once seen inside the rear fuselage of a Wellington he suddenly found himself posted to No. 75 (New Zealand) Squadron flying Wellington ICs at Feltwell in the wolds of Norfolk. His first flight in a Wellington took place on 25 January 1941. He said it wasn't until the middle of February that he flew his first solo in a Wellington, and that after only two and a quarter hours dual.

Shortly afterwards, on 21 February, he was off as second pilot to Sergeant White on his first operational flight, a raid on the German submarine bases at Wilhemshaven, recalling:

I wasn't particularly apprehensive about anti-aircraft fire coming up for the first time and then suddenly realised that it was possibly intended for me. There were 10 more trips as second pilot before I was given my own crew. I had also spent a considerable time as "OC Night" out in the cold, miserable flare path of Feltwell airfield.

I was very fortunate in being given the chance to learn something of the problems confronting the bomber crews before being sent off on my own. The most fortunate aspect of this period for me was being crewed with Pilot Officer Ron Simich, a New Zealander. Not only was he an extremely competent bomber pilot, calm, determined, patient, and knowledgeable, but also had a unique capacity for imparting that knowledge. Later in the war, this was considered an expensive unnecessary luxury. Also living in the Officers' Mess at Feltwell and in charge of ground defence of the airfield at that time, was a veteran Major of the Royal Artillery. I listened carefully to all he had to say on the subject of anti-aircraft defence. From these two sources then, I learned more than anyone else had to teach.

On 9 April they were sent off to bomb Berlin. Artie recorded his memory of that op:

The trip itself was comparatively uneventful and there could be no doubt that we located Berlin. For the return journey we were over a continuous cloud sheet and, unbeknown to us, there had been a dramatic wind change. With the very limited navigational aids

available to us at that time and not being able to see the ground we
went past our base. After descending below cloud we called 'Darky'
(the 1941 version of Mayday) on our primitive TRS radio and were
guided by searchlights to RAF Ternhill. On landing, Simich overshot the runway and we finished up in a nasty tangle of barbed
wire. A Polish crew who had landed just before us were not so fortunate, and their aircraft was extensively damaged. There had been
a mix up laying the flare path, which had been supervised by a
medical corporal! It was laid down-wind and was only 300 yards
long, so there was really little chance of a successful landing.

Artie's logbook for the 9 April Berlin raid stated: 'Very accurate searchlights and heavy AA Fire. Load 4 x 500, 1 x 250. Fighters encountered.'
On that operation, however, he was second pilot to Sergeant Faulkner.
It was on the operation of 17 April, when he flew second pilot to Simich,
that the aircraft was damaged and landed at Ternhill. His logbook again
recorded very heavy and accurate AA fire. Flight Lieutenant Simich
was awarded the DFC for the courage and skill he exhibited on this
particular raid.

Flight Lieutenant George Ronald Simich, RNZAF, DFC, MID

Ron Simich, as he was known, was born in Auckland on 3 September
1916. He served in the RNZAF from November 1939 until May 1945. He
was shot down over Germany when piloting a Stirling bomber on the
night of 26 July 1942. He was a prisoner of war until May 1945. In 1947
he took part in the ferrying of three Mosquitoes to New Zealand from
the United Kingdom and Australia. He was killed in an aircraft accident
at Himatangi Beach on 27 August 1947, during a test flight with No. 75
(NZ) Squadron. He was a passenger in the aircraft.

Citation, Distinguished Flying Cross (18 July 1941)

'This officer has completed 182 operational flying hours and 21 sorties.
He has proved an ideal captain and has done outstanding work. He has
attacked Berlin on four occasions, each time displaying outstanding

skill, determination and gallantry in successfully pressing home his attacks despite severe damage sustained at times by his aircraft. On the night of 17 April 1941, he ran into a fierce barrage of anti-aircraft fire and searchlight concentrations on the outskirts of Berlin. Despite his attempts to run on to his target, he was forced so low that he was unsuccessful and had to turn away. Regaining height he persevered until he was able to accomplish a successful run over his objective.' [50]

Citation, Mention in Despatches (11 June 1942)

'For Distinguished Service. Served as an instructor with 18 (Polish) OTU RAF (Wellington) June 1941–June 1942. In recognition of his service he was awarded the Polish Flying badge. Flt Lt Simich started his second tour with 214 Squadron RAF (Stirlings).' (Hanson, p. 439.)

On 3 May 1941 Artie celebrated his twenty-first birthday. It was also the wedding day of Sergeant Jimmy Blundell, the wireless operator in Simich's crew. The whole crew were present at the wedding, the reception and other jollifications, which occurred during their week's leave. This was not the most sober period of his life, he said.

On the 7th of that month they departed from Southport and travelled by overnight train via London so they could be back to rejoin the squadron on the 8th. Artie commented: 'After breakfast on the 8th of May, I was asked by Squadron Leader J.M. Southwell if I thought I was capable of taking a Wellington on operations that night. Being now 21, over-confident and big-headed, I told him I could and was promptly told to take his aircraft and crew that night.'

By an amazing coincidence the navigator in Johnny Southwell's crew was Sergeant Ted McSherry, who had been the stroke in the Wellington Rowing Club's Youth Four for two New Zealand championship regattas. Artie was bow in the same crew. On one occasion, Artie said: 'We were leading only a few lengths from the finish when, unfortunately, Ted "caught a crab", something he'd never done before.'

Inheriting an already established aircrew was fraught with risk. Bonding and good relationships among crew members were critical factors when it came to staying alive. They depended on each other. They needed to know

they could trust each other at all times, especially the first pilot. It seems
that Artie was able to establish himself with this crew as a competent and
skilled pilot who could be relied upon. Ted McSherry was to fly as navigator in Artie's crew on twenty operational sorties; mainly to targets in
Germany, but also on attacks of the German battleships *Scharnhorst*,
Gneisenau and *Prinz Eugen* at Brest, the naval base in occupied north-
west France.

Flying Officer McSherry was killed on air operations on 3 June 1943,
while en route to the Middle East. His body was never recovered and he
is remembered on the Runnymede memorial for all those British and
Commonwealth airmen who died and who have no known grave.[51]

Artie's record of this operation read as follows:

In the event the target was a submarine shipbuilding yard at
Hamburg and we duly arrived over the city at the appointed hour.
We were at 11,000 feet and had approached from the North having
crossed the coast just North of the western end of the Kiel Canal.
As frequently happened in those days, the German defences, decided
to lie 'doggo', presumably in the hope that if they didn't bother us
we wouldn't retaliate or the hope that if the defences were not
revealed, we would be unable to find the target. Because it was a
clear night and the river pointed like an arrow to our target in
Hamburg, we easily found the target and dropped our load. The
entry in my logbook is: 'Hit target, starting first fires. Badly beaten
up by flak.' I'm not certain what this means after this length of
time, as the logbook seems to contain a lot of references to 'blitz
on' and 'intense and accurate AA'. I do, however, recall that, as soon
as our bombs were on their way down, the searchlights came up,
although we were not coned,[52] and both heavy and light guns started
firing straight away. We returned home the way we had come to the
North and reached base after six hours and twenty minutes. The
whole way I had this niggling doubt as to my ability to put the aircraft safely back on the ground. In the event I needn't have worried
as Wimpy proved again what a lady she was and the landing was
almost perfect. The next night we veterans bombed Mannheim.

According to Middlebrook and Everitt's *Bomber Command War Diaries*, 188 aircraft took part in this raid on 8 May. These included 100 Wellingtons, of which 3 plus 1 Hampden were lost; 119 of these bombers aimed at the shipyards, the rest bombed city areas. Returning crews claimed good results and this is borne out by the Hamburg reports. Some 83 fires were started, of which 38 were classed as large. The then new 4,000-pound bombs were described by the Germans as causing many problems for the air-raid services.

The system of navigation in a Wellington in 1941 at night was, by today's standards, crude in the extreme. They used dead reckoning. Flight Lieutenant Simich supplemented this by visual pinpoints, bearings and drifts, using either the bomb sight or the tail turret. Artie recalled that although all navigators completed training in astro navigation, it was inaccurate and rarely used. This was in the days before such luxuries as 'GEE'[53] and the invention of VHF, by which a good wireless operator could get bearings from radio stations with known locations and it was possible to obtain bearings from base on return.

Bomber Command operations in 1941 were rather hit and miss affairs. Only the time of take-off, a suggested route to the target and a time to bomb were given at the pre-op briefing, along with the likely weather, the bomb load and some information, if known, of the German defences. During the early stages of the war, the direction of approach to the target and the height of the attack were left to the individual crews, especially the pilot. It transpired that during this period the actual damage being caused by these attacks was, for the most part, minimal, with comparatively little effect on the German war machine. Following a review of the bombing effectiveness, which had been ordered by the War Cabinet, the crews were given more intense instructions and squadrons flew together with defined approaches to the targets. The introduction of improved navigation aids also helped increase the accuracy. It was not until the establishment of the Pathfinder Force in late 1942, however, that the bombing accuracy and effectiveness began to improve significantly.

With the occupation of France and the Low Countries, the Germans were able to build a formidable defensive system. They established a radar early warning system that stretched from Denmark, down the North Sea coast, and further south to block an approach from the west across France. The 'Kammhuber Line' was made up of numerous boxes in which radar, searchlights and a night fighter co-ordinated an interception. When the coastal radar stations gave warning of approaching aircraft, the fighter in each box was directed to intercept any single bomber coming into its box. If a bomber force was scattered, many single aircraft would naturally be entering a large number of boxes at any given time. But if it could be arranged for many bombers to pass through one box at the same time, the fighter in that box would only have time to attempt the interception of one of them. A continuous searchlight belt covering the Ruhr in Germany made it easier for fighters to intercept the bombers passing through it, and here again it would be better for the bombers to get through this belt in a continuous stream, with the fighters only able to concentrate on one or two of them, rather than to go through it at long intervals and be picked off one by one. A few ground control stations were probably working at the beginning of 1941, but by the end of the year they had become numerous and efficient, and bomber casualties were rising faster.[54]

Chapter 10

Making of the Legend – Part 2

After the Wilhelmshaven raid, Artie flew on ten more operations as second pilot – Cologne (2), Haamstede, Brest, Kiel (2), Berlin (2), Bremen, Mannheim – before taking his first raid as pilot in command. On the night of 29–30 April they attacked Mannheim. His logbook recorded: 'Blitz on Mannheim. Bombs dropped on target area. Very intense and very accurate heavy flak in target area.'

On 10 June he participated in a daylight raid on the battle cruiser *Prinz Eugen* at the French port of Brest. The three German battle cruisers, *Prinz Eugen*, *Scharnhorst* and *Gneisenau*, were all based at Brest at that time. These formidable ships posed a constant threat to Allied shipping in the Atlantic and many attempts were made to destroy them. According to *Bomber Command War Diaries*, 104 aircraft were involved in this operation: 39 Hampdens, 38 Wellingtons and 27 Whitleys. No aircraft were lost.

The *Prinz Eugen* was captured at the end of the war and handed over to the US Navy. She was used as a target ship at the Bikini atom bomb tests. The *Gneisenau* ended the war as a block ship, sunk in the Gotenhafen harbour on 23 March 1945. She was raised by the Poles, broken up, and scrapped after the war.

According to author Hilary Saunders, to attack Brest was a particularly hazardous operation. With the possible exception of Berlin, it was at that time probably the most heavily defended place in Europe. Searchlights and heavy and light anti-aircraft guns abounded and it was constantly patrolled by fighters. Moreover, the target was very difficult to hit.[55]

The attack on the *Scharnhorst* was to earn Artie the Distinguished Flying Cross. He recorded this memorable operation:

On the 18th of June, we took off for an attack on Brest, this time trying to hit the *Scharnhorst*. We spent a considerable time over the target area and finally established by the light of one of our flares, that the *Scharnhorst* was not berthed where we had been briefed to find her. However, there was another ship in the harbour and this we attacked. On the way home we got ourselves lost by mis-identifying our place of landfall. As a consequence we flew through the balloon barrage at Bristol. It was just breaking daylight when this happened and there was quite a bit of anxiety in the aircraft until we were clear. My logbook recalls only that we were lost and came through the balloon barrage, but for this particular operation I was awarded the Distinguished Flying Cross.

By this time Artie had flown 125 hours 45 minutes on operations in twenty sorties.

Sixty-five aircraft took part in the Brest operation: fifty-seven Wellingtons and eight Stirlings. On this occasion none were lost. The official operations record said that haze and smokescreens prevented identification of the warship targets.

As is recorded in the citation for the award of the DFC, Artie showed great determination in trying to locate the target despite the haze and smoke. His logbook records the crew as Flight Sergeant McLaughlin, Sergeant McSherry, Sergeant Welby, Sergeant Hume and Sergeant Palmer.

At home in Alexandra, we first heard the news of the award from the BBC. I vividly remember the evening. My sister Edna was visiting at the time and we were sitting listening to the nine o'clock BBC news, a nightly ritual throughout the war. Suddenly we heard the name, Pilot Officer Ashworth, and the award of the DFC. There was great excite-ment. It was a great moment and my mother in particular was very proud of her son. Many congratulatory telegrams and messages were received from relatives and friends. The award was widely reported in the press, including the *Alexandra Herald* and the *Otago Daily Times*.

Citation for award of Distinguished Flying Cross

'On the night of 18/19 June 1941, Pilot Officer Ashworth was detailed to attack the *Scharnhorst* at Brest in Wellington aircraft T2747. On arrival over the area he found the target covered by a smoke screen. However, leaving nothing to chance, he set about his task in so painstaking and methodical manner that there is every reason to expect that the target was hit. Spending considerable time in surveying the area, he succeeded in dropping flares immediately north and south of the target, which enabled him to make his final run exactly over the ship. Altogether, he was over the area one and a quarter hours, during which time he made eight surveying runs at an extremely low altitude in face of intense anti-aircraft opposition. In addition, he aimed one bomb at an unidentified 10,000 ton vessel seen to be entering the docks.

Since February 21st this year, this Officer has taken part in twenty major operations including two successful missions over Berlin and one day operation. On other occasions, notably on the nights of 8–9 and 11–12 May, when attacking targets in Hamburg, he showed the same resource and infinite care and patience in locating and bombing precisely over his aiming point, and he rarely brings his aircraft home without showing some evidence of enemy action. By his undoubted courage, outstanding skill as captain of aircraft and devotion to duty, this Officer is worthy of the highest commendation.'

Covering remarks of station commander Group Captain M.W. Buckley

'Very strongly recommended. This Officer has at all times set an excellent example to other pilots in his Squadron.'

Covering remarks of air officer commanding, Air Vice-Marshal J.E. Baldwin

'I strongly support the above recommendation and consider that this Captain has at all times displayed the perseverance, coolness and courage which is so necessary if bombing operations are to be pressed home to a successful conclusion. I consider his example has undoubtedly influenced many individuals in his unit.'

Among many other congratulatory messages, Artie received a letter from the popular New Zealand High Commissioner Mr W. (Bill) Jordan. Mr Jordan took a keen interest in the New Zealanders serving with the RAF. He is said to have referred to them as 'his boys'.

The *Scharnhorst* operation was Artie's twentieth. He was destined to complete eleven more ops before the end of his first tour on 3 August 1941. These included two raids on the German city of Köln. His logbook for 21 June recorded: 'Intense, accurate heavy flak. Hit by flak. Bust geodetic and petrol pump!' For the second raid on Köln on 30 June, he reported that they had flown for three-quarters of an hour on one engine in Wellington T2747. Ted McSherry was the navigator. The logbook for the raid on Kiel on 24/25 June recorded: 'Forced to jettison when held in searchlights over target. Intense and accurate heavy and light flak.' Artie said this was the only time in his whole career that he ever jettisoned his bombs. The last operation in June was on the German port of Bremen.

July 1941 saw Artie participate in six operations: the Krupps works at Essen; a blitz on Munster – huge fires, no flak; Duisburg on the 15th; Mannheim on 21 July; and finally a daylight raid on the *Gneisenau* at Brest. Of this raid he reported 'fighters and heavy A.A. flak. Hit! 38 Wellingtons took part in this Op. Bombing was difficult because of cloud and flak. Four aircraft were lost.' Artie's logbook recorded: 'Bombed through cloud. Dive-bombed aerodrome with 2 x 500, 5 SBC.' Essen, Duisburg and Mannheim were situated in the heavily defended Ruhr Valley, the industrial heart of Germany.

His logbook entries for May, June, July and August 1941 were signed as correct by fellow New Zealander, Squadron Leader F.J. Lucas, DFC, as officer commanding 'A' Flight. 'Popeye', as he was popularly known by all, was a close friend of Artie's. He had a distinguished war career, rising to the rank of wing commander and was awarded two DFCs in addition to being mentioned in despatches. After the war Popeye founded Southern Scenic Airways, based in Queenstown. Southern Scenic was one of the earlier private airlines. He subsequently farmed Cecil Peak Station on the shores of Lake Wakatipu where, in addition to high-country farming, and in partnership with his wife Lorie, he promoted a successful tourist business. After retiring from his high-country sheep station, Popeye moved to Nelson where he died in 1993, one year before Artie.

They had kept in touch in the intervening years.

While on leave from the RAF in 1949, Artie spent quite a lot of time flying with Popeye as a despatcher dropping supplies to government deer cullers in the remote mountains of South Westland. Many stories are told of the high jinks of Popeye Lucas and Artie Ashworth in the Shotover pub near Frankton. One of the legendary stories about Popeye was the 'walking the ceiling' escapade. His book *Popeye Lucas, Queenstown*, recorded this now famous incident:

> After one night of 'relaxation' I found I'd 'walked' the ceiling making a path of black footprints across the anteroom ceiling, down the wall, and out through the ventilator. The effort was performed in an atmosphere of great hilarity and enthusiasm. By the time we'd had a few beers the chaps were ready for anything, and whether I was stripped or did it voluntary, I was soon down to my jockeys, spread-eagled on one of the enormous chesterfields, while someone industriously blackened the soles of my feet with shoe polish.
>
> Not long after, Air Chief Marshal Sir Arthur Tedder visited the station and wrote in the visitor's book, 'These footprints to remain for all time.' This put the seal of official approval on a prank that had been frowned on in some quarters.

When Popeye returned to New Zealand in 1942 after completing two tours, the prank was repeated at one of the RNZAF stations, but the footprints were later removed. Thankfully the legend lives on.

Squadron Leader F.J. Lucas: Citation, Distinguished Flying Cross (21 October 1940)

'Since the beginning of the year, this officer has completed one night reconnaissance and pamphlet raid of Germany and 35 major bombing attacks on enemy occupied territory. His consistently good work has been marked by a very definite devotion to duty, and his capabilities as captain of aircraft have produced excellent results. He has shown a marked ability to find and bomb his primary target.'

Citation Bar to Distinguished Flying Cross, (13 April 1942)

'Since being awarded the DFC this officer has completed a further 20 sorties. Throughout his second tour, Squadron Leader Lucas was in command of his flight and, by his outstanding keenness for operations, he did much to encourage and promote a fine fighting spirit. His courage and perseverance over heavily defended targets have been most marked. His enthusiasm is such that he was genuinely disappointed when taken off operations.'

Chapter 11

No. 75 (New Zealand) Squadron

This chapter provides a brief background to what became the famous No. 75 (New Zealand) Squadron. A description of one of the most famous bombers in the Second World War, the Wellington – with which No. 75 was equipped between 1940 and 1943 and in which Artie was to fly at least sixty-five ops – is also included.

No. 75 (motto: 'Ake Ake Kia Kaha'[56]) was established as a 'New Zealand' squadron in April 1940.[57] In the late 1930s, the New Zealand government had decided to equip the RNZAF with the latest bombers and ordered thirty Vickers Wellington Mark IC bombers. Aircrew of the RNZAF were sent to Britain to train on the new aircraft. It was intended that these pilots would ferry the Wellingtons to New Zealand on completion of their training.[58]

In the event the war intervened. When Britain declared war on Germany the New Zealand government made the aircraft and their crews available to the RAF, a gesture warmly welcomed by the British government of the day. Thus No. 75 (New Zealand) Squadron was formed on 4 April 1940. It was the first Commonwealth squadron to be so designated. After the war the squadron was transferred to the RNZAF and was finally disbanded in 1994.

The designation of 'New Zealand' squadron did not mean that it was made up entirely of New Zealanders. Throughout the war, however, the squadron personnel included a comparatively large number of New Zealanders and it had a distinctly 'New Zealand' flavour.

As part of Bomber Command, No. 75 Squadron performed with great distinction. It was regarded as one of the premier squadrons. Its operational record was one of the most impressive in the whole of Bomber

Command. According to the *Bomber Command War Diaries*, during the five years of war, it carried out a total of 8,017 sorties in 739 raids. In total, 193 aircraft were lost on operations and a further 8 fell victim to crashes. No. 75 Squadron carried out the fourth-highest number of bombing raids in Bomber Command and suffered the second-highest number of casualties: 1,139, including 452 New Zealanders.

Artie was very proud of having served in the squadron. He said No. 75 Squadron was much admired both in and outside the service. As this story will show, it was in this squadron that he was destined to establish an enviable reputation of daring, courage and skill. During his two tours in No. 75, he first earned the Distinguished Flying Cross (DFC) and later the Distinguished Service Order (DSO). No mean feat for a 22-year-old. The legend had begun.

From its formation until the end of hostilities in Europe, No. 75 Squadron operated as a heavy bomber unit in RAF Bomber Command. Equipped as it was with Wellingtons, it took part in the early bombing offensive against German, Italian and enemy-occupied territories. It also flew in the first 1,000-bomber raids. Towards the end of 1942 the squadron converted to Stirlings and thereafter made a significant contribution to the Battle of the Ruhr, the devastation of Hamburg, and the famous raid against the German V-weapon experimental station at Peenemünde.

A photo shows Artie with two crew members standing outside Wellington R1458. His logbook recorded that on 5 and 7 March 1941, he flew night-flying tests in this Wellington as second pilot to Sergeant White, the other members of the crew being Sergeants Harrison, Kelly, East and Campbell. He later flew as second pilot to Ron Simich in this aircraft for attacks on Bremen and Berlin, the latter being the attack on 17 April 1941 for which Simich was awarded the DFC.

In March 1944, No. 75 began to exchange its Stirlings[59] for Lancasters and was ready in time to participate in the preparation and support of the Allied invasion of Normandy in June 1944, the bombing of flying-bomb sites, and close support of the armies. In the later stages of the war, the squadron took a leading part in the offensive against German oil production and transport. No. 75 was also one of the foremost units in Bomber Command's successful mine-laying campaign.

Decorations won by New Zealand members of the squadron included one Victoria Cross (James Ward, later killed in action), eighty-eight Distinguished Flying Crosses (Artie included), six Distinguished Service Orders (including Artie), seventeen Distinguished Flying Medals, four Bars to the DFC and two Conspicuous Gallantry Medals.

From April 1940 to July 1945 the squadron was based at four airfields in Britain. These included Feltwell, Norfolk (April 1940–August 1942), where Artie joined the squadron; Mildenhall, Suffolk (August 1942–November 1942); Newmarket, Suffolk (November 1942–June 1943); and Mepal, Cambridgeshire (June 1943–July 1945).

A plaque commemorating the service of No. 75 (New Zealand) Squadron, RAF, was unveiled at Feltwell in 2003.

The following is an extract from a letter written by Gwyn Martin who was stationed at Feltwell during the early war years.[60] He later became a prisoner of war at Stalag Luft III, made famous by the 'Great Escape'.

I remember the security of Feltwell being permanently breached by everyone who was able to climb over the wall of the West End Pub behind the guardroom. Then meetings with the village policeman on his bicycle on the Feltwell–Hockwold road, when on many occasions he could inform us as to whether there were Ops on that night or not. He could tell us the bomb and petrol load for the night from which he could and did deduce successfully, the type of target and the length of the flight.

The Duke of Kent came to celebrate the VC award to Jimmy Ward. It happened to coincide with a fart lighting competition in the Sergeant's Mess snooker room where the consumption of beer had been greater than normal. The darkened room was periodically lit by sheets of blue flame as each fart was fired by a Ronson lighter. The contest for the most successful flame was in full swing when the Senior Warrant Officer appeared in the door of the darkened room and shouted: 'Room attention for his Royal Highness the Duke of Kent.' Someone answered from the safety of darkness: 'Tell him to f… off till I've lit this big bluey.' Without further comment there was a noise like thunder and the lit bluey was the best of the night. A right royal fart indeed.

I'm glad that I spent this period of my life at No. 75 Squadron. I
went from adolescence to manhood, bypassing youth in one year of
the company of a great bunch of guys. I am grateful for the direct
and indirect influences on my life exerted by such people as Group
Captain Buckley, Cyrus Kay, 'Popeye' Lucas and Dave Pritchard,
among so many others.

The Wellington bomber, the beloved 'Wimpy' as it was called, held a special place in No. 75's wartime service. It was the aircraft that flew the most
ops for the squadron. It was also the aircraft in which Artie served with
such distinction. He was piloting a Wellington when he won his DFC
and later his DSO. He remembered it with affection. A beautiful framed
painting of a Wellington in flight hangs in the lounge of his home in
Bournemouth.

Hon W. (Bill) Jordan, New Zealand's popular High Commissioner to
London during the war, made frequent visits to New Zealand service men
and women serving in Britain. A picture depicts Mr Jordan receiving
'three cheers' from New Zealanders in No. 75 Squadron in the early 1940s.

The Wellington was armed with twin .303-calibre machine guns in the
nose and tail turrets. It also had two manually operated .303 guns in the
beam positions and could carry a 4,500-pound bomb load. Slow speed,
limited ceiling and a comparatively small bomb load, soon made the
Wellington obsolete, although one significant design advantage was Barnes
Wallis's geodetic lattice-work fuselage construction. This made the Wimpy
extremely tough, and it often survived battle damage that would have
destroyed other types of aircraft.

Another wartime visitor to No. 75 Squadron was the Hon. Walter Nash,
a New Zealand government minister. Following a visit he made in 1942,
he kindly wrote to my mother recording how he had met Artie and saying
he was well and, along with other New Zealanders, 'doing splendid work'.

The visit of Mr Nash was reported in the *Otago Daily Times*. Among
other things it stated that he had seen remarkable photos taken on the
Hamburg operation for which Artie was to receive the DSO. The *Times*
reported Mr Nash as saying: 'A friendly tussle was ongoing in the
Sergeants' Mess when in strode a grinning Squadron Leader A. Ashworth,
DSO, DFC, with the words "On your feet fellows, I've got some dope to

read you." The day before he had been gazetted DSO, which he said he celebrated in the traditional manner thus: "Yesterday I got the DSO, today I've got apostrophies!"' Mr Nash said: 'This Ashworth is really a remarkable bloke. Debonair in appearance, he sports a beautifully long black "bomber command" moustache. He commands "A" Flight in the New Zealand Squadron and his truly terrific total of 63 operational flights includes the Middle East as well as Germany.'

The Wellington bomber was conceived by Barnes Wallis in the mid-1930s. He had previously designed airships and it was here that he first applied the geodetic construction to hold gas bags within the airship frame. The first geodetic aircraft was the Vickers Wellesley. All geodetic aircraft were to be given a W prefix. This was a private venture by Vickers and its performance exceeded all expectations.

The geodetic construction consisted of steel tubes or ribs being triangulated to each other. This gave the frame immense strength with a minimum amount of metal. The frame was then covered with canvas, sewn into place and treated to shrink and stiffen it into shape. This construction method enabled the aircraft to sustain enormous amounts of damage and still be able to return from operations.

The bomber prototype flew in 1937, with the first Wellingtons (named after the Duke) being delivered to RAF Mildenhall in 1938. From here the 'phoney war' was waged. This consisted of 'nickel' raids or leaflet drops over Germany as only warships out at sea were allowed to be bombed, leaving any civilian or military target untouched. During the phoney war, however, beer, wine and champagne bottles were deposited on military targets unofficially, to frighten personnel – a bottle hitting the ground from 10, 000–20,000 feet would be enough to alarm anybody.

When damaged, the offending part was cut out, a new piece made, covered, then fitted and painted later, with some repairs being carried out and the aeroplane re-entering service within a day. Crews found the Wellington fairly heavy on controls but also a very stable, reliable and satisfactory aircraft to fly, which inspired great trust and faith in it.

With delivery of the larger Lancaster and Halifax bombers, the Wellington was slowly withdrawn from the front-line bomber role that it had held previously. On the first of the 1,000-bomber raids, however,

500 Wellingtons were mustered, proving that it was not finished yet. The Wellington served in all Bomber Command groups. Alongside its bomber role, it is also remembered as that of a minesweeper. Some 11,500 were produced. Only two survive – one at Brooklands in England and the other in Bomber Command Hall, Hendon, London.

In 1980, Ken Moore of Waterville, penned the following moving memory of his comrades in '75'.

Comrades
New Zealand gave a Squadron of planes
When Britain's need was dire
Both countries' sons made up the crews
And they flew through hell and fire.

To the pommy lads the Kiwis made
A gesture that was grand
They gave them honorary citizenship
Of their own beloved land.

Under New Zealand's flag, they proudly flew
Comrades of the air
They lived and died, and side by side
Fates' lot they chose to share.

In Wellingtons, Stirlings, then Lancasters
To the foe they took the fight
On wings they soared through Europe's skies
In darkness and the light.

But a heavy price the Squadron paid
In five long years of strife
Of those who flew with '75'
One in three laid down their life.

On the East Coast of old England
The crumbling airfields stand

Where aircraft once left mother earth
Tractors till the land.

The era of the bomber war
Came, paused then passed away
But the bond between two nations' sons
Unchanged will ever stay.

PART 4:
MALTA AND THE MIDDLE EAST, 1941–42

YEAR: 1941		AIRCRAFT.		PILOT, OR 1ST PILOT.	2ND PILOT, PUPIL, OR PASSENGER.		DUTY (INCLUDING RESULTS AND REMARKS)
MONTH.	DATE.	Type.	No.				
—	—	—	—	—	—	—	— TOTALS BROUGHT FORWARD
September	28	V.Wellington	W5648	Self	P/O.	Ball	Shipping at Palermo (16) 250
					Sgt.	Watson	Second stick at 1000ft.
				P/O. Knowles	Sgt.	Jenkins	
					Sgt.	Holford	
September	31	V.Wellington	Z8797	Self	P/O	Ball	M.T. Yard at Tripoli. (6) S.B.C. (3)
					Sgt.	Watson	Direct hit on 3rd run at 500ft
				P/O. Knowles	Sgt.	Jenkins	(3) S.B.C. Machine gunned M.T.
					Sgt.	Holford	concentration in desert. Silenc
					Lt.	Gammidge	enemy gun positions. Hit.
				Summary for: September 1941			1. V.Wellington
				Unit: № 38 Squadron, Luqa			2.
				Date: 1st. October 1941			
				Signature: J.C.B.Davis			F/Lt D.E.C.
				for O.C. "B" Flight			
				Hallington ℓ			
							W/Cdr.
				O.C. 38 Sqdn. Luqa			
October	5	V.Wellington	X9693	Self	P/O.	Ball	Shipping at Tripoli (16) 250
					Sgt.	Watson	
				P/O. Knowles	Sgt.	Jenkins	
					Sgt.	Holford	
October	7	V.Wellington	R1139	Self	P/O.	Ball	Shipping at Tripoli (16) 250
					Sgt.	Watson	Blazing ship hit.
				P/O. Knowles	Sgt.	Jenkins	
					Sgt.	Holford	

× Afterwards D.F.C.
killed in 1943.

GRAND TOTAL [Cols. (1) to (10)].
694 Hrs. 40 Mins.

TOTALS CARRIED FORWARD

SINGLE-ENGINE AIRCRAFT.				MULTI-ENGINE AIRCRAFT.						PASSEN-GER.	INSTR/CLOUD FLYING [Incl. in Cols. (1) to (10).]	
DAY.		NIGHT.		DAY.			NIGHT.					
DUAL.	PILOT.	DUAL.	PILOT.	DUAL.	1ST PILOT.	2ND PILOT.	DUAL.	1ST PILOT.	2ND PILOT.		DUAL.	PILOT.
(1)	(2)	(3)	(4)	(5)	(6)	(7)	(8)	(9)	(10)	(11)	(12)	(13)
:15	125:05	3:00	6:55	13:45	263:30	11:15	3:05	129:10	69:25	60:10	11:35	13:00
								3:05				
								3:45				
					1:05			27:50				
								4:35				
								3:50				
:15	125:05	3:00	6:55	13:45	263:30	11:15	3:05	144:25	69:25	60:10	11:35	13:00
(1)	(2)	(3)	(4)	(5)	(6)	(7)	(8)	(9)	(10)	(11)	(12)	(13)

Chapter 12

The Siege of Malta

Artie was to experience the early stages of the Axis siege of Malta, which reached its peak during 1942. Before outlining his Malta and Middle East experience, this chapter presents a brief picture of the strategic importance of Malta and the role the island played in the battle for North Africa and beyond.

Artie arrived in the key Mediterranean island in August 1941, as part of No. 38 Squadron. He flew bombing operations from Malta until the end of October when he transferred to Egypt. He remained in Egypt until May 1942 when, much to his relief, he returned to England and his beloved No. 75 Squadron.

Malta's strategic position was clear. It lay astride the German and Italian supply routes to their armies fighting in North Africa. There were also the difficulties of provisioning the island through the Mediterranean from the British bases at Gibraltar and Alexandria in Egypt. It was 985 miles from Gibraltar and 820 miles from Alexandria across hostile waters.

In 1941 Royal Navy submarines and RAF and Fleet Air Arm torpedo-equipped aircraft operating out of Malta were wreaking havoc on Axis shipping carrying supplies and reinforcements to the German and Italian forces in North Africa. If the German forces were to succeed in North Africa and gain access to the Middle East oil, as was their objective, then they had to first eliminate the harassment from the Malta-based Allied air and naval forces. Thus the decision was made to invade the island. The German and Italian air forces were initially given the task of destroying the Allied capacity to resist invasion.

Preliminary attacks were made following the Italian declaration of war in June 1940. Prior to this date, fighters available to defend the vital island were virtually non-existent. The first modern fighters, a group of eight Hawker Hurricanes, were sent to the island in June 1940. Right through the spring of 1942, however, the Axis air forces blitzed Malta, such as no other island or city had experienced in the war. Malta became the most bombed place on earth. The distance of Malta from Gibraltar, the nearest base to support it, meant that fighter aircraft had to fly from aircraft carriers in order to reach the island. Thus the first reinforcement to the island's defence capability was twelve Hurricanes flown from the aircraft carrier HMS *Argus*. This got the island's defences up to strength until the Axis forces set their sights on a major attack in 1942.

British Prime Minister Winston Churchill was convinced of the island's strategic importance and that it had to be held at all costs. The need for more modern fighter aircraft for its defence was deemed vital. Subsequently, Spitfires were flown into Malta from the carrier HMS *Eagle* on 7 March 1942, to augment the few Hawker Hurricanes valiantly holding the fort.

The bombing of the tiny fortress island was intense. For example, in a twenty-four-hour period on 20–21 March 1942, 295 tons of bombs fell on Ta'Qali airfield, making it the most bombed Allied airfield ever. A total of 6,728 tons of bombs fell on Malta in April, thirty-six times the amount to fall on Coventry. Of these, 3,156 tons were dropped on the harbour at Valetta in April 1942. In March and April of that year more bombs were deposited on Malta than fell on London during the entire Blitz. There were 154 days of continuous raids in comparison to London's 57.

The anti-aircraft defences were very active. In April alone, the anti-aircraft gunners shot down 102 enemy aircraft. They destroyed 454 aircraft before the siege ended.

Following a direct request from Winston Churchill to US President Roosevelt, the US aircraft carrier *Wasp* was made available, and together with the Royal Navy carrier HMS *Eagle*, delivered forty-six and thirteen more Spitfires respectively. The addition of these fighters helped turn the tide. Day after day, outnumbered but dogged fighters climbed from their heavily bombed bases into the skies to defend 'the most bombed patch of land in the world'. By the end of the siege 30,037 buildings on Malta had been destroyed or severely damaged.

The suffering of the islands was not just due to the stresses arising from the air bombardment. The most notable memory of many on Malta during the siege was the hunger they endured. The re-supply convoys had to sail from Gibraltar through 'bomb alley'. Heavy losses were suffered by Allied shipping trying to get through. Many ships were sunk before reaching Valetta and, even when they did, they were often sunk in the harbour. The islands could not survive without provisions and at one stage were only two weeks away from having to capitulate. There was very little food for the 30,000 troops and 250,000 residents and almost no fuel left for the fighters defending the island. Operation 'Pedestal' became the turning point with the arrival of the *Port Chalmers, Melbourne Star, Rochester Castle, Brisbane Star* and the crippled aviation fuel-laden tanker *Ohio*, limping into Valetta harbour. These five merchant ships, the survivors of a convoy of fourteen, enabled the islands to carry on. Their Royal Navy escort had also suffered heavily in getting through to Malta.

Johnnie Houlton[61] was a New Zealand fighter ace who volunteered for service in Malta. He flew into Malta from an aircraft carrier in August 1942. In his book, *Spitfire Strikes*, he described the reception process as each Spitfire landed. He also talked about life on the island and his experiences in late 1942.

As each Spitfire came to the end of the landing run, an airman appeared out of the dust and, jumping onto the wing, directed the pilot into a blast pen built of stone block and dirt-filled petrol tins, each pen being already stocked with petrol and ammunition. The airman, assisted by soldiers, tore into the job of refuelling and arming the aircraft, while the pilot stretched his legs or was replaced in the cockpit by an experienced Malta pilot. Refuelling was done by hand, with four-gallon tins being passed along a human chain, while the armourers fed in the belts and drums of ammunition. The system was so well rehearsed that some of the new aircraft were airborne again within nine minutes. Some of the pilots had to land while a raid was in progress or under attack by German Me 109s hunting around the airfield. Several Spitfires were shot down when making their final approach.

Johnnie also described the grim living conditions on the island:

> While Malta was a fighter pilot's paradise as far as air fighting was
> concerned, the reverse was true of our living conditions. Food
> supplies were strictly rationed to a few ounces of bread – supposedly
> nine but more like five per day per man – with half a tin of bully
> beef. Tea, sugar, and butter were eked out between issues and
> staples such as potatoes were never seen. We slept in comman-
> deered quarters on the waterfront of Kalafrana Bay. An old,
> decrepit bus with no glass in the windows took pilots to and from
> the airfield. In a gully beside the road stood the burnt-out skeleton
> of one of the old Gladiators.[62] From daybreak each morning four
> pilots sat strapped into their aircraft on the line of the edge of the
> airfield, four more waited beside their aircraft in the blast pen, and
> four more waited in the crew room. As the first section was scram-
> bled the next one came on line and those in the crew room moved
> into the pens.
>
> Fresh water was in short supply and there was no hot water,
> which made hygiene a myth and helped spread the various
> complaints around. While we were half starved the mosquitoes,
> sandflies, bed bugs and fleas fed very well.

In July 1942, New Zealander Air Vice-Marshal Sir Keith Park,[63] the unsung
hero of the Battle of Britain, was appointed air officer commanding, Malta.
The situation at that time was desperate. Both military supplies and food
were critically short.

Alan Mitchell wrote in *New Zealanders in the Air War* that when Sir
Keith arrived at Malta the island was just about 'out'. It was his job to
develop it into an offensive springboard and he did it. The services were
short of flour and bully beef, and twice the RAF had only one week's
supply of petrol left. Fuel was so short that Sir Keith used to begin his day
by reading graphs showing the petrol position and how much had been
used the previous day. He worked on a quota, and if one was exceeded
one day then the following day's operations had to be restricted.

According to Mitchell, Sir Keith said: 'Malta from July to October 1942 was like the Battle of Britain in miniature, except that we were fighting against heavier odds. We had only a very small fighter force, added to which our men were hungry. We were short of food, and so short of petrol that we were unable to carry out engine-tests, which meant that the pilots had to take off and trust to luck that the servicing was efficient. It was, and there were very few accidents. The airmen had done good work again. They were first class, magnificent.'

In Sir Keith's view, Malta was not a bomb sponge, but a fortress that tied up superior forces of the enemy and made a valuable contribution to the campaigns of General Montgomery and General Eisenhower in North Africa and Tunisia, in addition to carrying on the war with the Luftwaffe in Sicily and Sardinia. 'First the RAF fighters crippled the German fighter force over Malta – on one occasion 40 German Aircraft were shot down in two days.' Then, despite petrol shortages, Sir Keith began attacking the Germans on Sicily, where they had amassed 700 fighters and bombers. He saw that if he could tie up that force it would greatly assist Eisenhower and Montgomery. He set out to obtain air superiority despite all Malta's disadvantages.

Sir Keith remarked that Malta would stand out as a shining example of the flexibility of air power, the adaptability of the British race to improvise, and the tremendous hitting power of a quite small air force when it is centralised and organised so that its striking force can be concentrated from hour to hour on targets vital to the campaign going on around. It was also an example of the cooperation of all three services working together as one.[64]

In August and September, the German and Italian air forces suffered heavy losses over Malta and in October they conceded defeat. At one stage in just a few days, the Luftwaffe lost about 50 aircraft, either destroyed or damaged. The defence of Malta was an all-arms maximum effort. Together with the people of Malta, the Royal Navy, Royal Air Force, Army and Merchant Navy all contributed to their limits as they battled in a fight to the finish, a fight in which they triumphed in the end.

The bravery and endurance of the Maltese people during the siege was formally recognised by His Majesty King George VI. On 15 April 1942, he awarded the George Cross[65] to the Maltese people: 'To the Island Fortress of Malta to bear witness to the heroism and devotion of its people during the great siege it underwent in the early part of World War Two.'

Chapter 13

His Second Tour – Malta and the Middle East

On leaving No. 75 Squadron Artie, having done thirty-one operational sorties in his first tour, went off to Harwell to the Middle East Despatch Flight where he teamed up with an entirely new crew, all volunteers, or, as he suggested, 'refugees from having become instructors at an Operational Training Unit'. He said that from Hampstead Norris (Harwell's satellite) they flew a Wellington Mark II to Gibraltar. 'The runway at Gibraltar was very short and started and finished in the sea. One of our Wellingtons overshot the runway and was a write-off. From Gibraltar we flew along the North African coast to Malta. Shortly before we reached Malta we passed an aircraft carrier, which we assumed to be ours, but one of the aircraft following us was attacked by an Italian CD425 fighter. The Intelligence Officer at Luqa (Malta) refused to believe us, as he claimed: "The Italians don't have an aircraft carrier."'

That was Artie's very matter-of-fact record of the flight to Malta. The reality was something quite different. His omission of what actually happened en route on 30 August 1941 reflects his reluctance to 'blow his own horn'. Or perhaps it was that he had been through so many narrow escapes that this was just another one that in comparison didn't need mentioning. His crew in this Wellington included Sergeant Cook as second pilot, Flight Sergeant Brown and Sergeants Smalley, Jenkins and Holford. Sergeants Jenkins and Holford were destined to fly nineteen operations out of Malta with Captain Artie Ashworth.

Sergeant Robert Holford wrote to his brother in New Zealand about the flight, telling him it was 'hair-raising'. In order to escape the attacking enemy planes, they flew so low they were almost topping the waves. He said they collected eighty holes from enemy fire on the way. Moreover, he believed their survival was due entirely to the skill of the pilot, Artie Ashworth. According to Robert Holford, several aircraft were shot down during this flight to Malta.[66]

As described in the previous chapter, Malta was an important island, positioned as it was across the supply lines of the German and Italian forces fighting in North Africa. Royal Navy submarines based at Malta were a constant threat to Axis supply ships, as were the RAF fighters and bombers flying from the island's airfields. As a consequence, the destruction of the Allied forces in Malta was crucial to the success of the Axis offensive in North Africa. A fierce air attack on the island's harbour and airfields was launched in 1941 as a prelude to invasion. It was into this cauldron that Artie and his crew found themselves on 30 August 1941.

On arrival in Malta Artie said that overnight the crew learned in the sergeants' mess that if they flew an aircraft to Egypt (they were actually on a delivery mission to Egypt), they would finish up in a tented transit camp in the Canal Zone where facilities were primitive, not to mention the sand, so they 'volunteered' to join the resident Wellington squadron, No. 38, whose home base was Shallufa in the Suez Canal Zone. The next night after landing Artie wrote that they had lost their navigator, who had been detailed to fly with another crew and had perished over Tripoli. 'From Luqa on Malta we flew mostly to Tripoli in North Africa, then later to Naples and Palermo in Italy where, at low level, we bombed a row of tethered submarines and escaped in the smoke screen round the harbour. This was the second time we were hit by shrapnel from our own bombs, the other being in the centre of Tripoli.'

The Wellington bombers were kept very busy. In the six months ending December 1941, the Wellingtons at Malta flew well over 1,000 sorties. 'It was an incredible achievement,' said Air Vice-Marshal Lloyd, the air officer commanding at that time. 'The crews never asked for a rest but continued to go out night after night despite the weather. In the autumn heavy rains played havoc with the taxi tracks and dispersal points at Luqa and it became impossible to move aircraft at night so that on their return the Wellingtons had to remain on the airfield until it was light enough to taxi away.'[67]

Artie's logbook details their operations in August and September while operating from Malta. Despite the hair-raising trip from Gibraltar described by Flight Sergeant Holford, they were sent into action two days after arrival.

The Malta George Cross Commemorative Medal was made available to veterans who served in Malta between 10 June 1940 and 8 September 1943. Commemorative medals were issued on the fiftieth and sixtieth anniversaries. In 1992 Artie was awarded the fifty-year memorial medal, which he wore with great pride on ceremonial occasions. On one side the medal depicts the George Cross awarded to the people of Malta in 1942 in recognition of their bravery and steadfastness during the siege.

Artie moved to Shallufa in Egypt on Guy Fawkes Day, 5 November 1941. He recorded that at Shallufa they became part of the 'milk run' to Benghazi. 'These raids were quite hazardous although not so much for enemy action as from the fact a fully laden Wellington in the heat would stagger off the ground after a long run and would climb with great difficulty towards the advanced landing grounds (ALG) in the Western Desert. From the ALGs we did raids mostly on Benghazi, but also Derna and Ain El Gazala.' The Wellingtons were refuelled by hand from four-gallon drums at the ALGs. Artie's last operation in a No. 38 Squadron Wellington was on 2 December 1941. By this time he had flown fifty-three operations against enemy targets.

Artie recalled: 'On one occasion the gunner (rear) said he wasn't going to Benghazi that night as flames from the port engine were going past his turret. On investigation, I found that this was so. The cause was a fractured collector ring – one of the cylinders had been forced through it.' He continued: 'One particular hazard at this time appears in my logbook. "Ran into Tobruk on the way home." This was not very advisable, as the inhabitants (who were on our side) were very sensitive about aircraft flying over their territory and were inclined to be hostile. Their anti-aircraft fire was intense and accurate.'

At this time the Axis forces had driven the 8th Army back to the border of Egypt. In the process the enemy had bypassed the Libyan port of Tobruk, which was occupied by the Australian division, the 'hostile inhabitants'. Artie remembered: 'From No. 38 Squadron I was posted to No. 216

Bomber Transport Squadron based at El Khanka in the Nile delta. This aerodrome of compound sand and gravel, was bounded by the triangle consisting on one side of the Egyptian Camel Corps, on another by a Cairo sewage farm and lastly, by Khanka village. So it didn't matter which way the wind blew it still smelled, the worst smell coming from the village.'

Rex Daniell, who trained with Artie at Wigram, was posted to No. 216 Squadron for a short period. He said that was where he met up with Artie for the first (and last) time since they landed in England in April 1940. He recalled that Artie was really 'brassed off' about being away from what he considered was the real action. Rex told the story of how he was actually instrumental in saving Artie's life one night after they had all had more to drink than was good for them: 'I was woken in the middle of the night to find Artie grumbling that he couldn't open the door. He was actually trying to open a window.' Rex said he managed to prevent him doing so for had he succeeded he would have fallen five floors to his almost certain death, or at least serious injury and most likely the end of his career.

No. 216 was essentially a transport squadron. Its job was to fly supplies in support of the Allied armies, including special groups operating behind enemy lines. They also transported seriously wounded soldiers back to base hospitals. In that regard Artie's logbook records such entries as: '30 December: El Gubbi to Whittaker Landing Ground. Whittaker L.G. to El Gubbi. Eight wounded.' This type of operation, sometimes three on the same day, continued throughout January 1942.

Artie remembered that the aircraft being flown by No. 216 Squadron were Bristol Bombays, a high-wing twin-engined monoplane, and DH86s, which were four-engined biplanes. 'I flew a DH86 mostly on casualty evacuation. Some of the wounded we carried from the Casualty Clearing Stations (CCS) to the advanced hospital were in a bad way. One feature of the DH86 was the very marked gyroscopic swing on take-off, so much so that the port outer engine was scarcely used. On one occasion I was able to exploit this feature when operating from a dried up salt lake. I was unable to start the port outer engine even after I had exhausted most of the batteries in the ambulances of the CCS. Anyway with a full load we took off on three engines and started the other whilst airborne. These flights were classed as operational. We had six DH86s and one was shot down.'[68]

When he came back from the Western Desert in late January 1942, Artie was sent off to Iraq to act as the personal pilot to the American general who was in charge of double tracking the railway line from Basra to Teheran in Persia as it was then called (now Iran). The purpose of this railway was to facilitate the transport of supplies through Persia to Russia. Artie said, 'Quite rightly the General complained that the aircraft stank of gangrene. So we scrubbed the inside with a gallon of Jeyes fluid and water. He then quite rightly complained that the aircraft smelt of Jeyes fluid and gangrene.'

Artie commented that when their aircraft were due for an inspection, they went back to Khanka, where the remaining DH86s were transferred to another squadron and he became a second pilot and later a captain of Bristol Bombays.

Artie finished his tour in the Middle East at the end of April 1942. By this time he had flown 423 hours as captain and 26 hours 40 minutes as second pilot in multi-engined aircraft. The so-called 'mis-employed' experienced Wellington crews were recalled to England in support of the 'Newmarket' maximum effort raids, the first of which was the 1,000-bomber attack on Cologne.

They were flown clear across Africa and from Egypt to Takoradi in West Africa in a Pan American Airways DC3 (Douglas Dakota). Artie sailed from Sierra Leone to Scotland where he arrived some time in May. His 'mis-employed' Wellington crews comment reflected his general unhappiness with his posting in the Middle East. Along with others, he felt his experience, and no doubt his skill as a bomber pilot, were being wasted. He was, however, soon where he wanted to be, back with No. 75 Squadron and once more flying into the hell of the heavily defended Ruhr Valley.

SINGLE-ENGINE AIRCRAFT.				MULTI-ENGINE AIRCRAFT.							PASSEN-GER.	INSTR/CLOUD FLYING [Incl. in Cols. (1) to (10).]	
DAY.		NIGHT.			DAY.			NIGHT.					
DUAL.	PILOT.	DUAL.	PILOT.	DUAL.	1ST PILOT.	2ND PILOT.	DUAL.	1ST PILOT.	2ND PILOT.			DUAL.	PILOT.
(1)	(2)	(3)	(4)	(5)	(6)	(7)	(8)	(9)	(10)	(11)		(12)	(13)
4:45	134:35	3:00	6:55	15:55	425:40	26:40	3:05	221:25	69:25	86:20		11:35	13:00
	:25												
	:20												
								5:50					

3 copies.

28.

OC 75

ZL

FELTWELL   GPC NR GPC 8/30 NOT WT
PASS SELF

TO FELTWELL
 FROM 3 GROUP
 A1/417 30/7
 THE A. O. C. CONGRATULATES F/O ASHWORTH C/75 SQDN ON HIS
PHOTOGRAPHS OF HAMBURG NIGHT 28/29 JULY === 0930

KM VA XV./ R 1013/30 TDC VA

54:45	135:20	3:00	6:55	15:55	426:20	26:40	3:05	237:15	69:25	86:20	11:35	13:00
(1)	(2)	(3)	(4)	(5)	(6)	(7)	(8)	(9)	(10)	(11)	(12)	(13)

Chapter 14

His Third Tour, 1942

In his personal memoir Artie commented that somewhere in West Africa (probably Sierra Leone) he picked up recurrent malaria, which dogged him for the rest of his life, contributing as it did, to his severe eyesight and hearing loss in later life and eventually to his early death in 1994.

On arrival in England Artie observed: 'We reached England at the end of May 1942 and I went straight to No. 75 Squadron at Feltwell. Here I was welcomed with open arms by Ted Olsen, the CO, who arranged for my posting back to the squadron. No. 75 was now equipped with the improved Wellington Mark III.'

He was back in his element and was to remain with No. 75 Squadron until the end of August when, having finished his third tour, he was posted to the headquarters of the elite Pathfinder Force (PFF) at Wyton. In the meantime, he was to complete a further eleven operations, mostly to heavily defended targets in the Ruhr Valley, the heartland of Germany's military industrial complex.

'It wasn't long before I was back in the swing, starting with four flights to Duisburg. Partly by accident we developed a way of getting back through the German defences at low level,' he said. Duisburg, situated in the heart of the Ruhr Valley, was one of the most heavily defended targets in Germany. The 'partly by accident' comment belies the reality of the 'accident'. Pilot Officer Taylor was the second pilot in Wellington BJ584 on the night of 13–14 July when the squadron was detailed to attack Duisburg. Taylor recorded what actually happened:

I suppose Essen in the Ruhr was the most feared target but for my

money Duisburg ran it close. My pilot was the legendary Artie
Ashworth and I was flying as navigator/bomb-aimer and second
pilot, which was common during this phase because of casualties.
We did have a front gunner, however, and he was to prove very
useful as it turned out.

I had just dropped the load on target and was on the flight deck
on my way back to my chart table when we were 'coned' in a box
barrage. This was a frightening experience but not my first. The
only way to survive is to go down, but quick! This immediately
relieves you of the heavy flak but not the six searchlights. On the
way down I happened to glance at the speedometer – it was in
excess of 300 mph but the wings stayed on. We were now being
engaged by light flak, which was tracer, but sustained no hits and
we gradually lost the searchlights.

We finished up missing the chimney pots and I suddenly realised
that we were over the Rhine and very nearly in it. I signalled to
Artie to turn to starboard, which in hindsight was a good decision.
As we proceeded up-river virtually at nought feet, we were engaged
by tracer from the right bank and this is where the front gunner
came in useful because the Krauts didn't like the return fire.

Then we came to Düsseldorf and leap frogged over a few bridges,
which we could just make out. I don't think there were any bridges
at Leverkusen but then we came to Cologne and Bonn, where there
were several. There was no more tracer and once we were in the
Moselle valley we were safe.

Regaining operational height of 12,000 feet, I was able to get
some GEE[69] fixes and plot a course for home but not, of course, by
the prescribed route.

For this raid on 13–14 July 1942, Artie's logbook recorded the crew of
Wellington BJ584 as Pilot Officer Taylor, Flight Sergeant Albert, DFM,
Flight Sergeant Thistle and Pilot Officer Lunn. It was his fifty-fourth
operation and the first after returning from his tour in the Middle East.
His logbook merely reads: '36 x flares, 6 x 500' (500-pound bombs). The
time of flight was 4 hours 10 minutes. This operation was one of five,
three on Duisburg and two on Hamburg, that led to him being awarded

the Distinguished Service Order, of which more later.

The *Bomber Command War Diaries* reported that the force on this particular night encountered cloud and electrical storms and that the bombing was scattered. The Duisburg authorities recorded only housing damage. Of the 194 aircraft that took part in this raid, 6 were lost and 4 more crashed on their return in England.[70]

Artie also went to Hamburg on the night of 26–27 July, about which he made no comment in his memoir. Terry Kearns, a fellow New Zealander from Reefton on the west coast, also serving in No. 75 Squadron, was on that raid. Kearns and Artie were close friends. Artie was to be best man at Terry's wedding in 1946. Kearns also helped with the arrangements for Artie's funeral in 1994. He was one of New Zealand's most decorated Second World War pilots. He completed a tour with No. 75 Squadron, immediately after which he joined No. 156 Pathfinder Squadron where he was one of the first to be awarded the coveted Pathfinder badge. After this tour he instructed at 11 OTU, RAF, before returning to operations for a third tour, this time with No. 617 Squadron, flying first Lancasters and then Mosquitoes. Kearns was awarded the Distinguished Service Order, the Distinguished Flying Cross and the Distinguished Flying Medal. After eighty-eight operations he resumed instructing and was later seconded to BOAC.[71] After returning to New Zealand in 1947, he took up a permanent commission with the RAF. He retired in 1963 and died in England in 1995, one year after Artie.

Artie's personal memoir recorded: 'An attack on Hamburg on the night of the 28–29 July was successful and, without much support from the other aircraft, we crossed the city three times and three times we took photographs of the centre. Losses were said to be heavy that night due to icing, but we didn't see any [the reference is to icing], probably because we were not high enough. My logbook shows that Flying Officer Ashworth was congratulated by the Air Officer Commanding (AOC) 3 Group for these Hamburg photos. It wasn't long after that I was promoted to Acting Squadron Leader and again not long after, I was awarded the Distinguished Service Order (DSO).'

This was the second time Artie had been to Hamburg which, in addition to being a large port, was an important industrial target where most of Germany's submarines were built during the war. The super battle-ship *Bismarck* was also constructed in the Hamburg shipyards. In 1943, by which time Artie was flying fighters in a RNZAF squadron in the Pacific, Hamburg was the target for the infamous 'firestorm' raids, which resulted in huge fires and heavy loss of civilian life. According to Martin Middlebrook in *The Battle of Hamburg*: 'The city had gained an evil reputation among Bomber Command aircrew for the strength of its defences. These were situated in a wide circle up to twenty miles from the city centre and it took a bomber fifteen minutes to fly through the full spread of the city's guns and searchlights.'[72]

The first raid on the night of 26–27 July 1942 was reported to have caused considerable damage. Losses were high. Of the 403 aircraft despatched on that night, which included 181 Wellingtons, 29 were lost – 7.2 per cent of those sent. No. 75 Squadron lost 2 Wellingtons and 10 aircrew.

New Zealander Pilot Officer Frank Chunn of Te Awamutu (later Flight Lieutenant, DFC) had joined Artie's crew as the rear gunner on 20 July. He was substituting for the normal rear gunner who was away on some course. Frank wrote in his diary: 'Did an N.F.T. [night-flying test] with Artie Ashworth DFC, a New Zealand pilot, and a good one.' Frank was to fly a total of six operations with Artie for whom he had a high regard. He was the rear gunner on the Hamburg operation on the night of 28–29 July. Of that raid he said that once more they managed to slip in and out through the flak and the searchlights and get three photos. 'A long stooge trip and we got home short of petrol but made it. A hellish night for 75 Squadron. We lost six kites tonight', were the words in his diary.

The Operations Record Book of No. 75 Squadron for this raid noted that seventeen Wellingtons were despatched and that six aircraft failed to return. Thirty spaces would be empty at the post-op breakfast and thirty messages would be sent to the respective parents, wife or fiancée, that their loved one was reported missing on operations. While the crews and ground staff tended to give the impression it was just one of those things that happened in war and there was no point in dwelling on the loss of friends, all would have been affected to a greater or lesser degree. They all knew that it could well be their names that went up on the losses board next time. Meanwhile, large numbers of family and friends would grieve and feel the losses deeply.

What Frank Chunn and Artie didn't say about the second Hamburg raid was that it took real guts, determination, great skill and a good dose of luck to fly three times through this hell. Once their bomb loads had been dropped, hopefully on the target, the huge majority of captains and crew couldn't get out of it all fast enough. But not Artie Ashworth. He was determined to get the photos that Bomber Command required and, against all odds, he succeeded.

Artie's logbook records the three Duisburg raids and the first Hamburg raid. Frank Chunn was the rear gunner on all four operations. The logbook also records the second Hamburg op.

Shortly after this operation, on 30 July, the officer commanding No. 75 Squadron at Feltwell, Group Captain Olsen, received a signal from the air officer commanding No. 3 Group, congratulating Flying Officer Ashworth on his photographs of Hamburg on the night of 28–29 July.

Bomber Command War Diaries recorded that 403 aircraft were despatched from No. 3 Group on this second Hamburg operation. A total of 29 aircraft were lost, including 15 Wellingtons, which embraced 6 from No. 75 Squadron. The crews encountered a mixture of cloud and icing at some place on the route but the weather was clear over the target according to the war diaries. Hamburg reports show that severe and widespread damage was caused, mostly in housing and semi-commercial districts rather than the docks and industrial areas.

By this time Artie was the officer commanding 'A' Flight, and had completed 61 operations over enemy territory and flown almost 1,000 hours. Shortly after these memorable raids the following sign appeared on the door of the OC 'A' Flight:

Ashworth & Co. – Aviators
Trips to Happy Valley at Government Expense

'Happy Valley' was the bomber crews' name for the Ruhr Valley, one of Germany's most heavily defended areas. Artie noted that, subsequently, some 'low type' inserted below the sign: 'Return trip not guaranteed.'

Chapter 15

The Distinguished Service Order

Artie was granted an 'immediate award' of the DSO soon after the Hamburg raid. He was twenty-two and now sported a DSO in addition to his DFC. During the Second World War eight officers serving in No. 75 Squadron were awarded the DSO.

The Distinguished Service Order was instituted in 1886 by Queen Victoria. It was established for rewarding individual instances of meritorious or distinguished service in war. It was a military order and, until recently, for officers only. It is normally awarded for service under fire or in conditions equivalent to service in actual combat with the enemy. The honour is often regarded as an acknowledgement that the officer has only just missed out on the award of the Victoria Cross. In 1942 the award was extended to officers of the Merchant Navy who had performed acts of gallantry while under enemy attack.

Citation for the Distinguished Service Order

'Arthur Ashworth, Acting Squadron Leader, No. 3 Group, No. 75 (NZ) Squadron. Total number of hours flown on operations 338. Number of sorties 61. Recognition recommended: Distinguished Service Order.

The above named Officer is now on his third operational tour, having so far completed 61 operations. He commenced his first tour in this Squadron on February 21, 1941, finishing in August 1941, having completed 32 sorties. During this tour he was awarded an immediate Distinguished Flying Cross. He then proceeded to the Middle East, where he completed a tour of operation of twenty two trips.

Since commencing his third tour he has consistently displayed courage and devotion to duty of the highest order. He never fails to reach the target in spite of all odds, pressing home his attack at heights of 8–9,000 feet and invariably obtains photographs of the aiming point. On recent raids on Duisburg and Hamburg he has secured the following photographs on the aiming points.

13–14 July 1942	Duisburg	1 Photograph
21–22 July 1942	Duisburg	1 Photograph
25–26 July 1942	Duisburg	1 Photograph
26–27 July 1942	Hamburg	1 Photograph
28–29 July 1942	Hamburg	3 Photographs

Flying Officer Ashworth shows exceptional keenness to operate at all times and his great courage, skill, and efficiency as a pilot, Captain of aircraft and Officer, are a splendid example and stimulus to the entire Squadron. I consider Flying Officer Ashworth worthy of the highest consideration and strongly recommend him for the award of the Distinguished Service Order.

Signed: E.G. Olsen, Wing Commander, Commanding No. 75 (NZ) Squadron, RAF.'

Covering remarks, station commander

'It is impossible to speak too highly of this Officer's great courage and determination to reach his aiming point in the target area, his utter fearlessness and his great enthusiasm and devotion to duty. Every one of his sorties is carried out in such a manner as to earn a decoration if they were carried out by the more ordinary control. I would like to see this Officer receive an immediate award.

The recommendation was strongly supported by the Air Vice-Marshal Commanding No. 3 Group. An Immediate Award[73] was approved by the Air Marshal, Commander-in-Chief, A.T. Harris.'

Chapter 16

Two of Artie's Rear Gunners

The life of a rear gunner in Bomber Command was both lonely and highly dangerous. Casualties were high. The extra danger came from the enemy fighters which too often went for the rear gunner in order to silence his guns. When being attacked by fighters, it was the Wellington's rear gunner's responsibility to instruct the pilot on what evasive actions to take. It was lonely since the gunner faced backwards and had no visible contact with the rest of the crew. Moreover, he was hemmed into a very limited space. He was literally crammed in with little or no room to move. And, invariably, it was very cold.

Ken Rees, a wartime bomber pilot, commented that he always had great admiration for the rear gunners, cooped up in their freezing, cramped turrets, staring for hours out into the dark, hands often frozen to their guns, feet frozen in their boots. Other crew members busy with their respective jobs could always get up and move around. But the gunners had no such luxury. He said they were tough characters and he never knew one who showed fear or the slightest reluctance to fly. Mostly, they just had to sit there chilled to the bone and staring into the darkness, waiting for that sudden burst of gunfire which, unless they got their guns to work on time, meant almost certain death.[74]

Given the high casualty rate among rear gunners, the records of two New Zealand gunners who flew with Artie in 1942 is remarkable. Both survived a large number of sorties. Frank Chunn successfully completed sixty-nine and Ken Crankshaw a massive seventy-nine. And all over some of the most heavily defended targets in Germany. Both were awarded the DFC and Ken Crankshaw a DFM as well. Chunn flew six operational sorties as part of Artie's crew and Crankshaw three.[75] Both expressed great respect for Artie's skill as a pilot and both commented that he had a 'dare-devil' streak in him!

Flight Lieutenant Frank Chunn, DFC. Frank joined the RNZAF in March 1940. He first served with No. 5 OTU, carrying out twelve 'unofficial' day-light patrols during the Battle of Britain. He then joined No. 255 Squadron, RAF, on night fighters. During the German 'Blitz' in 1940, he flew thirty-two night patrols, shooting down three He 111s. For the 'rest' of the tour he flew with No. 231 Squadron, RAF, flying Lysanders[76] on Army cooperation in Northern Ireland before joining No. 75 (NZ) Squadron and flying a further sixty-nine sorties in Wellington bombers.

He survived two crashes in Wellingtons. The first was at RAF Sutton Bridge when, with twelve air gunners on board, one motor failed but they all got out safely. The second was on a No. 75 Squadron sortie when his aircraft was hit by flak on a night operation to Essen. The navigator was injured, one 500-pound bomb 'hung-up', and the undercarriage would not lower. Due to fog, they were diverted from their home base, eventually crashing in sand dunes. All the crew survived. After a spell as the RNZAF liaison officer in Canada, Frank returned to New Zealand in July 1944 and was discharged in November of that year.[77] Flight Lieu-tenant Chunn died in Te Awamutu in 2007, aged ninety.

Flight Lieutenant F. Chunn, Citation for DFC

'Flying Officer Chunn has completed many sorties as a rear gunner and has destroyed at least two enemy aircraft. He has consistently shown excellent leadership and a thorough knowledge of gunnery. His courage and keenness to engage the enemy have been most marked.

21 October, 1942'

Flight Lieutenant Ken Crankshaw, RNZAF, DFC, DFM. West coaster Ken was one of life's great characters. According to his cousin Morry Deterte of Wellington, he rebelled against authority and discipline from an early age. He had no time for what he regarded as the 'bullshit' of military pro-tocol. Morry claimed that shortly after arriving in England Ken was severely reprimanded one day for not saluting some British officers. Ken's defence, he said, was that he had come 12,000 miles to kill Germans, not to go round saluting stuffy British officers no matter how senior. All that notwithstanding, Ken Crankshaw was a brave and skilled air gunner, who proved his worth where it counted – in the hell of bomber operations over enemy territory.

While serving in No. 75 Squadron, Ken became known as 'Ring-the-bell Crankshaw'. Apparently at one stage his crew were billeted in a stately home near their airfield. Ken took a liking to a bell, used no doubt to summon servants in better times. Having little regard for that sort of upper-class stuff, the wild west coaster decided to 'borrow' the bell and henceforth carried it with him on operations. Legend has it that while over the target, and when the bomb doors were open, the pilot would call: 'Ring the bell Ken.' According to Max Lambert the sound would then be boomed out via the transmitter to the accompaniment of the song 'Oh, the Bells of Joy Go Tinga-linga-ling', supposedly a trick to convince the Germans that a new secret weapon had arrived![78] When Ken returned to New Zealand in late 1944 he brought the famous bell with him. Today it adorns the entrance to his former home in Tallon, Australia, where it serves as the front door bell.

Following another of his pranks, Ken was court-martialled and sent back to New Zealand in late 1944. It appears that the protocol in the officers' mess was that the group captain (the station commander) had the right to stand in front of the fireplace. This didn't suit Cranky Crankshaw at all, so he arranged that one day, when the concerned officer took his place, crackers would explode in the fireplace. The explosion was such that the group captain suffered the indignity of having the seat of his trousers blown off! Legend has it that the offended group captain considered Ken to be 'crackers' and should be sent home. This, after he had done seventy-nine operations. By this time he was serving in one of the more famous Pathfinder squadrons, No. 156.

While stationed at the RNZAF base at Ohakea, Ken first met his future, very talented wife Valerie, then in the Women's Auxiliary Air Force (WAAF). Val said that at that time he was a mental wreck, which is not surprising for someone who had been through his harrowing experiences. They married in 1947. After living in Cambridge and Coromandel for many years, they went to live in Australia where Ken died in 2009.

In the latter years of his life, Ken suffered from dementia. Val cared for him until the last month of his life. In that sad period, during which his memory failed almost completely, two precious things remained deep in his faded memory: his logbook and his medals. Until the day he died he insisted they be under his pillow every night.

Citations for DFM and DFC

Distinguished Flying Medal

'Flight Sergeant Crankshaw has taken part in many operational sorties, the majority of which have been over the most heavily defended area of Germany. He has always displayed the utmost keenness to attack the enemy's searchlights and gun positions. His skilful fire against enemy fighters and excellent instructions to the pilot have contributed largely to the safe return of his aircraft. His constant cheerfulness and high example of courage and determination have been an inspiration to all.'

Distinguished Flying Cross

'As air gunner Pilot Officer Crankshaw has taken part in a very large number of sorties and has displayed outstanding determination and devotion to duty. One night in August 1943, during a sortie to Berlin, his aircraft was attacked by a Ju88. Coolly and skilfully, Pilot Officer Crankshaw engaged the attacker and accurate shooting caused the aircraft to dive away apparently on fire. This officer has displayed courage and confidence, setting an excellent example.

19 October, 1943'[79]

Chapter 17

Saarbrücken: Operation Sixty-five

Following the completion of his third tour and his second with No. 75 Squadron, by which time he had survived a total of sixty-four operational sorties, Artie found himself posted as a staff officer to the headquarters of the Pathfinder Force at Wyton. His next operation, for which he volunteered, was to be perhaps the most memorable of all.

The story as recorded by Artie continues: 'Before I left 75, I was sent by Group Captain "Speedy" Powell to lecture at the Wellington Operational Training Unit. This was a daunting experience as, at each station, the entire flying people, both instructors and pupils, were assembled. I like to think I was able to instil some "know-how" to both sections.' So wrote Artie Ashworth; surely a massive understatement if ever there was one. Those who were privileged to hear someone who had flown sixty-four operations, wore the DSO and DFC ribbons, and who, by that time, had become a living legend, were not going to miss the opportunity of learning all they could from him. 'I continued to fly with 75 Squadron until August 1942 when I was sent for by Group Captain Don Bennett, who was establishing his Pathfinders. As a result I was posted as a founder member of his staff.'

He took up his role at the Wyton headquarters of the Pathfinder Force, on 28 August 1942. An interesting incident occurred before he left No. 75 Squadron, however. His logbook for 11 August merely states 'test-crashed'. He was testing Wellington BJ773 with Sergeant Melbourne as the second pilot and Sergeant McAlpine the only other crew member. The group captain commanding RAF Mildenhall took a dim view of this episode and endorsed his logbook for 'bad airmanship'. Quite a comment about a pilot who had flown sixty-four operational sorties, most of them as captain, and at that time had 1,001 hours 55 minutes' flying time.

Artie's sixty-fifth operation proved to be more than a 'normal' experience. His bravery and skill on this operation received wide publicity. A number of variations of the story have been recorded, all of which include some inaccuracies. The following is the story as recounted by the man himself. Hopefully this will set the record straight:

> My 65th sortie was flown in September 1942, which began as a normal working day. The target came through from Bomber Command to the operations room at Pathfinders Headquarters, Wyton, where I was now one of Don Bennett's merry men. The target was Saarbrücken and I got permission from the Group Captain to fly that night. So I rang Wing Commander T.S. Riott-Carnac (known as "Nuts & Bolts") the CO of No. 156 Pathfinder Squadron at Warboys, and asked for the loan of a Wellington and crew. This was readily agreed. Unexpectedly, later that morning, my brother Corran, a fighter pilot in the RNZAF, phoned from the railway station at Huntingdon to say that he had arrived to see me. We took off from Warboys with a load of 12 three-inch flares and six 250 lb bombs. The flares were used to illuminate the target for the rest of the bombers. I'd never seen the crew before and it was to be quite a long time before I wanted to do so...!
>
> The first sign of trouble was a smell of burning; no smoke, or at least none where I was. We were somewhere near the target at the time and had been for quite a while, flying up and down, trying to get the reflection of the moon in the river. There was haze on the ground and we needed the river to pinpoint our objective. A few seconds after I'd noticed the smell of burning, the Wireless Operator came through on the intercom with the information that sparks were coming through the floor. I wasn't at all worried, it might have been anything, say an electrical fault.
>
> All sorts of odd things happened to one in the air over wartime Germany. So we went round again still searching for the river, which took five minutes, then the Wireless Operator came through that there were more sparks coming through the floor. He also said

he was standing by with a fire extinguisher. I realised then that we must be on fire somewhere and guessed it was one of the flares. These being in the bomb bay under the floor and unreachable from inside the aircraft, I decided to jettison the flares.

The bomb aimer let them go and suddenly there was a blinding light all round the aircraft and what appeared to be flames underneath us. Looking over my shoulder through the window it seemed to me that the whole of the rear of the aircraft was on fire. I had enough experience, this being my 65th Op in a Wimpy, of watching Wellingtons being destroyed by fire in the air. They seldom lasted long so right away I said 'OK bale out.'

I felt the rear gunner go at once because his turret turned. The rest seemed to take a devil of a long time. I yelled and swore at them to get on with it but I doubt if they heard me. It was possible that here the confusion over parachutes arose, and one of them may have got the impression that I was letting him take mine. At last all the others were clear. I saw a couple of them sliding out in the light from underneath me, just for an instant I could see their bodies falling.

It was now my turn and I came dashing out of my seat to follow, but horror of horrors, my parachute had gone. It should have been in the stowage just forward of the cockpit on the starboard side, but I quickly realized that one of the others had taken it in the confusion.

I went back along the fuselage – it's amazing how quickly one can move in an emergency – to see if I could find a parachute. The glare was still with me and now a great deal of smoke. I looked in the Navigator's and Wireless Operator's stowages and the rear stowage above the bed – nothing – and all I could do was return to my seat.

At first I could not think of anything to do. I'm sure this was due to a state of numb fear.[80] Then I had an inspiration; if I could get to the ground very quickly, I might be able to crash-land the aircraft before it broke up, so throttling back, I did the classic action to be taken in the event of 'fire in the air', sideslipping violently from side to side. I was down to 800 feet when suddenly the fire went out. The burning bit of flare caught in the bomb bay had broken off, though

I didn't know this until much later.

After all the glare my eyes weren't much use to me and it took quite a while before I could see the instruments properly, but I still had control. It seemed pretty hopeless to try to get back home alone, but then I hadn't a lot of alternatives.

Climbing to 5,000 feet I left the controls and went back to the Navigator's position to see what I could find. I found a map but most of the Navigator's stuff was lying about all over the floor. His log would have been useful, but I couldn't find it – it was found next morning on the floor.

Popping back from the controls again to the Nav's position and using his protractor, I marked out a course and drew a line to England. I didn't really know where I was until I hit the French coast. There some flak and searchlights marked the position of Dieppe, recognizable by the angle of the coast to North. From there on it was plain sailing. [Plain sailing indeed![81]] From a quarter of an hour before the French coast there was nothing showing on the petrol gauges, so I had the engines running as economically as possible. I didn't care what part of England I hit and when I was halfway across the Channel I switched the IFF[82] to the 'Distress' position. It was very dark.

I had just sighted the English coast when both engines cut. I ran back down the fuselage to turn on the nacelle tanks. Normally this was done by simply pulling a piece of wire in the side of the fuselage, but in this aircraft a trap for young players had been incorporated so that in order to pull the wire it was first necessary to slide a ring on the end of the wire so that it would slip through a slot in the aircraft's side. Using strength born of wild desperation index [sic], I pulled the angle-poise light from the Wireless Operator's position round a strut to find out this fact, then pulled the wire. This started the port engine and I raced forward desperately to the cockpit. There I pulled the cross-feed cock to start the other engine.

After a few minutes I was over England and was guided to West Malling in Kent by searchlights, for which I was very grateful. After landing, I was directed to a parking spot on the edge of the airfield.

The engines now wouldn't stop so I left them running and opened the bomb door. After climbing down the ladder I moved aft and there I found the parachute caught in one of the bomb racks. Pulling the cords of the parachute I could see that there was a round object at the end. At first I was distressed when I imagined it was part of the crew but it turned out to be the broken flare that had caused all the trouble. The 'missing' parachute I eventually found on the bed below the rear stowage.

The crew on this mission comprised: Flight Sergeant Nobles, Flight Sergeant Cordock, Sergeant McGeown and Sergeant Durham. Artie never recorded just what happened to them nor did he ever talk about it, suggesting he may have felt some guilt at having ordered them to bale out and then surviving himself. According to Errol Martyn, author of *For Your Tomorrow* (three vols), and the HMSO publication *Prisoners of War, Naval and Air Forces of Great Britain and the Empire 1939–45*, all four survived and were made prisoners of war. Oliver Clutton-Brook, author of *Footprints on the Sands of Time*, thought it possible that Sergeant McGeown was slightly wounded, but all four were imprisoned at Stalag VIIIB, Lamsdorf, Germany.

After landing Artie called Wyton to ask that they let his brother Corran know that he was okay. Artie wrote: 'A couple of days later I flew Corran back to his fighter base at Hibaldstowe. I never saw him again.'

The last comment is especially poignant. Artie and his brother were very close.[83] Having been born a little over twelve months apart, they had grown up and shared many of the adventures of youth together. Corran was flying Mustang fighter-bombers in No. 65 Squadron, RAF, in Normandy, when he was killed on 3 August 1944. At that time Artie was a fighter pilot serving in the Pacific.[84]

Artie's lone flight home received widespread publicity. He was interviewed by the BBC and a number of British and New Zealand newspapers, including the *Otago Daily Times*.

There have been different stories about how exactly Artie was treated at this time by the RAF top brass. According to Lorie Lucas, wife of Artie's friend from No. 75 days, Squadron Leader Fred (Popeye) Lucas, RNZAF, DFC, and author of *Popeye's War*, Artie told one of the crew to take his parachute (p. 152). She also wrote: 'When he taxied in to his parking place, he was asked where the hell is your crew? "Oh, the crew", he answered, "well as a matter of fact they've gone off on a long leave."'

Lorie also claims that Artie was put on charge and reduced in rank for a short period for the parachute incident, since as captain he had not made sure sufficient parachutes were aboard. She went on to say that despite this he was awarded the DFC for this operation. Apart from Artie's comment about his crew going on a long leave, both claims are incorrect.

The newspaper report includes a little more detail of this historic operation in Artie's own words. It erroneously gives his rank as wing commander.

Nick Carter of Hamilton, at that time serving in No. 75 Squadron and later in No. 156 Pathfinder Squadron, thought Artie had been disciplined due to negligence and was sent home to New Zealand as a result. That assertion is only partly accurate. Artie did return to New Zealand in early 1943 but not for the reasons claimed by Nick.

Some believed he should have received the Victoria Cross for his bravery and skill in flying a bomber back single-handedly. In the event, he was awarded a Mention in Despatches (MID). Pathfinder Nick Carter also said he thought Artie should have received higher recognition.

In his book *Strike Hard – A Bomber Airfield at War*, John Hilling wrote about Artie and his sixty-fifth operation:

> One-time Air Staff Officer at PFF HQ, Artie Ashworth, was a
> famous pilot with 635 Squadron. Also ex-35 and 156 Squadrons,
> he was one of the founder members of the original PFF. Artie was
> one of a select few captains, who, upon finding his aircraft on fire
> due to heavy flak over the target area, ordered the entire crew to
> bale out. As the fire appeared to intensify, and he was very near the
> highest part of the Alps, he put the aircraft into a dive and found
> to his surprise the slipstream put the flames out. Then, without a
> crew, he managed to navigate to the French Coast and hence to the
> UK, and by following the identification letters being flashed in the
> Morse of RAF airfields he found his way back to base.
>
> Oddly enough the CO of No. 35 Squadron, Wing Commander
> Robinson, did exactly the same thing very shortly afterwards and

was awarded an immediate bar to his DSO for his effort. Ashworth only remembers a right royal rocket he received from Don Bennett and he was never able to understand what the difference was between his solo effort and that of Wing Commander Robinson.

Hilling has a couple of his facts wrong but his comments illustrate how remarkable courage and skill went unrecognised.[85] Much depended on the mood of the responsible CO at the time. Upon being told this story, Oliver Clutton-Brook commented that receiving a 'right royal rocket' from Bennett was itself a badge of honour. One possible explanation for Bennett's fury could be that Artie was not officially detailed to fly on this operation. He was a staff officer no longer posted to operations and not part of No. 156 Squadron. He had no need to participate, other than some keen desire to fly on an operation, which I believe had some secret objective. But the truth will never be known.

When visiting the RAF museum at Hendon, London, I read the citation of a high-ranking RAF officer who had received the VC for managing to fly his damaged bomber back to England on his own after the crew had baled out. This award only serves to make one ponder exactly why Artie was treated as he was.

Artie had been posted to the HQ of the Pathfinder Force at the request of Don Bennett, the officer commanding. Artie's story continues:

In the early part of 1943, Headquarters Pathfinder Force (PFF) became Headquarters No. 8 (Pathfinder) Group and eventually all my jobs were taken over by some high priced help. I like to think that I had some influence and was partly responsible for the early operational PFF tactics. I had on many occasions to make the decisions on route, height, timing and bomb load for the entire Force. Please remember I was 22 years old. The residue of my stay with the Pathfinders can be found in code names for two of the types of attack we used. After discussing with Group Captain Bennett[86] how we were going to use the new air and ground markers, I went about writing the two operations orders for their original use. I named the two types of attack first 'Wanganui' – I had a brother living there at the time – and 'Parramatta' in deference to

Don Bennett (an Australian).

The first or 'Wanganui' attack was to use coloured flares as air markers and the second used coloured cascading target indicators to mark the target on the ground through haze or thin cloud. I know this is contrary to what Don Bennett wrote in his book *Pathfinder* about code names he claimed to have named. He claimed that Wanganui was my birth place. The nearest I have ever been to Wanganui is the RNZAF base at Ohakea, some 40 miles distant.

The story now shifts to New Zealand where Squadron Leader A. Ashworth, DSO, DFC, MID, was welcomed home as a local hero.

PART 6:
THE PACIFIC, 1943–44

YEAR: 1944		AIRCRAFT.		PILOT, OR 1ST PILOT.	2ND PILOT, PUPIL, OR PASSENGER.	DUTY (INCLUDING RESULTS AND REMARKS).
MONTH.	DATE.	Type.	No.			
—	—	—	—	—	—	— TOTALS BROUGHT FORWARD
September	14	Corsair	5331	Self		Bombing & strafing. 1 x 500
September	15	Corsair	5326	Self		Bombing & strafing. 1 x 500
September	17	Corsair	5338	Self		Test
September	18	Corsair	5331	Self		Squadron formation
September	20	Hudson	2039	F/Lt Durning		Henderson ~ Torokina
September	21	Corsair	5392	Self		Bougainville patrol
September	22	Corsair	5313	Self		Bombing- S. of Bonis. 1 x 500
September	23	Corsair	5313	Self		Dawn Patrol
September	24	Corsair	5324	Self		Sweep- Put Put ~ Keravat. 1 x 500
September	25	Corsair	5315	Self		Bougainville patrol
September	26	Corsair	5313	Self		Strafing ~ Shortlands. 1 x 500
						Summary for: September 1944 1. Corsair
						Unit: Nº 17 (F) Squadron 2. Hudson
						Date: 1st October 1944
						Signature: *R.J.Proulka* F/Lt.
						O.C. "B" Flight.
						[signature] S/Ldr.
						O.C. Nº 17 Squadron.
October	2	Corsair	5299	Self		Bombing ~ Numa Numa ~ 1 x 1000
October	3	Corsair	5324	Self		Bombing ~ Kanakadran ~ 1 x 1000

GRAND TOTAL [Cols. (1) to (10)].

1273 Hrs. **15** Mins.   TOTALS CARRIED FORWARD

Chapter 18

A Hero Returns

On leaving the Pathfinder Headquarters, Artie later recorded: 'By various means I managed a posting back to New Zealand and went across the North Atlantic by liner, across the North American Continent to San Francisco by train, then by troopship across the Pacific to Brisbane, by train to Sydney (to be repeatedly short-changed), by train to Melbourne, across Bass Strait to Launceston, by Noddy [sic] train to Hobart, and finally on the *Dominion Monarch* to Wellington.' Artie commented that in 1948 when en route to New Zealand on leave from the RAF, he was a passenger on the same liner on her 'maiden voyage'.[87]

From Wellington, he made his way to Dunedin, which in those days was quite a journey. There were no air services, which meant taking the overnight ferry from Wellington to Lyttleton, then ferry train into Christchurch where one breakfasted at the railway station, and then took the 'express' to Dunedin, an all-day journey. He would have stayed overnight in Dunedin and then travelled on the 'Central Otago Express' to Alexandra. The train would leave Dunedin at 10 a.m. and arrive in Alexandra around 3 p.m., assuming it wasn't late that is, which it invariably was.

My mother and I travelled by train to Ranfurly to meet him. The small town on the Maniatoto Plain was roughly halfway between Dunedin and the terminal at Cromwell. Passengers to and from Dunedin would lunch in Ranfurly. I vividly remember seeing this uniformed air force officer with the huge 'Bomber Command' moustache, striding down the platform, arms outstretched, to take his very proud mother in his arms. It was an emotional moment. I was eleven years old at the time and was somewhat overawed by the event. I recall just standing and staring with great admiration at my hero brother.

The arrival at the Alexandra railway station was a huge event for the small town. It was mid-1943. The country had been at war since September 1939. Artie was the first man in Alexandra to volunteer for the air force in 1939. He was one of the most decorated Second World War servicemen in New Zealand at that time and Alexandra was very appreciative of their hero, someone who had been part of their tight-knit community. He had been a keen Scout, a rugby player, a good student, and was well known and popular with his peers. He had shown leadership qualities at an early age. In short, he was one of their own. His exploits had received wide publicity in the local media. And here he was, their home-grown man of courage.

As the train approached the station, the engine sounded 'hip-hip-hooray' with appropriate blasts on the whistle. It seemed that the entire population of the town had turned out. David Ellis, a school contemporary of mine, said that the whole school were marched up to the station.

My mother and Artie were greeted by the Mayor and Mayoress and the President of the local RSA. The Mayor gave a short speech of welcome and then Artie made his way through the admiring crowd to walk the short distance to our home in Station Street. A rather embarrassed hero was persuaded to make a short speech, thanking all and sundry for their welcome. Along with my mother and two sisters, Iris and Edna, he then made for home as quickly as possible. But more was to come.

The local Scout troop had formed a guard of honour at the front gate of our house. The boys saluted as he approached and Artie shook hands with each as they were introduced by the Scout leader, Mr Duncan. Then finally he was home. I recall being completely overawed by the whole occasion. Here was my hero and all I could do was continually stare at him in admiration.

Throughout the war, the local community always held a public 'welcome home' for returning service men and women. Artie's official welcome was duly reported in the *Alexandra Herald*: 'The Alexandra Town Hall was filled almost to capacity on Thursday night last, when representatives of practically every home in Alexandra as well as many visitors, gathered together to show their appreciation of the services rendered to the Empire[88] by Squadron Leader A. Ashworth, DSO, DFC, who is on loan to the

New Zealand Government. Residents of this town from Central Otago as a whole, have every reason to be proud of Squadron Leader Ashworth, as few airmen in the country have shown the skill and courage to win the distinction he has. For his mother too, everyone has the warmest admiration for her courage, there being three of her sons serving with the RAF.'[89]

At a suitable interlude, the Mayor, Mr A. McKellar, took the opportunity to make a presentation to the guest and to express the gratitude of the Alexandra citizens for Squadron Leader Ashworth's brilliant service. Messrs J.R. McKissock, RSA, D.W. Moorhead, Fruitlands Patriotic Committee, and E.J. Iversen, Earnsclugh Patriotic Committee, all spoke in glowing terms of the young man.

According to the *Herald*: 'In rising to reply, Squadron Leader Ashworth was received with great applause, which marked the esteem in which he was held. Speaking in his modest vein, he thanked those who had made his welcome such a pleasure and said his achievements were due to the fine instruction he had received.' Artie was quite embarrassed by the whole affair.

In many respects, Artie must have considered Alexandra a rather dull place. I imagine he would have found it difficult to adjust, given the experiences he had been through and the life he was now used to living. I suspect most returning service men and women had the same problem. The only people who would have had any understanding of what these men had been through would be those who had fought in the First World War.

Local people, probably including members of my own family, rather expected him to be the same young man they had known before the war. But now he was a different person. I suspect my mother in particular found it hard-going to adapt to this change. For example, she was a strict teetotaller. Alcohol was forbidden. In her eyes, anyone who drank more than one beer must be a drunkard. And here was her own son, somehow smuggling bottles of beer into her house and then each night sitting down and drinking a whole bottle, if not two. As many of his comrades testified, Artie liked his 'grog'.

During his stay at home and before he reported to RNZAF Headquarters in Wellington, Artie spent much of his time visiting old friends and families. Most of his contemporaries were now serving in the armed forces.

But he took the time to visit their relatives, including the Lunns, Nightingales and Smiths among others.

He also spent time with our sister Edna who lived in Queenstown where her husband, David Galbraith, was a plumber. Our Aunt Margaret, older sister of my late father, also resided in Queenstown. Auntie Mag, as she was known, was by then the family matriarch whom all held somewhat in awe. She was tall, regal and very proper. One had to be on one's best behaviour when in her presence. But like all of us, she was very proud of her now-famous nephew.

Artie presented the RNZAF with a dilemma. There was no post available at that time for a squadron leader in the RNZAF, let alone one with sixty-five operations behind him, not to mention a DSO and a DFC. He was on 'loan' to the RNZAF, being as he was a New Zealander commissioned in the RAF rather than the RNZAF. He said his role was uncertain so he was conveniently despatched to the Army Staff College at Massey College (now Massey University) near Palmerston North. He found the army people a 'grand bunch' and felt he was able to use what he learned at the college to subsequent advantage, although he never said what that was.

He mentioned that one of the other students, John Albert Axel Gibson, was a fighter pilot and survivor of the Battle of Britain who had already completed a tour as fighter pilot in the South Pacific. He subsequently proved a remarkable fighter leader in Europe. During the gap between the Army Staff College and his posting to the Pacific, Artie flew as second pilot to John Gibson on a number of occasions. The next step in Artie's career was serving as a staff officer with No. 1 Group, RNZAF, in the Pacific, first at Espiritu Santo and then Guadalcanal.

Squadron Leader John A.A. Gibson, RAF, DSO, DFC

John Gibson was born in Brighton, England, in 1916. He joined the RAF in 1938 and was on loan to the RNZAF from June 1942 until December 1944. He returned to the RNZAF for one year ending December 1946. He then rejoined the RAF in 1948 and retired in 1954.

John Gibson was a Second World War fighter ace. He was credited with the destruction of fourteen enemy aircraft plus eleven damaged while serving with No. 501 Squadron, RAF, in France and during the Battle of Britain, and No. 15 Squadron, RNZAF, during the Solomons' campaign. He completed four operational tours, was shot down five times, crash-landing once and baling out four times, twice in the English Channel – thereby qualifying for membership of the 'Caterpillar' and 'Goldfish' clubs. He was CO of No. 15 Squadron, RNZAF, from December 1943 until July 1944, while on loan to the New Zealand government. He also flew during the Biafran war in 1970 and with the Rhodesian air force in 1971 through 1979. He died in England in July 2000.

Citation, Distinguished Flying Cross
30 August 1940: No. 501 Squadron, RAF (Hurricanes)

'In August whilst on an offensive patrol over Dover this officer engaged and destroyed a Junkers 87 and was afterwards shot down himself. Although his aircraft was in flames he steered it away from the town of Folkestone and did not abandon the aircraft until it had descended to 1,000 feet. Pilot Officer Gibson has destroyed eight enemy aircraft and has displayed great courage and presence of mind.'

Citation, Companion of the Distinguished Service Order

'Since the award of the DFC for his achievements as a fighter pilot in the Battle of Britain, this officer has further distinguished himself both in England and more recently in the Pacific, where he made three Tours in the Solomons' area. He has destroyed a total of $14^{1}/_{2}$ [sic] enemy aircraft adding to his earlier record of one Japanese fighter, which was fiercely attacking him and an Allied formation over Rabaul Harbour. Acting Squadron Leader Gibson, as a brilliant pilot and born leader, has to his credit the exceptional total of 669 hours of operational flying covering 382 missions. On his two latest Tours in the Pacific, he commanded a squadron and his fearless leadership has been outstanding. His personal courage, both in aerial combat and ground strafing and fighter-bomber missions, and his long experience have been of inestimable value to his Squadron and earned high praise of Allied Commanders.'

Chapter 19

Fighter Pilot – the Pacific Theatre

The Army Staff College recommended Artie for 'regimental duties'. He was posted to No. 1 (Islands) Group where he served on the Air Staff on Espiritu Santo [in what is now called Vanuatu] and Guadalcanal. Artie reported for duty in May 1943, but did not arrive at Santo until early in September. Prior to this he seemed to do a lot of flying between RNZAF bases.

During May and July he undertook several flights as second pilot in Harvards between the various RNZAF airfields including Whenuapai, Ohakea, Milson (Palmerston North), Rukuhia (Hamilton), Rongotai (Wellington) and Hastings. On twelve of these the first pilot was none other than Flight Lieutenant Gibson, DFC, with whom he had attended the Army Staff College. He also met up with Bob Spurdle again at Ohakea. He flew as second pilot with Bob on one occasion. Like Artie, Bob had returned to serve in the RNZAF, having distinguished himself in action in England.

On 14 September 1943, he flew to Espiritu Santo in a C47 transport aircraft.

Artie did not record anything of his time as staff officer in the Pacific. His logbook does not report any flying during December 1943. In February 1944 he was stationed at Henderson airfield, Guadalcanal, the main island of the Solomons group. Guadalcanal was the scene of very bitter fighting as the Americans fought to drive the Japanese from the island.

While stationed at Guadalcanal he engaged in one of his passions – gardening. He somehow had obtained some vegetable seeds from New Zealand, which he proceeded to plant. I remember him writing home saying it was like 'magic'; 'plant the seeds and they germinate almost overnight'.

Artie's logbook pages records the last month at Wyton, his flights with John Gibson and his subsequent arrival in Espiritu Santo.

On his return to New Zealand in April 1944, Artie asked for and was given the opportunity to train as a fighter pilot. Before embarking on instruction, he paid a short visit to my mother in Alexandra. His logbook records flying from Taieri to Alexandra as second pilot to Wing Commander Matheson in a Tiger Moth on 23 April 1944. He spent two days in Alexandra before returning to Taieri. He was then flown to Tauranga where he was intensively coached on Harvards. Artie said he trained first on Harvards at Tauranga and Woodbourne, then Kittyhawks and Corsairs at Ardmore. He commented that the OTU at Ohakea on Kittyhawks was one of his only two Operational Training Units to which he was posted in the whole of his service. The other was at Benson in 1940, flying Fairey Battles.

Instruction on Harvards continued unabated during April and May 1944. Activities included low-level bombing, aerobatics, medium dive-bombing, air-to-ground combat and so on. At the beginning of June he changed to Kittyhawks, which he flew throughout July. The next move was to Ardmore near Auckland, in preparation for transferring to the Pacific. Early August saw him flying Corsair fighter-bombers, but this time with No. 17F Squadron, RNZAF, in the Pacific at Espiritu Santo. Artie commented: 'At Ardmore I joined No. 17F Squadron as a Supernumerary and we moved to Bougainville in the Solomon Islands via Espiritu Santo and Guadalcanal. At each place we took over the Corsairs left by the rotating squadron ahead of us. Our main task on Bougainville was to contain the encircled and by-passed Japanese forces in the area. Practically all our air opposition had already been wiped out so we spent the days, either on individual hunts for the opposition or attacking with bombs and our 6.5 inch machine guns, specific targets set by the Command through the intelligence sections.'[90]

Artie recorded the following story: 'My aircraft was damaged on only one occasion when, as I was trying to land a bomb on a Japanese armoured car, I heard machine gun fire coming from my right. I gave the position of the gun a quick spray and then called my section to return to Bougainville; we were over Rabaul area of New Britain at the time. Quite a long way out to sea my engine stopped then by dint of judicious diving, started again, and I headed for Green Island. All the way to the Island it kept stopping and starting but by the time I reached the Island, I had gained a bit of height and was able to make a dead stick landing on the coral strip. An American aircraft fitter devised the fault as a damaged ignition harness to one bank of cylinders, caused by a single bullet. He replaced the harness and back I went to Piva south of Bougainville.'

Artie engaged in his first action as a fighter pilot on 1 September 1944, a Corsair dawn patrol flying this time out of Henderson airfield on Guadalcanal. During September and October operational sorties were flown on most days. He took the time to enter interesting unofficial notes in pencil in his logbook. Some of these are as follows (pencilled entries in italics):

21 September: Bougainville patrol: *strafed huts and cooking fires.*
22 September: Bombing South of Bonis: *had a shot at some huts on East Coast.*
23 September: Dawn patrol: *strafed fires on East Buka.*
24 September: Sweep – Put Put–Keravat, 1 x 500: *across Tobera and Keravat. Strafed fires and huts. Shot at B.N. Warornai.*
25 September: Bougainville patrol: *strafed huts and cooking fires.*
26 September: strafing Shortlands. 1 x 500: *killed first son of Heaven on Faisi. Burnt two barges and 1 tent. Bombed village opp. Ballalae. S/L St. George wounded.*

Throughout October the action was just as intensive, with operations on nineteen days.

4 October: bombing Faisi – 1 x 500: *Jap strong point. First trip as division leader.*
5 October: Bombing Buka. 1 x 1000: Hahela mission.
6 October: Bombing Mu. 1 x 1000: *bivouac area. Many casualties.*
7 October: Bombing Shortlands. 1 x 1000: *Jap strong point.*
8 October: Bombing Numa Numa. 1 x 1000: *bivouac area.*
9 October: Numa Numa. 1 x 1000: *bivouac area.*
10 October: Bombing Ralum. 1 x 1000: *stores and bivouac.*
11 October: Bombing Numa Numa. 1 x 1000: *bivouac area.*

16 October: Bougainville patrol. 1 x 500: *probably killed 1 Nip.*

17 October: Bougainville patrol. 1 x 500: *probably killed 2 Japs.*

18 October: Scramble: *radar tracking.*

19 October: Bombing Waitavalo. 1 x 1000: *bivouac and stores.*

21 October: Bombing Shortlands. 1 x 500: *Jap strong point. Strafed huts.*

24 October: Bombing Keita. 1 x 1000: *Jap Company.*

25 October: New Britain sweep. 1 x 500: *destroyed 1 truck, odd huts.*

26 October: New Britain sweep. 1 x 500: *destroyed 1 truck. Killed 2 Nips.*

27 October: New Britain sweep. 1 x 500: *killed 2 Nips. Direct hit on petrol dump. Landed Green, duff motor, strafed 9–10 trucks, 1 tank.*

28 October: *dawn patrol.*

29 October: *Bougainville patrol: strafed huts, odd Nips, got none!*

Trevor Pearce, later warrant officer, maintained that Artie never quite mastered flying fighters. When the squadron returned to Ardmore in preparation for flying to the Pacific, Trevor wrote:

Now we had one great character with us. He was seconded from the RAF and he sprouted a huge moustache and of course was known as 'Auntie'.[91] He had received a DFC[92] for action over Germany, but was very heavy handed when it came to handling fighters as he was used to flying heavy bombers, which of course were not as responsive as a fighter.

… When we were re-equipping with Corsairs it was general practice for the CO to fly the new type first, and then the senior NCO. After that it was the next senior officer, which was 'Auntie'. Well he took it up alright but on landing he had the misfortune of selecting the dive brake position instead of the undercarriage down and so landed with his tail wheel still retracted but the Corsair has a skid ram just for such an occasion. For that mistake he paid a hefty fine to the Squadron drinking fund.

Now when flying with 'Auntie' it was an experience in itself. He was used to flying heavy bombers and all his movements were over-correcting which made you keep on your toes as one minute his aircraft was over there and next he was heading straight for you and so you reacted very fast and let him pass underneath. To the best of my knowledge he never did get it right but he was well liked by one and all.

Frank Ferrier was a member of No. 17F Squadron. He said he remembered Artie as a supernumerary flying Corsairs operationally out of Green Island. 'I was a Pilot Officer at the time but even with the NCO ranks he wished to be called Artie and not sir.' Frank recalled that 'he liked his grog and had an eye for the ladies'. He described Artie 'as a great unassuming guy.'

'From Bougainville we returned to New Zealand (2–3 November) – quite a lot lighter than when we had left mainly due to dysentery. I was offered command of one of New Zealand's fighter squadrons in the Pacific, but declined on the grounds that they faced very little opposition.' So wrote Artie Ashworth. He wanted further participation in the real action with Bomber Command in Europe. By this time the end of the war was in sight, although there was still much hard fighting, destruction and loss of life before Germany finally surrendered in May 1945. Artie wanted to be in the thick of it again before it all ended. It's also possible that he was by this time thinking of life after war. A career in the RAF would be more likely to be achieved if he was back in England.

Before leaving New Zealand on 7 December 1944, he made a quick visit to my mother in Alexandra. Artie was always concerned for his dear mother. He appreciated the hardships she had endured in her life and he was worried for her welfare. At that time my mother and I were the only family living at home. Having turned eighteen, my brother Donald had been conscripted into the air force and was in training. He made the fourth Ashworth brother to serve in the air force during the Second World War. I remember Artie buying me some new clothes. I think he was appalled at what he perceived as some of the rags I wore. He also realised that my mother and I were at that time living in poor circumstances. He determined to help and upon his return to England arranged for £5 (around NZ $400, 2011 value) to be sent to my mother each month. I know it was a big help.

PART 7:
PATHFINDER, 1945

YEAR: 1945		AIRCRAFT.		PILOT, OR 1ST PILOT.	2ND PILOT, PUPIL, OR PASSENGER.	DUTY (INCLUDING RESULTS AND REMARKS
MONTH.	DATE.	Type.	No.			
—	—	—	—	—	—	— TOTALS BROUGHT FORWARD
April	1	Lancaster	PB926	Self	Crew	Training
April	2	Lancaster	PB926	Self	Crew	Practice bombing
April	11	Lancaster	PB979	Self	F/L. Melling & Crew	to Oakington & return
April	12	Lancaster	PB926	Self	Crew L.A.C. Boily	X Country
April	13	Lancaster	PB926	Self	Crew	Ops. ~ Kiel 3 x 1,000 T.I. 6 x 1,000, 4 x 500 (75)
April	12	Oxford	HN768	F/O. Cardinal	Self	B.A.T. 3 x 1,000 T.I., 4 x 1,000, 4 x 500 (76)
April	14	Lancaster	PB926	Self	Crew F/L. Bresslof	Ops.~ Potzdam
April	16	Lancaster	PB926	Self	Crew	Training
April	19	Lancaster	PB913	Self	Crew	Training 6 x 1000, T.I. 4 x 500
April	22	Lancaster	PB913	Self	Crew	Ops.~ Bremen 4 x 1,000 T.I., 3 x 1,000, 4 x 500 (77)
April	26	Lancaster	PB913	Self	Crew	Ops. ~ Berechtesgaden 2 x 250 T.I. (78)
April	30	Lancaster	PB913	Self	Crew	Supply dropping ~ Ypenburg
				Summary for: April 1945	1. Lancaster	
				Unit: № 635 Squadron	2. Oxford	
				Date: 1st. May 1945		
				Signature: a ashworth S/Ldr.		
				O.C. "A" Flight		
May	2	Lancaster	PB989	Self	Crew	to Wyton
May	2	Lancaster	PB935	F/O. Rowland	Self & Crew L.A.C. Franks	return 2 x 250 T.I.
May	5	Lancaster	PB913	Self	Crew Cpl. Hall	Mercy mission ~ Rotterdam 2 x 250 T.I.
May	8	Lancaster	PB913	Self	Crew	Manna to the Hague

GRAND TOTAL (Cols. (1) to (10)).

1462 Hrs. 40 Mins.

TOTALS CARRIED FORWARD

SINGLE-ENGINE AIRCRAFT.				MULTI-ENGINE AIRCRAFT.						PASSEN-GER.	INSTR/CLOUD FLYING [Incl. in Cols. (1) to (10).]	
DAY.		NIGHT.		DAY.			NIGHT.					
DUAL.	PILOT.	DUAL.	PILOT.	DUAL.	1ST PILOT.	2ND PILOT.	DUAL.	1ST PILOT.	2ND PILOT.		DUAL.	PILOT.
(1)	(2)	(3)	(4)	(5)	(6)	(7)	(8)	(9)	(10)	(11)	(12)	(13)
65:25	413:40	3:50	16:45	18:20	503:20	26:40	3:35	294:45	69:25	308:40	15:40	13:40
					2:15							
	Crew				2:05							
Visual ~ F/L. Morgan, D.F.C.					:45							
					2:40							
								5:10				
				1:00								
								8:15				
					2:25							
					3:00							
					4:05							
					7:40							
					2:20							
					27:15			13:25				
				1:00								
					:20							
										:20		
					2:25							
					2:30							
65:25	413:40	3:50	16:45	19:20	535:50	26:40	3:35	308:10	69:25	309:00	15:40	13:40
(1)	(2)	(3)	(4)	(5)	(6)	(7)	(8)	(9)	(10)	(11)	(12)	(13)

The Pathfinder Force

On returning from his Pacific tour Artie was appalled when, after first completing a course at the Officers' Advanced Training School at Cranwell, he was told he would be remaining there as an instructor. That didn't fit with his ideas at all. Artie Ashworth wanted back in the real action. He felt he had missed a great deal of it during his sojourn in the Pacific. So, as we will see in the next chapter, he hurriedly arranged to be posted back to a Pathfinder squadron. He was to finish his wartime career serving in No. 635 Pathfinder Squadron, of which he was immensely proud. Before moving to that part of the story, however, there is a need to understand something of the Pathfinder Force, including its role and techniques.

Charged with the formidable task of locating and marking German targets for attack by the main force of Bomber Command, the Pathfinder Force (PFF) became perhaps the most experienced and highly trained elite unit within the RAF during the Second World War. Its aircrew members were almost wholly volunteers and – despite the terrifying odds against any individual or complete crew ever completing the forty-five or more sorties in a tour of operation with the PFF – the most feared punishment for PFF members was to be sacked and posted away to other units.

The PFF role was to locate and mark targets with flares, which the following main bomber force could aim at, thereby increasing the accuracy of the bombing. While the majority of Pathfinder squadrons and personnel were from the Royal Air Force, the group also included many from the air forces of Commonwealth countries. In January 1943, the Pathfinder Force became No. 8 (Pathfinder Force) Group.

It was the ineffectiveness of Bomber Command's bombing campaign in the early stages of the war that led to the formation of the PFF. At the start of the war, RAF Bomber Command carried out daylight raids, but the losses incurred from lack of escorting fighters when operating over Europe were unacceptably high. This led Bomber Command to switch the majority of its strategic bombing missions to night-time. This reduced fatalities, but made identifying and then hitting a target accurately very difficult. The formation of the Pathfinder squadrons was seen as at least one way of remedying this problem. Don Bennett, who became the commander of the force, had been thinking and planning something like the PFF long before it was finally established. In 1941 he was invited to address the Directorate of Bomber Operations at the Air Ministry to give his views on how to improve the then current standards of navigation and bombing.

He later wrote: 'I looked at the assembled company and I simply asked a question: "You are all experienced general duties officers; you have been flying a lifetime. Could you get into an aircraft on a pitch-black night, fly for 3 or 4 hours on a compass and an air-speed indicator, find a pinpoint in central Germany, avoid the spoofs and dummies, not be put off by night fighters, flak, and searchlights and guarantee success?" They looked at each other and replied: "Of course not; we are pilots not navigators." I pointed out that they had 20 years or more in the air, whereas those boys they were sending out over Germany had had no practical experience whatever of genuine operational flying.'[93]

Formation of the PFF was not without controversy. The idea met with strong opposition, which included that of the formidable air officer commanding, Bomber Command, Air Marshal 'Bomber' Harris. It was the source of one of the bitterest arguments of the Second World War. It was initially the brainchild of Group Captain S.O. Bufton, a staff officer for whom Bomber Command's chief had special contempt. Harris believed an elite group would breed rivalry and jealousy, and have an adverse effect on morale. Sir Henry Tizard, however, one of the chief scientists supporting the war effort said, 'I do not think the formation of a first XV at rugby union makes little boys play any less enthusiastically.' Eventually, Harris was forced to accept the idea by a direct order from no less authority than Prime Minister Winston Churchill. And when the Prime Minister spoke one didn't argue.

But Harris persisted with his own idea. In order to minimise any adverse effects on the wider Bomber Command, he wanted every group to have its own pathfinders, but, again, a sharp disagreement ensued. Eventually Harris lost and a separate group was formed. Harris selected the highly regarded Australian officer, Don Bennett, to command the Pathfinder Force. Aged just thirty-two, Bennett was almost two decades younger than most of the other group leaders, but he had proved himself one of the most skilful and dauntless pilots in the RAF, with an unrivalled mastery of the arts of flying and navigation. His knowledge of navigation was to play an important role in the success of the Pathfinders.

Harris was to tell Prime Minister Winston Churchill that Bennett was by far the most efficient and capable young officer he had ever met. His appointment was a great success. He was feared by many for his brusque manner and he didn't suffer fools easily. Tolerating only the best and the highest standards, he also had a very high opinion of his own ability and views and was constantly striving to develop new tactics and ideas for improving bombing accuracy. Bennett was, though, highly respected by all who served under him.[94]

The PFF was initially formed in August 1942 by creaming the best squadrons from the existing Bomber Command groups to make up the force, a tactic that understandably did not go down too well with the other group commanders. Initially the Pathfinder Force had no better tools than the rest of Bomber Command, flying its fair share of Stirlings, Halifaxes, Lancasters and Wellingtons.[95] When new aircraft, such as the De Havilland Mosquito, became available, PFF got the first ones, and then made good use of them by equipping them with ever more sophisticated electronic equipment, such as OBOE, a highly accurate radio navigation and bombing aid.[96]

Bennett set high standards for PFF aircrew recruitment. He wanted, and in most cases got, only the best. All members of the PFF were volunteers. In comparison with the normal twenty-five to thirty operations per tour, Pathfinders were required to complete tours of forty-five or more operations. The reasoning behind this requirement was that the extra experience and skill of longer-serving PFF crews was essential for the success of the whole programme.

From 1943 until the end of the war, Pathfinder crews found themselves given increasingly sophisticated and complex tasks that were constantly modified and developed tactically during the bombing campaign. Some of the more usual tasks are described below:

Finders were No. 8 Group aircraft tasked with dropping sticks of illuminating flares, firstly at critical points along the bombing route to aid navigation and keep the bomber stream compact, and then across the approximate target area. If conditions were cloudy then these were dropped 'blind' using H2S navigational radar.

Illuminators were PFF aircraft flying in front of the main force, which would drop markers or Target Indicators (TIs) on to the designated 'aiming point' already illuminated by the Finders. Again, if conditions were cloudy, H2S navigational radar was used. These TIs were designed to burn with varying colours to prevent the German defences lighting decoy fires. Various TIs were dubbed 'Pink Pansies', 'Red Spots', and 'Smoke Puffs'. Illuminators could include Mosquitoes equipped with OBOE if the target was within the range of this highly accurate bombing aid.

Markers would drop incendiaries on to the TIs just prior to the main force arrival. Further Markers called 'Backers-up' or 'Supporters' would be distributed at points within the main bomber stream to re-mark or reinforce the original TIs as required.

Visual centrers had to estimate the mean point of impact of all the primary markers and drop their TIs on this point. Their TIs were usually a different colour from those of the primaries to help the main force distinguish between the primary and secondary markers. It was their job to see that the target was illuminated at all times.

As the war wore on, the highly dangerous role of 'master bomber' was introduced as a sort of master of ceremonies. The appointed Pathfinder (usually a highly experienced senior officer) continuously circled the target broadcasting radio instructions to both Pathfinders and main force aircraft, correcting aiming points and generally coordinating the attack. The 'deputy master bomber' was, according to author Gordon Musgrove, a sort of 'man Friday' who took over control in the event that the master bomber was unable to control the operation.[97] These roles were especially dangerous. Circling the target at a low level while the raid was in progress, vulnerable to bombs falling from above, and flak below, was not one that held out good life insurance prospects.[98]

The proportion of Pathfinder aircraft to main force bombers varied enormously according to the difficulty and location of the assigned target; one to fifteen was common, although it could be as low as one to three. By the start of 1944, the bulk of Bomber Command was bombing within 3 miles of the PFF indicators, a huge improvement in accuracy. The success or failure of a raid now depended overwhelmingly on the Pathfinder's marker placement and how successfully further marking was corrected.

There was some rivalry between the 'Pathfinder' groups. This was mainly between No. 8 and No. 5 Group, which was driven by the personal rivalry between Bennett and the air officer commanding of No. 5 Group, Sir Ralph Cochrane. Cochrane was an advocate of precision low-level marking, and lobbied heavily to be allowed to prove himself, and that No. 5 Group could attempt targets and techniques that No. 8 Group would not.[99]

Cochrane's specialist No. 617 Squadron proved his point when they attacked the Ruhr dams (Operation 'Chastise' – the Dam Busters), requiring bombing from a height of 60 feet (20 metres), and, later, at high altitude, using the new Stabilizing Automatic Bomb Sight, achieved an incredible and very necessary accuracy of only 94 yards (86 metres) at the V-weapon launch site at Abbeville. No. 5 Group invented various techniques, such as the '5 Group corkscrew' to evade enemy fighters, and the '5 Group quick landing system'.

From the time of its formation in August 1942, the PFF flew a total of 50,490 individual sorties against some 3,440 targets. The cost in human lives was high. At least 3,727 members were killed on operations.

Three main techniques were used by the PFF to identify the targets of the main force bombers:

Parramatta: The first technique was known as 'Parramatta'. Target Indicators (TIs) were dropped by aircraft using H2S or OBOE to identify the exact location. The target was continuously marked by TIs dropped by a secondary marking force, referred to as 'backers-up', used when the original markers were either bombed or went out over time. This technique was used when the target was large.

Newhaven: The second technique was known as 'Newhaven'. First, an aircraft would drop flares over the target to illuminate it. When the aiming point had been visually identified by other aircraft, they would accurately drop their TIs on to the objective using the Mark XIV bomb sight.

Wanganui: This method was used if the target was covered by cloud or a smokescreen. The Pathfinders identified the target using H2S or OBOE, then dropped TI flares suspended below parachutes. The suspended flares provided the main force with suitable aerial aiming points.[100]

All three methods could be used by aircraft utilising either H2S or OBOE. If Pathfinders were using OBOE the different techniques would have the prefix 'Musical' such Musical Parramatta, Musical Newhaven or Musical Wanganui. The TIs could either be red, yellow or green and were specified in the briefing for each raid to identify primary and secondary targets.

Despite his deep misgivings about its establishment, when Bomber Command chief Harris appointed Don Bennett to command the PFF, he promised him all his support. He was as good as his word and gave Bennett his full backing for the rest of the war.

While Artie received no credit from Bennett in his book *Pathfinder* for his role in developing these various techniques, other authors, notably McKinstry and Thompson, recorded that Artie had played a major role in developing the PFF strategies and attack methods when he served at PFF Headquarters in late 1942. Artie's version of the role he played in developing the original Pathfinder operational techniques was previously described in Chapter 17.

Chapter 21

Pathfinder No. 635 Squadron, Downham Market – Part 1

The sixth year of hostilities, 1945, dawned to a war-weary world. With the breakout of the Allied armies in Normandy and the relentless advance of the Soviet armies in the East, the defeat of Germany and the end of the war in Europe was now in sight. But sadly too many lives were to be lost and huge damage incurred, before Germany finally surrendered in May.

Bomber Command had now reached the zenith of its power. It had become the most formidable force of its kind that the world had ever seen. It was now largely equipped with the redoubtable four-engined Lancaster bomber, claimed by many to be the finest bomber of the Second World War. It could fly higher, carry a greater bomb load, and was equipped with the latest navigation aids. Its flying characteristics were superb, it was easier to service, and its enormous bomb bay accommodated 'Tallboy' and, when modified, the 'Grand Slam' bombs. It was the only aircraft capable of carrying these huge bombs.[101]

Bomber Command attacks had become more accurate and the losses decreased. While the German ground defences were still daunting obstacles, the capacity of the air defence had fallen considerably. This was due, among other things, to a growing shortage of experienced pilots to man the fighters and a decreasing number of replacements for the fighter aircraft being lost.

Perhaps the most important constraint, however, was the growing shortage of oil and fuel due to the devastation inflicted on the synthetic oil plants and the Romanian oil production facilities by the Allied air offensive. By this time the German aircraft industry had also suffered severe damage. This notwithstanding, in the latter part of 1944, the first German jet-fighters made their appearance. They were faster than any of the Allied fighters and had they been produced in quantity, they would have presented a major challenge.

Another factor contributing to the reduced losses, especially on daylight attacks, was the advent of the Mustang fighter which, with its longer range, provided support for the attacking bombers. These aircraft operated from advanced landing grounds in newly liberated areas of France. In addition, RAF Mosquito night fighters were lessening the dangers posed by German night fighters attacking raiding bombers.

The controversy about Bomber Command target priority continued. According to the Allied High Command, the prime concern was to attack transportation infrastructure and oil installations. However, as air officer commanding, Sir Arthur Harris continued to insist that the real precedence should be the continuing destruction of German cities. He regarded anything else as peripheral, convinced as he was that the way to bring an early end to the war was to destroy the morale of the German people through widespread destruction of towns and cities along with the inevitable loss of civilian life. The RAF was also required to attack the V1 and V2 rocket production and launching sites situated mainly in north-west Europe. At this time these lethal weapons were causing considerable damage and deep public concern in England.[102]

As a senior RAF officer, however, he knew his duty and reluctantly obeyed the order (although not entirely, as area bombing of German cities continued) to give priority to the disruption of transportation infrastructure – roads, railways, bridges – and oil installations.

Artie returned to England in mid-December 1944. He recorded: 'From New Zealand I was flown across the Pacific, across the United States, then from Canada to Scotland.' It wasn't as simple as it sounds and was actually a long tortuous trip flown in cold, noisy, uncomfortable converted military aircraft. It took eighteen days in total, as follows: 29 November 1944: Rongotai–New Plymouth–Whenuapai; 7 December: Whenuapai–Nandi; 8 December: Nandi–Canton–Hickham (USA) (over dateline); 8 December: Hickam–Oakland–Hamilton–Lyndbergh; 9 December: Lyndbergh–Love; 13 December: Love–Washington–Dorval; 15/16 December: Dorval–Gander–Prestwick. All in a C87 transport aircraft.[103] Some journey. Artie noted: 'On arrival in England I reported to the Air Ministry and was sent to the Officers Advanced Training School at Cranwell on a course. On finishing this at the end of January, I was supposed to remain as an instructor but a hurried visit to Don Bennett at Huntingdon and a plea to re-join his Pathfinders, changed all that.'

So in February 1945, Artie was posted to No. 635 Pathfinder Squadron based at Downham Market in Norfolk. No. 635 Squadron was equipped with Lancasters, which aircraft Artie had not previously flown. Before being sent on operations, Pathfinder crews were first required to pass through the exacting Pathfinder Training and Navigation Unit (PTNU). Having assembled a new crew, he spent all of February training on Lancasters. By the time he had completed his PTNU training he had flown nearly twenty-four hours as a Lancaster first pilot, which included just over seven hours of night flying. He continued: 'So from leading a Section of four Corsairs to land on Piva South[104] on the 29th October, 1944, my next operational sortie was as Captain of a Lancaster in No. 635 (Pathfinder) Squadron on the 7th March, 1945.'

But it was a different war to the one he had experienced when he last flew heavy bombers on operations in 1942. The aircraft were better, the navigation techniques greatly improved and, as observed previously, the German defences at least a little less formidable. As the Allied armies liberated more of France, sorties to Germany and beyond had diminished enemy-occupied territory to negotiate both on the outward and homeward legs of their journey. Additionally, Allied fighter squadrons were now based in Advanced Landing Grounds in France, which enabled them to provide fighter protection for the bombers during daylight operations.

During March and April 1945, Artie participated in thirteen Pathfinder attacks on German cities: Dessau, Kassel, Wuppertal, Zweibrücken, Dortmund, Nuremberg, Bremen, Bottrop, Osnabrück, Kiel, Potsdam, Bremen again and finally Berchtesgaden in that order. The last is situated in the Bavarian Alps and was the site of Hitler's mountain retreat.

His crew for almost all these operations included Flying Officer Calton, engineer; Flying Officer Parry, navigator 1; Flight Lieutenant Jarry, navigator 2; Flight Sergeant Hailey, wireless operator; Flight Sergeant Snowdon, mid-upper gunner; and Flight Sergeant Sindle, rear gunner. Flight engineer Ken Calton said: 'We were a very neat crew and we had a truly great skipper and Flight Commander in Squadron Leader Artie

Ashworth. Our crew was very experienced.'

Artie later wrote: 'Starting as a new crew, assembled from "odds and sods", we finished as Primary Visual Markers. It would have been nice to be able to boast that we became Master Bombers or even Deputy Master Bombers, but one must be honest and anyway, the war ran out on us.' This comment reflects his disappointment at not receiving the promotion he no doubt thought he had earned, a task he felt fully qualified to handle. Given his previous operational experience in Bomber Command and his reputation for competence, his regret is understandable. Artie also said that while the crew were inexperienced,[105] he was no stranger to operational flying on bombers, having previously taken part in some sixty-five sorties in Wellingtons, some of which were in the Middle East theatre.

The new crew's first Pathfinder operation was an attack on the German city of Dessau on the night of 7–8 March 1945. In his operational report, Artie recorded: 'We arrived on the target at 2155 hours and then made an orbit to starboard. As we made a second run we saw a green TI burning on the ground and bombed on this. Sky marker flares appeared rather scattered. Incendiary fires were visible behind the cloud and appeared to be well confined to the target area. Several spoof[106] red and green TIs were seen north of the target.'

Although that's what Artie Ashworth reported, flight engineer Flying Officer Ken Calton said that there was much more to this raid than Artie's official account: 'We were lucky to survive on this trip as several times we were nearly taken down by night fighters. The skipper knew the only way out of the situation was to weave the aircraft and then hope they would leave you alone. It seemed to work. We were 10 miles away from the target area when the rear-gunner shouted "Dive to port skipper." Artie gave the aircraft such a shift to port that we nearly did a 180° flip. I went flying towards the bomb-aimer's section, but lucky for me Parry stopped me. When we levelled off the skipper came on the intercom and said "Sorry chaps, everyone okay?" We all settled down after that, we didn't see any more fighters and set our course for base.'[107]

After the war Artie commented about this raid: 'On two occasions we were given up for lost. The first was on our first sortie which was to Dessau when we religiously followed our briefing instructions, speed, height and times and arrived back after nine hours, we thought right on time. The rest of the squadron had returned some time before and had already debriefed. We were greeted by Tubby[108] with "We'd given you up."'

On 8 March the crew participated in the attack on the industrial city of Kassel. This sortie required almost seven hours' flying, mostly over enemy-occupied territory. Artie reported: 'Several fighters had a go at our aircraft, air gunner quick to respond, slight heavy flak, it must have been our lucky day to return back to base, nearly collided with another Lancaster in the landing circuit coming out of cloud (flight very bumpy).'

His sixty-ninth operational sortie on 13 March, and the third in No. 635 Squadron, was a strike on the German industrial city of Wuppertal. On this operation the crew were designated as 'support bombers'. The *Bomber Command War Diaries* reported that some 354 aircraft participated in this raid, 24 of which were Lancasters, including 12 from No. 635 Squadron. Artie's operational report read:

At 1547 hours we heard the Master Bomber giving height as per flight plan and warning that the cloud base figure given might be different. He called the 'Visuals' down to 12,000 feet. We could see the marshalling yards and bomb bursts were well concentrated in that area. Smoke rose from the estimated position of the aiming point. We flew alongside Tubby to and on the return trip acting as wing-man supporter on this important operation; it was a good prang.[109]

As a crew we had the honour of being a supporter for Tubby's 100th sortie to Wuppertal, just south of the Ruhr. We flew in formation to the target, which required a lot of concentration as we had a full load of fuel and 18 x 500lb bombs. I think the task appeared more difficult because Tubby and his Flight Engineer seemed to have a container of some sort in the cockpit and every now and then raised tankards toward us with 'good health' gestures! The cloud base of the target was about 5,000ft and Tubby dropped below this and called down the bombers of the main force. As far as I remember he wasn't very polite about it! On the run in to the target we were required to be about 1,000ft below Tubby and some way in front. No bombs were to be dropped on our first run to obviate the possibility of obscuring the target with bomb debris. As Tubby attacked at 3,000ft it didn't leave a lot of room for us to manoeuvre and of course we had to drop our bombs on a second run. We dropped 18 x 500lb HC bombs.

Artie later wrote:

> When I joined the Squadron, the Commander was Tubby Baker (Wing Commander S. Baker, RAFVR, DSO and Bar, DFC and Bar). Our crew were selected to act as Supporters for his 100th sortie, which was to Wuppertal. Tubby was the Master Bomber for this raid.
>
> The cloud base over the target was about 1,000 feet below Tubby and some way in front. This was one of the most impressive demonstrations I saw of Pathfinder operations as the bombers, almost all Canadians, came hurtling down Pell Mell [sic] through the clouds, almost all with their wheels extended and flaps down so as to lose height rapidly. Shortly after this sortie, Tubby was awarded a well-deserved bar to his DSO, to join the DFC and bar he already had.

Tubby Baker. This was a very special op for the squadron commander, Wing Commander Sidney 'Tubby' Baker. Squadron COs did not normally fly on operations, but Tubby wanted to go on this one. He obtained the authority of Pathfinder commander Don Bennett to fly as master bomber. The whole group knew just how important it was for him.

On their return to base there was a big crowd gathered outside the flying control and briefing room. They had come to congratulate him on his 100th trip. Tubby said that he later found out that Artie Ashworth had told the WAAFs in the signals room and they in turn told everyone else. 'It was quite amazing really to know you are respected like that.' And respect it was indeed. Anyone who had survived 100 trips, flying through the hell of enemy flak, searchlights and fighters, deserved all the respect and admiration shown him, together with his 'well deserved bar to his DSO'. It took real courage, daring, great skill and not a little luck to survive 'going over the top' 100 times.

Following Wuppertal on the 13th, Artie went to Zweibrücken the very next day. On this operation he was designated as 'visual illuminator'. His operational report read: 'OBOE red TIs were seen cascading at 2011 hours and we dropped our flares on these, other flares went down at the same time and the target was well illuminated. Mixed red and green TIs followed and these overshot the aiming point by approximately 400 yards. The Master Bomber was first heard calling for illuminators and after he had marked he instructed aircraft to undershoot red and greens by one second, and later by 100 yards. The Main Force bombing was very well concentrated on and around the aiming point. At 2025.02 hours a large sheet of flames were [sic] seen just south-west of the aiming point and our own bombers went very close to these. We dropped 40 flares and 3 x 1,000lb HC bombs on the target.'

The next operation was an attack on the German city of Nuremberg on 16 March 1945. Bomber Command was still mindful of the heavy losses incurred in the assault on this city in March 1944 when 95 aircraft were lost. For this, the last raid on the city by Bomber Command during the war, a total of 293 aircraft, including 16 from No. 635 Squadron, were detailed by Bomber Command; 25 aircraft were lost, a reminder that German defences, including night fighters, were still formidable and that fighter escorts were necessary to protect the bombers. The operational report stated that the main force bombing appeared to be well concentrated on the markers, resulting in a large area of fires, which were visible for 100 miles on the return journey.

Copies of Artie's meticulously kept logbook covered the PFF operations in March 1945, his sixty-eighth to seventy-fourth bomber operations. The log for the early part of March also lists the members of his 'odds and sods' crew.

On 21 March there was a raid on a vacuum oil refinery plant situated in the German port city of Bremen. A total of 133 aircraft were detailed for this, including 16 Lancasters from No. 635 Squadron. The squadron operational record stated that there was intense flak over the target area. Several aircraft were hit but all managed to return to base. For this raid Artie was designated as 'visual centrer'. He reported: 'We heard the Master Bomber broadcast the height and flight plan. Later at 1000hrs he broadcast instructions not to undershoot the yellow TIs. The yellow TIs were right on the aiming point, fires were burning around the aiming point and there were explosions in the same area. Black smoke billowed up to 3,000 feet. We dropped 4 TIs and 8 x 1,000lb bombs.'

Bomber Command was very active on 24 March when the Allied armies successfully crossed the River Rhine, the last major physical obstacle to the march on Germany. A total of 537 sorties were flown on this day including the operation to Bottrop in which Artie was again in action. This time the attack centred on the Matthias Stinnes oil plant. This was a daylight raid in which 173 Lancasters and 12 Mosquitoes participated. The defences were reported as 'Slight light flak and some heavy flak in places. No fighter activity.' Three Lancasters were lost but all of No. 635 Squadron aircraft returned safely.

On this raid Artie was again designated as 'visual centrer'. He reported: 'On the run up to the target a red TI was burning on the ground. This appeared to be short by a quarter of a mile. Our aircraft did not back-up. On the second run up the Master Bomber was heard instructing "to bomb on second red TI" but this must have been covered by smoke as it was not seen. Our aircraft did a third run and bombed the up-wind edge of the smoke. Bombing appeared to be somewhat scattered in the early part of the attack. As we left the target area bombing seemed to improve. We dropped 6 x 500lb TIs, 4 x 1,000lb and 1 x 4,000lb cookie blast bomb.'

This raid was the second occasion when he was given up for lost. He later wrote: 'The laid down route was over the target, turn right across "Happy Valley", before turning South West to cross the Rhine. We duly turned right and after a very short space of time found ourselves almost entirely alone in a cloudless and very unfriendly sky. It was not until after the war that I found that the Pathfinders were notorious for returning direct from their targets.' Apparently, his was the last aircraft to return, all the others having flown straight home rather than following the prescribed return route.

Artie's final wartime operation was as part of an attack on Adolf Hitler's mountain retreat of Berchtesgaden. This was a big operation for the participating aircrews. A total of 359 Lancasters and 16 Mosquitoes of Nos 1, 5 and 8 Groups were detailed for this raid, 15 Lancaster aircrews coming from No. 635 Squadron.

In the early hours of 25 April 1945 the aircrews from No. 635 Squadron attended one of the last operational main briefings at the base. It was a briefing that would lift the morale of all attending. They were told that the target for the day was special. The bombing leader spoke about how particular attention must be made when making the bombing run – destroying the target was vital. At that point no target had yet been revealed. The bombing leader built the occasion up very nicely by pulling back the operational curtains and announcing: 'Your target is to knock out Hitler's Eagle's Nest chalet and the German SS Guard barracks. With any luck Hitler himself will be there, then one of you could be the lucky aircrew to drop a 1,000 pound bomb on his lap.' This brought forth a big cheer from all those attending.

McKinstry reported that excitement spread through the briefing as crews burst into noisy chatter. Everyone knew the war in Europe was drawing to a close but to be going after Adolf Hitler and his henchmen as the target, made this operation different. Targets didn't usually have identifiable faces attached to them but this time they knew the names and what they looked like. This time it was personal. But they also realised the location was going to be heavily defended and they would have to be on their toes if they weren't going to get the 'chop'.[110]

There were three main targets at Berchtesgaden: the Berghof itself, the SS barracks and the Eagle's Nest, Hitler's personal retreat high in the mountain where in 1938 he had negotiated the dismemberment of Czechoslovakia with Neville Chamberlain.

The sixteen OBOE-equipped Mosquitoes detailed for the operation were unable to get the correct fix on the aiming point, due to the mountain range interfering with the relay signals. This surprised the RAF as the OBOE crews had been instructed to operate from 39,000 feet, supposedly a sufficient height to allow the relay signals to be received. However, the Mosquitoes were able to drop 'Window'[111] ahead of the Pathfinder main force.

According to the squadron's operational record, all aircraft were able to identify the aiming point in relation to the lake and the town of Berchtesgaden. No Mosquito red TIs were seen, so the master bomber dropped his red TIs with a slight overshoot. The main force bombing was quickly concentrated on the aiming point, which soon became covered by smoke. The master bomber then instructed the main force to bomb the upwind edge of the smoke. Only a few aircraft actually saw the red TIs about 100 yards north-west of the aiming point. The main force bombing was well concentrated throughout the attack and a pall of smoke was visible when aircraft were 50 miles away on their return journey.

There was the predicted heavy flak but no fighter activity, which surprised most crews. All No. 635 Squadron aircraft returned back to base safely. Most of the bombs dropped on to the target had numerous messages written in chalk on them from the ground crews.

Artie Ashworth's 'visual centrer' report stated: 'On approach to the target the red TI was seen at 0947 hours which appeared to be well on the aiming point. The Master Bomber was heard at 0948 hours instructing the main force to bomb the upwind edge of smoke. Our aircraft bombed the red TIs at 0948 hours. On leaving the target area smoke appeared to cover the whole aiming point.'

Squadron Leader George Hitchcock, DFC, MID.[112] New Zealander George Hitchcock was on the Berchtesgaden show. He said it gave Bomber Command a chance perhaps to show off; a daylight raid with little fighter opposition:

> When we took off on the 25th it was a beautiful clear day. Flying out of Downham Market, I was tasked that day as Deputy Master Bomber flying Lancaster F2-U (PB922). Approaching Germany some of the Master Bomber's gear went u/s so we took over. The Alps were a great sight but we were now head of the team so things were pretty busy. Our H2S equipped Lancasters carried an eighth crew member to look after some of the electronics.
>
> Our approach was good then out of nowhere came heavy and accurate AA fire. We were briefed that the area was being fortified for Hitler's last redoubt and the many German defence forces were well-trained SS regiments. Well, they certainly knew how to shoot! So much so that after dropping the target indicators I put Uncle into a vertical bank and a photo taken at 16,600 feet shows just how

vertical we were. I believe we missed Hitler's Eagle's Nest but clobbered the SS barracks and Goering's mansion. Good enough for me![113]

Flight Lieutenant L.J. Melling, DFC. The Berchtesgaden operation stayed in Melling's mind despite the passing years. 'We took off before dawn and one of my strongest memories is the exhilarating sight of the Alps as we flew over in the clear early morning with the sun shining on the snowy peaks. I have never again seen anything to equal it.'

Flight Lieutenant David Ware. David Ware was the captain of No. 635 Squadron Lancaster PB931 and designated as 'visual centrer', the same role as Artie. He recalled the sense of ease compared to previous raids: 'We were bristling with the Allied fighters all over us. There was complete air superiority. There was no fear of anything. We found Berchtesgaden and were the first to drop flares as we were the primary visual crew. Not that you really needed flares because you could see the target. Berchtesgaden was on a mountain and you could see it very clearly. We had a great run in and we did some great marking very accurate. Then we turned for home.'

Author Leo McKinstry recorded that the raid only had limited success. The SS barracks and the Berghof were hit, but the Eagle's Nest remained untouched. Worse still, two Lancasters were shot down, a tragic outcome of what was almost the last trip of the war. Some of the crews felt bitter about the poor planning of the mission, which, to them, seemed little more than a public relations exercise. But on the way home to England, and back at base, there was a mood of celebration. David Ware recalled that 'We only had to worry for about half an hour because we were soon back over Allied territory. This was wonderful. This was the end of the war, no more living with that gnawing fear, am I going to survive? When we got back the ground crew had got a big table out with lots of glasses and champagne. They had been our ground crew throughout the campaign and we were pretty close. But we could not get too pissed now because we had to go to debriefing. That night, we were a bit over the top.'[114]

Artie remembered the trip to Hitler's lair:

The next time we were given up for lost was the last raid of the war, the final attack on Berchtesgaden. About half way across Bavaria on the outward journey we had to feather the starboard engine because of a glyco leak. Because of some fault in the mechanism, the propeller would not feather completely and kept windmilling. This meant that we couldn't climb to our specified height and we had to cut a large corner off the allotted route to make the target on time. In the event, we did our bombing run along a valley with the AA guns firing at us almost level and, as we came to the target, the Main Force suddenly appeared above the 'Eagle's Nest' and started dropping their bombs. This meant that, had they been accurate, we would undoubtedly have had it, but fortunately for us, the first bombs were all overshot and slightly to starboard. Nevertheless it is a very impressive sight to see bomb after bomb, from 500 to 4,000 lbs and strings of gaggle of other bombers raining down just outside one's starboard wing tip. Because of the non-functioning engine and the windmilling propeller we were late home. In celebration I did a low pass over the station buildings on arrival which was not viewed with any favour by the Station Commander who had words to say on the subject!

Hitler's Eagle's Nest

The Eagle's Nest was designed and built for Adolf Hitler's fiftieth birthday in 1938 by his personal secretary and head of the Nazi Party Chancellery, Martin Bormann. According to the legend the beautiful green marble fireplace was a gift from Mussolini. It was more than an alpine chalet. It was a huge compound of some eighty buildings, all of which were closed to the public. It is believed that much of the planning for the Second World War was done at this location. It was there that Hitler hosted world leaders, bragging to them about his aesthetics and the engineering of his mountain palace, the adoration of his people and the glories of National Socialism.

While a fortune is believed to have been spent building the Eagle's Nest perch, Hitler made only fourteen official visits to it. To get there from the base of the mountain, a finely crafted tunnel led to the polished brass elevator that zipped visitors to the top.

A strange irony of history is that Hitler designed much of his Second World War campaign of terror from the Eagle's Nest, and Bomber Command's last heavy raid of the war was to strike this German fortress, thus bringing a certain redress for wrongs committed there, and closure to the air war. (Adapted from Coverdale, *Pathfinders 635 Squadron*)

Chapter 22

Pathfinder No. 635 Squadron,
Downham Market – Part 2

Squadron Leader I.W. Bazalgette, VC, DFC. According to Coverdale's *Pathfinders 635 Squadron*, the 1945 award of the Victoria Cross to Squadron Leader Ian Bazalgette resulted from research conducted by Artie Ashworth. Based on interviews with the surviving crew members and eyewitness accounts, Artie produced a report that led to the honour. The award was made posthumously. While participating in an attack on a V1 rocket storage site near Trossy St Maximin in France, both the master and deputy master bombers were put out of action and Squadron Leader Bazalgette found himself in command of the operation.

When aiming the bombs, pilots had to fly straight and level so the bomb aimer could obtain a fix on the target. This of course made them comparatively easy targets for anti-aircraft fire, which on this day was heavy and intense.

As they made their second run over the target the Lancaster was hit by heavy flak, shaking it violently. The flak had ripped through the plane's starboard wing, setting the fuel tanks on fire and taking out both starboard engines. Flight engineer Turner cut off the fuel pumps to the starboard side with the aid of the bomb aimer, who had been badly injured. Turner called for the wireless operator, Chuck Godfrey, to help him get the injured bomb aimer, Hibbert, to the rest bed where he could be treated. Hibbert was in great pain and deep shock, with his right arm barely intact.

Meanwhile, Bazalgette was over the target and released the markers. With the release of the bombs the aircraft went into a spin and lost height but the pilot managed to regain control, albeit with only two engines running. He then asked the navigator for a course to fly them to the nearest airfield. The Lancaster was rapidly losing height and they were 'living on borrowed time'. George Turner, the flight engineer, told Bazalgette: 'You will have to put her down skipper. We have no chance. We need to go now.'

The captain then gave the order to bale out. They were down to 1,000 feet and he was struggling to keep control of the aircraft. Bazalgette was left, along with the injured crew members, Hibbert and Leader. He understood the odds of crash-landing under these conditions and also knew he could have baled out, leaving the two crew members to their fate. He had crash-landed before and could do it again. As Godfrey drifted down on his parachute he watched his skipper pull off a fantastic manoeuvre with only one engine and the aircraft on fire. It looked like the blazing aircraft would crash into the village of Senantes but somehow Bazalgette managed to touch down some distance away. As it landed the aircraft exploded, killing all on board. Two corpses were afterwards dragged from the wreckage by the local villagers and later on, as the wreckage was being removed, some of the remains of Ian Bazalgette were recovered. He is buried in a military plot in the Senantes churchyard.[115]

Upon attaining the requisite number of operations, aircrew were given the right to wear the Pathfinder badge. Operations served prior to joining the Pathfinders were taken into account. Along with the badge, a special certificate was issued. Initially, the right to wear the coveted badge was temporary, to be worn only while the holder remained a Pathfinder. Once the full number of required operations was completed, the holder was given the right to wear the badge permanently. Artie later qualified to wear the badge permanently, but regretfully the certificate saying so has been lost. The raid on Hitler's mountain retreat was Artie's final operational sortie of the war. The last time he would fly through flak and face the ever-present risk of death from enemy action. By that time he had accumulated just under 1,400 hours as first pilot and participated in 78 bombing missions over enemy territory.[116] No mean record.

Flight Lieutenant Ken Calton, RAF. Ken Calton was the flight engineer in Artie's No. 635 Lancaster crew. He flew all thirteen operations, which Artie completed in 1945. Ken said that the aircrew in No. 635 Squadron had to be considered higher than average. Most of them had already finished tours of operations before transferring to the Pathfinder squadron. Artie formed his own crew when he joined in February 1945. There were two Canadian navigator/bomb aimers, a wireless operator, two air gunners and Ken as flight engineer, who acted as second pilot if necessary. He recalled: 'I considered Artie to be an exceptional pilot. During my previous service I had flown with many pilots and there is no doubt that Artie was the best. He was cool in emergency situations, very confident and very disciplined. He gave all the crew the same attitude to the job in hand; to do the very best first time. ... I consider myself very fortunate to have been a member of his crew. I always held him in high respect. He was a credit to New Zealand.'

The war in Europe ended on 8 May 1945, with the unconditional surrender of Germany. By this time No. 635 Squadron had flown 2,453 Lancaster sorties since its formation as a Pathfinder squadron in March 1944. It had lost 34 aircraft on operations, while an additional 7 were destroyed in crashes. A total of 207 aircrew were killed in action and a further 28 were captured and made prisoners of war.

With the war in Europe over, Bomber Command's attention turned to the Far East and the war against Japan. A number of No. 635 aircrew were detailed to prepare for posting to a Lancaster squadron in the Far East, which was being established to support the US Air Force attacks on Japan. Ken Calton was one of those who expected to be posted to this region. The war against Japan ended in August following the dropping of the atomic bombs on the Japanese cities of Hiroshima and Nagasaki. VJ (Victory over Japan) Day was celebrated on 15 August 1945. It was declared a public holiday and the squadron paraded under the command of Squadron Leader Artie Ashworth and attended a thanksgiving service in No. 1 hangar. The war was finally over.

The Price Was Too High

'Not a day goes by that I don't relive mentally my operational experiences. Even after all this time, my heart still bleeds for the boys I knew who were killed, especially my pilot. So many of them died unnecessarily, especially over Berlin. They were the cream of the nation. We paid too high a price.'

Flight Sergeant R.E. Buck, Pathfinder, Nos 207 and 97 Squadrons, from a plaque displayed in the Pathfinder Museum, Wyton.

Chapter 23

Operations 'Manna' and 'Exodus', and 'Cook's Tours'

While operations attacking targets in Germany were over, there were still important tasks to be done. During late April and early May 1945, Artie was to carry out food drops to starving Dutch people in Operation 'Manna'; ferry released prisoners of war back to England in Operation 'Exodus', and make tours of devastated German cities in 'Cook's Tours'.

The first of these missions was known as Operation 'Manna'.[117] The advance of Allied armies in late 1944 had cut off the German forces in western Holland. By January the five million Dutch people within this area were in grave danger of starvation. Their daily calorific food ration had been reduced to 500. Relief food shipments by the Swedish International Red Cross were hopelessly inadequate to prevent a looming disaster. By mid-January the situation was critical. Queen Wilhelmina addressed a note to King George VI, President Roosevelt and Prime Minister Winston Churchill: 'Conditions have become so desperate that it is abundantly clear that if a major catastrophe, the like of which has not been seen in Western Europe since the Middle Ages, is to be avoided in Holland, something drastic has to be done now. That is before and not after the liberation of the rest of the country.'

Up to this time, the Allied leaders had insisted that nothing could be done until the country was set free. All knew, however, that this would involve heavy Allied and civilian casualties and massive destruction to the Dutch cities and towns.

After protracted negotiations, first among the Allied leaders and then the concerned military chiefs – including the commander of the German forces in the occupied area – a truce was finally agreed that would allow RAF mercy food drops to commence on 29 April 1945. In preparation for this, the Dutch people had been warned to stay away from the identified drop sites since there would be considerable danger from falling containers.

On 30 April, eight Lancasters from No. 635 Squadron were detailed to aiming points in the Hague region. Flying Lancaster F2-D PB913, Artie and his crew dropped food supplies in the Ypenburg area. He recorded his memory of the operation:

> On the 30th of April[118] we were briefed to lead a small force of Lancasters to drop supplies at a place called Yppenburg [sic] in South West Holland. Until then we were unaware that the Dutch people were starving. One food drop had been successfully done the previous day. We were a bit apprehensive about this, as the flight was to be made along a track and height and speed laid down by the Germans – and the war was not yet over. So, in some ways we were prepared for German guns (all manned and aimed and following us as we passed overhead), and we were prepared for the possibility that some would open fire.
>
> But nothing could have prepared us for the Dutch people. They went mad with excitement, which was almost contagious. Everywhere one looked there were people waving things – flags, sheets, tablecloths, aprons – you name it, and leaping and jumping for joy. We did two more of these sorties before the official end of the war, but Dutch enthusiasm didn't wane.

Despite the truce agreement, the aircrews were conscious of the risks involved. They were to fly straight and level at rooftop height, even though they would be sitting ducks should the Germans decide to take advantage of the situation and open fire. As it was, many aircraft were hit by small arms fire from angry Germans. This brought forth a strong message from the Allied Commander-in-Chief, General Eisenhower, to the German commander: 'Order your troops to stop this practice or suffer the consequence!' It apparently worked.

For the men carrying out this mission it was a relief to be greeted with cheers rather than anti-aircraft fire. David Ware, a pilot of No. 635

Squadron, remembers the experience of flying over Rotterdam harbour at 200 feet: 'On the ships and the quayside you could see everybody waving. It was a wonderful experience, flying so low, which you could because Holland is so flat. We flew down a canal and reached a town where there were hundreds of people waving at us.

Harry Hooper of No. 115 Squadron said they flew as low as was safely possible, between 100 and 200 feet. 'The Germans knew we could not bomb from that height so they felt safe. The dropping zone was marked with a very large white cross. We dropped the food and a lot of it burst but most got through. What stands out in my mind was seeing all the Dutch people in the streets and on the rooftops waving and cheering as we flew by. Messages were set out on sheets on the ground, "thank you". It was marvellous. One minute I had been dropping bombs to kill people now I was dropping food to save people.'[119]

Inside the Lancasters, Britons, Poles, Canadians, Australians, New Zealanders and one Dutch airman looked down upon the excited masses below. 'The skipper said to us "God, look at the poor buggers. They've gone mad. They just run across the drop zone. If they don't take care they'll be smashed by the food." When we flew home across the North Sea it was dead silent inside the Lancaster. Seeing the British coast ahead of us the skipper said: "These bloody Jerries, we should line them up against the wall and shoot them all."'[120]

Another humanitarian exercise carried out by Bomber Command was the repatriation of prisoners of war from Germany and some of the occupied territories, in Operation 'Exodus'. Some forty Lancasters were stripped of everything except essentials, thus accommodating up to thirty-five passengers. Artie did one flight to Lübeck in Germany on 9 May, returning with twenty-four ex-POWs.

David Ware, the Pathfinder pilot of No. 635 Squadron, said he was very moved when he had a squadron leader POW sitting beside him with tears rolling down his cheeks as the Lancaster crossed the English coast.

Thomas Treadwell described the scene on the base where he operated: 'Some of the prisoners were in danger of collapse. When they went into the hangars they were sprayed with DDT – and this was a little undignified. Many of them having been in German hands less than 24 hours earlier were in a state of complete confusion. Some of them had been in the POW camp for four years and they had had their little pile of belongings, like a small bar of soap, which they had to put down while they were deloused. To begin with, their eyes would never leave these little piles on the floor. After a while they began to relax and they would just walk straight past their possessions, which they had jealously guarded and now had completely forgotten. It was all rather pathetic.'

When the war ended it was decided that the ground staff who had supported aircrews throughout the long campaign, should be given the opportunity to view some of the effects of the bombing on German cities. Artie participated in four of what were titled 'Cook's Tours'. What they witnessed was total devastation. Few had any idea of the level of destruction resulting from the Bomber Command campaign.

Before leaving No. 635 Squadron Artie said they flew a mission to Italy to help bring back some of the 8th Army. Then on 3 September, the anniversary of the outbreak of war, he was posted to No. 35 Squadron, a PFF squadron based at Graveley.

Chapter 24

Memories of Downham Market and No. 635 Squadron

Artie paid tribute to No. 635 Squadron:

I was one of the fortunate ones who lived in the Vicarage adjoining the church on the station, which Lee Boyd and I attended regularly. Considering the Vicarage was built for one family, it was huge. Most of the Squadron were accommodated in Nissen huts spread over a wide area. As dispersed stations go, Downham Market was a good one with little of the normal dampness and mud.'[121]

No. 635 was a superb Squadron. It was thoroughly efficient in every way except possibly dress and discipline on the ground and excepting every department where it mattered. Not the least of the Squadron's many assets was the ground crews – and not only those directly on the Squadron strength but also the support services. The same went for the ground crews of No. 608 Mosquito Squadron on the Light Night Striking Force, which was also stationed at Downham Market.

The aircrew were a polyglot mixture from many parts of the world, but they all had one thing in common – they were all volunteers, and not only to be aircrew but, having proved themselves, to be members of a Pathfinder Squadron.

A No. 635 Squadron WAAF[122] remembers – Mrs J. Pointer:[123]

I was posted to Downham Market in October 1944, when they were starting operations and I didn't leave until they were disbanded, which as far as I can recollect, was October 1945. My job was in

signals. We worked in a hut at the edge of the runway, so when
operations were on life was very hectic. The noise for one thing was
terrific, and the ground used to literally shake as the Lancasters
took off.

I think of one of the worst memories I have is the night one
blew up on take-off fully loaded. It's very difficult to describe how
we felt. It was simply dreadful waiting to hear which one it was.
From what I can remember several Australians were on board, and
I believe that they are buried in Saint Edmunds churchyard in
Downham Market.

Another difficult task was notifying relatives when aircrew didn't
return. Sometimes the telegrams would come up in batches, there
were so many. I remember after Nuremburg it was particularly
unpleasant.[124]

Of course there was a lighter side. We had our favourite meeting
places. Slys Café was always packed out with aircrew and WAAFs,
and of course we had our dances in the town hall.

Looking back I wouldn't have missed any of it. There was no life
outside until I joined up. People were thrown together from all
walks of life and it's amazing how once we were all in uniform we
were all on the same level, if only life were as easy today. The day
I arrived at Downham Market a full crew was waiting for transport
at the station, so naturally we were picked up together. Crews were
very superstitious and on being dropped at the guard room made
me promise to meet them later at Bexwell church and say a prayer
before they started their stint. Of course I was a bit wary about this
as the place would be in darkness by the time we had arranged to
meet. However I needn't have worried because when I went to
report there was a friend I had known before so we went together.
Maybe they were justified in saying the prayer, because they were
shot down later, but made their way back through the escape route.
I can remember the night Bazalgette didn't return. He later got the
Victoria Cross.

I recall how they used to report back from operations looking
as if they had been sweeping the chimney, their faces covered in oil
and soot. The first time I saw a crew in this state I just couldn't

believe it. I particularly recall one engineer who would come in and bring in the remainder of his chocolate and fruit and nut ration to the girls on duty, no doubt again tied up with superstition.

I well remember that on our off-duty days we would cycle over to Denver past the Mill and on to the Jenyn Arms where we could always obtain refreshment. This was a favourite, ranking along side Slys café and the Crown.

Mrs Moorcroft was a WAAF watchkeeper:

Wing commander 'Tubby' Baker used to breeze into the operations room with a 'what's cooking good looking?' He took me up in a Lancaster 6 for a flight test once. Going around the perimeter track in his car was slightly unnerving, let alone the flight.

Downham Market was always an extremely chilly place. It was by the side of a ditch and at one time I had to sweep the water from under my bed. Curiously in the summer months there was an acute lack of water when baths were forbidden, and only one cup of tea per meal allowed, dished out of a pail with a ladle so that the size of the cup couldn't help. Working a watch system (24 hours on, 24 hours off) for a short time when one of the watchkeepers was on leave, I would often be the only WAAF Sergeant in the Sergeants' Mess and would eat with NCO crew members and watch them play cards etc. Their faces are a very faint memory now so many of them went missing. I never got to know any well. They would sometimes ask 'What's the target for tonight?', knowing I wouldn't tell them.

The parties in the Sergeants' Mess were pretty wild affairs, with a lot of beer thrown about, the floor a-swill with it. If you didn't want to have your tie cut off at the knot, it was wise to get away early.

Flight Sergeant Paddy Cronin, flight engineer, recalled:[125]

We saw the German jet-fighters long before it was published in the press. We saw a lot of them towards the end of 1944. We used to see them shoot past us. We were only doing 100 miles per hour or so.

The poor old rear-gunner was on his own in the cold so far back there whereas the rest of the crew were in some sort of proximity to each other but he was on his own. A lonely job stuck out there in the tail but they had to be wide awake all the time.

Even when we were resting there were always training flights, bombing practice in the Wash. The commanders made sure the standards were kept up. We would have a navigator come and tell us about the stars. If you were lost and your instruments were out of operation, how you could get a course get to back to base. My role was flight engineer. The bomb-aimer was also capable of flying as well and we used to keep our hand in on the link trainer, 30 minutes or an hour during our rest period.

The winter of 1944 was so cold that our tortoise stoves in the huts were always short of kindling wood. Colonel Pratt's sheds down the road had a lovely lot of wood on the side. Some of the boards were loose so we helped them off! The Colonel went to the Group Captain and complained about the loss and told him to stop his men doing it. Group said 'Yes of course I will see to it' but he could not do anything. We were here today and may be gone tomorrow. We could not have cared less. Once we heard that he had complained it only encouraged us to take even more so eventually there was not a lot of wood left on the sheds.

When Warrant Officer New came from Norwich, he wanted us on parade at nine the next morning. That night we got him pickled in the mess and then carried him back to his hut and gently laid him on his bed. Then we nailed up the windows and doors. In the morning some went on parade some did not. Of course when he was sent for he was found nailed up! The parade was dismissed. On another occasion he was put in the horse trough. He must have threatened us again so we gave him a warning. He might as well have talked to the Moon. We would rather go flying than on parades. That was the last thing we wanted to do.

WAAF Corporal Eleanor Bignal remembered that 'Downham Market was undoubtedly the happiest station I stayed on during my five years of service. We had lovely dances in the NAAFI and I guess we just lived for the day or night as I suppose everyone did in those days.'

Flying Officer B.J. Sherry, DFC, said that bomber crews raiding over occupied Europe led a strangely schizophrenic existence:

> By day in the quiet of the English countryside; by night engaged in a running fight in the cold and dark over enemy territory; then coming back from this bad dream to the calm of the Fenlands. It was two totally different worlds that they moved between. If the dark side could be hell, then daytime became a bit of heaven. Morning came; you were still alive, and very conscious of being alive. Everything tasted better; jokes were funnier; nature lovelier; all girls were beautiful. There was a heightened intensity about the daytime half of the equation as well as the night-time part. Very little excuse was needed to have a celebration. The unspoken reason was that we were still here, still in the land of the living. We had some memorable parties both on the station and in the pubs of the surrounding villages, and enjoyed the marvellous hospitality of the local people.[126]

Perhaps the most memorable return was that of Lancaster D-Dog of No. 635 Squadron on 6 October 1944. The squadron had despatched six of its aircraft from RAF Downham Market to bomb an oil plant at Gelsenkirchen, and all six planes were hit by flak. D-Dog had been hit over Holland on its way to the target and trouble developed in the port inner engine so the plane could not gain any height. Over the target, just after releasing its bombs, the aircraft was hit again and the port inner engine caught fire. The fire was extinguished and the pilot, Flight Lieutenant Alex Thorne, DSO, DFC, set course for home with only three engines working. Over the Dutch coast the Lancaster was struck yet again by flak. This time the starboard rudder was shot away and the port outer engine failed. The aircraft rapidly lost height and an SOS was sent out to warn the coastal patrol that they intended ditching in the North Sea. When the English coast was eventually sighted, the SOS was cancelled and Thorne headed for the emergency airfield at Woodbridge. As they approached the airfield at about 500 feet the starboard inner engine packed up, leaving only one engine working. D-Dog swerved to port but the pilot managed to put the plane into a glide and made a successful landing in a meadow near the airfield.

As the crew climbed out, the ammunition started to explode and soon the aircraft was burning furiously. All managed to escape from the blazing inferno except the wireless operator, Sergeant Jim Crabtree, whose body was later found among the charred remains.

Thorne lost consciousness immediately after staggering on to the ground. The next thing he remembered was waking up in a wood to which the crew had carried him. With them was a lady who had hurried over from her nearby farmhouse, undeterred by the explosion still erupting and asking if they would like a cup of tea. She duly arrived back with what must have been her best tea set on a silver tray with white lace cover.[127]

A Lancaster station generally comprised two squadrons, each of them led by a wing commander. The squadrons themselves were made up of two or three flights, each of them normally equipped with eight to twelve heavy bombers under the control of a squadron leader. Artie became the officer commanding, 'A' Flight, No. 635 Squadron.

Within the flight, every individual Lancaster was given its own title such as G-George, or Q-Queenie, names that would be easily identifiable over the radio-telephone when preparing to take off or coming into land. Aircraft often had, on one side of the fuselage, mascots and symbols indicating the number of operations.[128]

The aircrews themselves were just one part of the system. A typical Lancaster airfield at the peak of the war contained about 2,500 personnel, with the airmen only making up one-tenth of that number. The rest included armourers, mechanics, clerks, drivers, caterers, RAF service police and WAAFs.

There was nothing luxurious, however, about life on most of the bomber airfields, which had sprung up rapidly during the early part of the war and whose predominant architectural feature was the squat, primitive Nissen hut. For those who served in Bomber Command, the prevailing memories were often of icy winds blasting across the Fens, of dark nights shivering around a stove, of rough beds with rough blankets, and of dirty washrooms and tepid showers. There were much better quarters in pre-war stations like the wood-panelled splendour of Petwood House near Woodhall Spa in Lincolnshire, which was used by No. 617

Squadron, but these were the exception.[129]

Fred Grantham was a wireless operator with No. 635 Squadron from 7 April to 22 August 1945: 'I will never forget the moment I clapped eyes on so many legendary bomber pilots at once in the Officers' Mess when we first arrived. My pilot, Flight Lieutenant Derek Fowler, DFM, introduced us on this occasion to Alex Thorne, Artie Ashworth, Dennis Witt, Emile Mange and Pat Connolly.'

Fred recalled that his crew were called up for briefing just hours after arriving; it was to see the flight commander of 'A' Flight, Squadron Leader Artie Ashworth. He was known throughout the base and Pathfinders for his attention to detail; plus, he was someone who required the very best from aircrews under his command:

This guy got respect from everyone on the base and in fact we learnt very quickly how much respect. We later learnt that Group HQ also in turn gave Ashworth huge respect and that the 635 Squadron was lucky to have him aboard.[130]

Following one Saturday evening at the Crown, we returned to base and climbed into our beds. Our Mid-Upper Gunner, Dovey, had been left in Downham Market with his girlfriend, both of whom had apparently reserved rooms at the Castle Hotel. Early on Sunday morning I was woken by Dovey's voice saying 'Fred, I'm in the mire.' During the night he had needed to go to the toilet and leaving the shared bedroom in complete darkness had negotiated the bedroom landing towards the loo. Unfortunately he had forgotten the two stairs at the end of the corridor and noisily stumbled down both. The return journey proved disastrous. In the corridor he was confronted by the landlady in her nightgown with one hand on the light switch. Dovey said he was 'starkers'. In the morning he was told not only to leave the hotel but that the episode would be reported to his station CO. As he was leaving, Dovey was stopped at the doorway by none other than the CO who said: 'Flying Officer Dovey, I have to remind you for ignoring King's regulations in so much as you should be suitably attired for all eventualities – you may go.' Relief would hardly be the appropriate word.

Accompanied by former Flight Engineer Ken Calton and author Christopher Coverdale, in 2011 my wife and I were taken on a guided tour of the former Pathfinder station RAF Downham Market. The land has now been returned to productive farming and little remains to show that this was once a hive of Pathfinder activity. Many of the old buildings remain, however. Some like the former Guard House are being used but most are in various states of disrepair. A busy road now dissects what was the main airfield and runways. St Mary's church and the vicarage remain as they were when Artie served at the station.

It was an emotional thrill to stand in the former office of the 'A' Flight commander, Squadron Leader A. Ashworth, as it was for Ken Calton to enter the office of the flight engineer leader's former office.

Chapter 25

Frank Prebble Remembers No. 635 Squadron

In 1944–45 New Zealander, Flight Lieutenant Frank Prebble, DFC, served on fifty operations in No. 635 Squadron as a bomb aimer. On a number of occasions his crew were designated as master or deputy master bombers, even more hazardous tasks than normal. He participated in most of the thirteen operations that Artie flew as a Pathfinder in 1945. These included raids on Dessau, Kassel, Dortmund, Wuppertal, Zweibrücken, Nuremburg, Bremen, Bottrop, Osnabrück and Berchtesgaden.

The Dessau raid was the one where Artie's flight engineer, Ken Calton, said they were lucky to survive and Artie merely commented that they were last home and had been given up for lost. Frank wrote in his diary that his crew were the master bomber on this op. They took off at 1720 hours and returned at 0200 hours, a total of 6 hours and 40 minutes of flying. He recorded that they orbited the target at low level as the main force bombed. 'A good attack,' he said. 'The rum and coffee tasted good.'[131]

The next raid was Dortmund when he flew with the squadron commander, Wing Commander 'Tubby' Baker. As evidenced by the devastation shown in a photograph, it was, Frank stated, 'a good operation'.

After a raid on Nuremburg on 16 March, in which Artie was also involved, Frank wrote that in the last five days they had carried out five operations: two daylights to Germany and three long night trips. These made forty-two operations as a crew and they were the top visual markers in the squadron. As a result they were given the best jobs, such as master or deputy master bomber, or primary visual markers.

Five operations in five days would have been hugely stressful. It reflected the sort of pressure these young men endured, facing as they did the possibility of a one-way trip each time. As the bomb aimer lying in the front of the aircraft, Frank commented that he had a bird's eye view of the target – and the flak!

On 24 and 25 March, both Frank and Artie took part in raids on Bottrop and then Osnabrück. Frank said the benzol plant at Bottrop was heavily defended by a box barrage. As they came up to the target it was a black cloud of flak bursts in the air: 'It was a little intimidating but we were too busy to worry about it. We were the Master Bomber and we orbited the target and directed the raid.' They left behind a scene of total destruction.

His diary for 4, 9 and 10 April recorded raids on Harburg, Kiel and Plauen:

Although the war was drawing to a close we were still bombing German targets. On April 4 we targeted the oil refinery at Harburg across the river from Hamburg. It was a night operation and we were the Master Bomber. It was a successful operation.

On the 10th of April I flew my last operation with Peter Mellor and crew. We had been a good team but they had completed their two tours as Pathfinders. The target was Plauen and even at this late stage it was heavily defended. We were the Primary Visual Markers. It was a long trip, 7 hrs 35 mins.

By the time I flew my next operations my old crew, with whom I had flown 48 operations, were grounded and posted from the squadron. It was to be 45 years before I saw any of them again.

Frank's last operation was participating in Operation 'Manna', dropping food to the Dutch people. On returning from that final sortie, Frank and his crew went to the mess for lunch and listened to the BBC giving the news of the end of the European war. A public holiday was declared on VE (Victory in Europe) Day, 8 May 1945. 'That evening there was a party at the station and also a great gathering in the town square in Downham Market where the townspeople and airmen celebrated together. The pubs were all overflowing. Two searchlights made a V over the aerodrome,' he said. 'One was still geared to operations and all the partying was a bit of an anticlimax. I suppose one gradually unwound. It was certainly the end of an experience one would carry through life.'

After the war Frank recalled some of his memories of Downham Market and the station:

About 1 mile from Downham on the Swaffham farm road, is the small 12th century Norman church of Bexwell with its rectory and Bexwell Hall nearby. Essentially this was the centre of the station complex. The aerodrome was on the north side of the road and the living quarters on the south. When I arrived I moved into a Nissen hut close to the rectory. There were eight officers in the hut with a couple of batmen to make the beds, bring the tea in the morning, and look after our kit and keep the place clean.

The winter of 1944–45 was extremely cold and the corrugated iron Nissen huts were like refrigerators. To keep them warm we had a pot-bellied stove in the centre fired by coal. Coal was rationed and invariably scarce so there was a constant search for fuel or anything that would burn. Eventually one of the engineering officers came up with a scheme where a perforated metal plate was set in the stove and a mixture of used engine oil and water was dripped on to it. The fire was started with paper and wood and once the plate was hot the oils splattering on the plate burned well. By contrast, the huts were like ovens in the summer. Ablutions were all within another hut in the complex.

The Officers' Mess consisted of two large Nissen huts joined by a smaller one. This formed the bar called Fingerwell Inn while one of the larger huts was the dining room and the other the lounge. The most popular place was the bar. Like many, I had my own silver beer mug hanging above the bar counter. Many a line was shot over a pint of beer.

I remember one time before lunch Margaret Wilkinson, our intelligence officer, was bending over poking the fire when the Squadron Commander 'Tubby' Baker took a bottle of soda water, shook it up and put it under her skirt. She nearly killed him with the poker.

Many a good party as well as dances were held in the mess. We had on the squadron Leading Aircraftman (LAC) Sam Costa who later became the radio celebrity in *Much Binding in the Marsh*, a very popular BBC comedy show after the war. Sam ran the station orchestra and provided us with some good music.

There were the usual RAF capers in the mess such as footprints on the ceiling and the singing of many raucous songs. Another favourite in the mess was to take the star package out of a Verey [sic] cartridge and quietly drop it in the open fire. The result was a brilliant red or green flash which rocked people out of their chairs.

On one occasion Air Vice Marshal Bennett, the Pathfinder Force Commander, came to the mess for a formal occasion. When he went to leave his car was in the middle of the ornamental pond in front of the mess. This type of activity was a way of letting off steam especially following a string of operations.

In the town of Downham Market there were three pubs. The Crown, the Swan and the Castle. There was also Slys coffee shop, a favourite haunt for morning coffee. The town hall sat in the Market's square. Here Saturday night dances were held if one was not on operations that evening or next day. We usually cycled down to the village for the evening. My favourite pub was the Crown run by Mr and Mrs Crump. Most of the ground crews and junior officers and sergeants frequented the Crown.

The Castle was usually the haunt of senior officers such as Squadron Leaders (such as Artie) and above. The piano in the Crown was always in use and many a song not for tender ears was sung by both WAAFs and Airmen. When the pub closed we wandered up Swaffham Road to the station. I always said that every hedge row and every straw stack whispered.

The relationship between the villagers and station was always good. The town hall dances reminded me of the dances in New Zealand. They were well attended by all WAAFs, Land Army girls, and nurses from the local hospital. A few of the aircrew had cars and one did not ask where the petrol came from. Peter Mellor, my skipper, had a car and when he was not out with his WAAF girl-friend, Jerry Shaw our navigator and I would sometimes be invited and go along to King's Lynn,[132] providing finances allowed.

I arrived at the station as a Flying Officer earning sixteen shillings and six pence (NZ$1.65) per day. I was later promoted to

Flight Lieutenant earning 22 shillings and six pence per day (NZ$2.25). We had a monthly mess bill to pay for extras in the mess and a compulsory allotment of pay was made home to New Zealand. I usually had about 15 shillings (NZ$1.50) per day to spend or save.

We were given a week's leave every six weeks. During the operational six weeks activity was pretty intense and we made the most of our week's leave. I usually headed for London as there was always a chance of seeing my old mates or lads I had trained with in Canada. The New Zealand Forces Club was the centre of activity. I made a serious attempt to see some of the sights of London. During the evenings, however, as the blackout was in force, the nearest warm pub was the place to be. I was not in London during the blitz but I did experience the 'buzz' bombs, V1 and V2 rockets. Londoners were once again sleeping in the Tube stations and bomb shelters.

On VJ day [Victory over Japan, 15 August 1945] I went into London to join in the celebrations and stood in the Mall outside Buckingham Palace. The King and Queen, and the two Princesses along with Churchill, appeared on the palace balcony. After all the high jinks I met up with some of my old cobbers at the New Zealand Forces Club in Charing Cross Road where we continued the celebrations well into the night. I returned to Graveley[133] but within a few days I was posted to Blyton in Lincolnshire along with other New Zealand aircrew. From Blyton we returned to number 12 PDRC[134] in Brighton where we had started out 18 months earlier. It was time for going home.

Fifty years later, in 1995, on the anniversary of the end of the war in Europe, Frank and his wife, Terry, stood in the Mall and witnessed the ceremony of Thanksgiving, conducted by the Archbishop of Canterbury. This time it was the Queen and the Duke of Edinburgh, along with other members of the Royal family, who appeared on the balcony of Buckingham Palace.

Frank said that one of the celebratory events was the traditional Beating Retreat ceremony on Horse Guards Parade. He described the whole ceremony as a magnificent musical event. The bands marching and the singing of a huge choir he considered unsurpassed. After an hour's music the Queen, who arrived in an open carriage, escorted by the Blues and Royals on horseback, addressed the crowd. This was followed by two minutes' silence and then the words from the Kohima Memorial in Burma – a message from those who died in that campaign – were spoken by a young officer: 'When you go home, tell them of us and say, for your tomorrow we gave our today.'

PART 8:
RAF SERVICE, 1945–53

YEAR:		AIRCRAFT.		PILOT, OR 1ST PILOT.	2ND PILOT, PUPIL, OR PASSENGER.	DUTY (INCLUDING RESULTS AND REMARKS).
MONTH.	DATE.	Type.	No.			
—	—	—	—	—	—	TOTALS BROUGHT FORWARD
		Total Flying as at 1st January 1951 :-				
		Tiger Moth				
		Vildebeeste				
		Avro 626				
		Gordon		Total Experimental Flying as at 1st January 1951 :-		
		Battle				
		Lysander				
		Hart				
		Whitney Str.				
		Mentor		Day :	169 Hrs. 00 Mins.	
		Hornet Moth				
		Harvard		Night :	33 Hrs. 50 Mins.	
		Kearwin		Total :	202 Hrs. 50 Mins.	
		Moth Minor				
		P40				
		F4U				
		Argus				
		Proctor				
		Auster				
		Tempest				
		Spitfire				
		Youngman-Baynes				
		Seafire				
		Vampire				
		Firefly				
		Sea Fury				
		F. Junior				
		Storch				
		Athena				
		Vega Gull				
		Hudson				
		Anson				
		Wellington				
		Oxford				
		Bombay				
		D.H.86				
		Dakota				
		Mosquito				
		Liberator				
		Ventura				
		Dominie				
		Lodestar				
		Lancaster				
		Valetta				
		Devon				
		Viking				
		Lincoln				

4,000 bi B/5/44—1588]

GRAND TOTAL [Cols. (1) to (10)].

_____ Hrs. _____ Mins.

TOTALS CARRIED FORWARD

Chapter 26

1945–49, Middle East Command, Test Pilot

The end of the war coincided with Artie's twenty-fifth birthday. During the previous four years he had experienced more than the great majority might do in a lifetime. His was indeed a distinguished record of which anyone could be justly proud. As the story will tell, there was more to come. Artie was pleased with his achievements but he never flouted or even mentioned them. It was just part of his life and it was time to think of the future. He loved the air force life, especially as a RAF officer. In 1945 he decided to continue his RAF career and applied for a permanent commission.

With the end of the war, what to do in the future was an important question for Artie. He did not relish the idea of returning to New Zealand and resuming his career as a draughtsman in the Public Works Department.[135] Given the life he had led over the previous five years one can understand that reluctance. As so many found, settling back into pre-war life after the experiences of war, was not easy. Artie was granted a permanent RAF commission (with a drop in rank to flight lieutenant). He said that solved the problem and might go some way to explaining to his many relatives and friends back home in New Zealand why he stayed on in England.

Of another honour, in a typical matter-of-fact way Artie merely stated in his memoir: 'I was awarded a Bar to my DFC.' At first he was unaware of the award. A friend at RNZAF Headquarters in London told him the news. Artie said it would have been for his work in No. 635 Squadron and his service in the Pacific. The award was gazetted on 6 November 1945. The citation read as follows: 'Since the award of the Distinguished Service

Order, Flight Lieutenant Ashworth has completed numerous sorties. He has been employed on operational flying since 1941 and, however arduous the task allotted to him, this officer has completed it in a cheerful and confident manner, often making several runs over heavily defended targets to ensure accuracy. Flight Lieutenant Ashworth's fine fighting spirit and devotion to duty has set an inspiring example to all.'

On 3 September 1945, the anniversary of the outbreak of war, Artie was posted to No. 35 Squadron based at Graveley. This squadron was part of the Pathfinder Force and at the time he arrived was being prepared and trained as part of 'Tiger Force' to be used against the Japanese. His time in No. 35 Squadron was, however, short. With the end of the war against Japan, the PFF was disbanded in October 1945.

In January 1946 he was sent as an instructor to the Middle East Officers' Advanced Training School at Amman, in what was then known as Transjordan. There he taught many subjects such as public and non-public funds, accounting for equipment, and air force law. He was the drill instructor as well as being in charge of all the messes. 'At the school was a Fairchild Argus and an Anson and I flew both locally and to Egypt. There was duck shooting at Qasr Azrak and pleasant interludes in a Basha at Aquaba,' he said. 'After I thought I had done long enough at this I was posted with a drop in rank to Command the Iraq & Persia Communications Flight at Habbaniya in Iraq, which was then one of the largest (and hottest) RAF Stations in the Middle East. Here I had Ansons, Whitney Straights, Ventura and Lodestars on my flight. Our main task was to keep the Gulf Stations supplied with mail, fresh rations and, of course, people. The Stations concerned were Shaibah, Bahrain, and Sharjah, but there were other tasks and flights to Egypt, Karachi, and to most parts of Iraq. The weather could make some of this quite risky, but I enjoyed the work. Then out of the blue I was selected to attend the Empire Test Pilots' School at Farnborough at the beginning of 1948.'

As Artie said, selection for attending the Empire Test Pilots' School came as a big surprise. Perhaps it shouldn't have, as a staff flight engineer at the school, Don Briggs, said: 'Only exceptional pilots were "long listed", with possible hundreds being whittled down to 40 or so. Artie was one of those exceptional pilots. I flew with all the student test pilots in the Avro Lincoln and many other types. I had the pleasure of flying with Artie on an exercise which called for extremely accurate flying. Artie demonstrated this with smoothness of "feel".'

When writing to me Don concluded: 'Your late brother Artie was "truly a great bloke!" I can still picture him at the cosy little bar in the mess with his own tankard (woe betide anyone else who used it! Our faithful barman knew the tankard well). Artie would smoke his cigarette from a long holder clenched between his teeth, some of which I seem to remember had either gold or silver fillings. One of his drinking principles was to ensure that when raising the tankard to drink, the elbow had to be higher than the pot and he made sure everyone else did likewise. What a character!'

Don said they were both model aircraft enthusiasts and Artie produced some really superb flying models (rubber driven and then early power driven). This was something I never knew. I don't recall him ever mentioning it.

Artie recorded his experience at the school: 'The Test Pilots' School was a revelation to me. Apart from classroom work and studying, we flew a fairly wide variety of aircraft types, sometimes under supervision from test-flying instructors. I made a lot of lasting friends. I flew my first jets in the shape of the Vampire and Meteor. On only two aircraft – the Mosquito and Lincoln – was I given limited dual instruction, the rest were flown from reading pilots' notes. … I finished the Test Pilots' School in December 1948 and went off to New Zealand on leave. I paid a visit to all my relatives and among other flying, flew as dispatcher in an Auster with my old friend "Popeye" Lucas,[136] dropping supplies to deer cullers.'

Chapter 27

The Last Visit Home, 1949

I'm not sure how Artie travelled to New Zealand, but seem to recall him mentioning the *Dominion Monarch*, a passenger liner, which at that time provided a regular service between England and New Zealand. His homecoming this time was not the 'royal welcome' the returning hero had experienced in 1943. He was a private citizen who slipped into the country unnoticed except, of course, for his family. I recall his arrival in Alexandra. He came by bus from Dunedin and my brother Donald and myself met him at the bus stop outside Gourley's the chemist in Alexandra's main street. My mother, naturally, was greatly excited by his return. It had been five years since we had seen him. This notwithstanding, he must have found life back home rather dull. Our mother frowned on any drinking and alcohol was forbidden in the house. Artie was renowned for his drinking escapades so my mother's rule was not exactly to his liking to say the least. However, her love for her famous son allowed some relaxation. Soon Artie had a 'secret store' in the bathroom, which he would tap late in the evening after my mother went off to bed.

I recall Artie one evening inviting some of his old school friends who were still around to join him for a game of cards at our home. Arthur Gladstone (known as Arthy Quack since he was the son of the local doctor), Ron 'Big George' Smith, who stood over 2 metres tall with the other dimensions to go with it, and Johnny Nightingale were among the players. Much to my dear mother's disgust, a lot of beer from the 'secret store' was consumed. She went off to bed early with the command to myself to do likewise. The party continued!

Artie made every effort to visit his sisters as well as brother Archie (Tex) who lived in Dunedin. Tex had served in the RNZAF as a bomb aimer in the UK and Italy for two years during the war. At that time brother Donald, who lived in Christchurch, made a special visit home.

On one occasion, first cousin Marjory Ashworth came to visit with her husband one Sunday afternoon. Marjory was the daughter of our Uncle Archie. Her parents were strict Presbyterians. Alcohol, cigarettes and philandering were all forbidden. Marj was great fun and indulged in all these forbidden activities with almost reckless abandon. During her visit the 'secret store' supplied the refreshment and Marj partook along with the men. My dear mother was shocked and later remarked to me: 'Did you see that Marjory. She had two glasses of beer!'

After a couple of weeks in Alexandra Artie went off to see people in other parts of the country. These included sister Margaret Koberstein, who at that time was living at Kio Kio near Otorohanga.

After visiting friends and relatives in the North Island, Artie returned to Alexandra and then went on to stay with his pal of No. 75 Squadron days, 'Popeye' Lucas. Popeye had founded his own airline, Southern Scenic Airways. One of his jobs was supply dropping to government deer cullers in the remote mountains of south-west New Zealand. As the 'despatcher' he was responsible for seeing the supply packages exited from the air-craft.[137] He much enjoyed his time with Popeye. I recall him saying that Popeye had tried to persuade him to join the partnership. Artie declined the invitation but commented that had he done so they would not have made much money, if any, but would have had a lot of fun trying!

David Lucas, son of Popeye, related that many were the stories told of the hilarious escapades of Artie and Popeye at the Shotover Pub, a country hotel overlooking the Shotover River. Today, the pub is bypassed by a new road and bridge across the river.

Before departing, Artie spent a few days with Tex in Dunedin before embarking on the *Saxon Star* for England from Invercargill. The ship was a mixed cargo–passenger type, which provided apparently comfortable berths for around twelve passengers. At that time several similar Star Line ships regularly plied between New Zealand and England.

During the three-week voyage to England, Artie struck up a friend-ship with fellow passenger, Mr W.R. Brugh, a Dunedin resident. To pass the time they engaged in furious cribbage competitions. During one such game Mr Brugh scored the perfect hand, twenty-nine points, which is the highest score possible. To attest to this milestone a special certificate was duly prepared and signed by both Artie and Mr Brugh. The chief and second stewards confirmed the score as witnesses.

Twenty-one years were to elapse before I was to see my brother again. We did correspond somewhat spasmodically and Artie always replied, saying what he was doing at the time. He corresponded quite regularly with my mother, who invariably passed on his letters.

Artie's next posting was to the Royal Aircraft Establishment at Farnborough.

Chapter 28

Test Pilot, Royal Aircraft Establishment, Farnborough

On his return to England in June 1949, Artie was posted to the Instrument and Photographic Flight at the Royal Aircraft Establishment at Farnborough. He remained at Farnborough until the end of December 1951. Commenting on his work he later wrote: 'This covered a multitude of sins. At first the only test flying I did concerned automatic pilots and flight instruments, the latter mostly in the Spitfire in which I did a lot of spinning. Then came photography in all sorts of forms. All this in a wide variety of aircraft. Some of the auto-pilot testing was, to say the least, exciting. I did quite a lot of glider winching in the Fleischer Storch, the only German aircraft I have flown.'

Artie continued: 'Towards the end of 1950, after our photo flashes had caused wide-spread panic on the East Coast, together with a specialist crew, I flew the high altitude Lincoln out to Woomera, Australia. The Woomera operation seemed to be all hush-hush. Britain had been conducting atomic tests in the closed area. Testing of the early rockets was also carried out at Woomera.

A lighter note was recorded as a result of his flight to Australia in the Lincoln bomber. Having traversed the equatorial line while in the heavens, he became a member of the Winged Order of Line Shooters.

Artie was promoted to squadron leader at the beginning of January 1950 and returned from Woomera at the end of November of that year. A February flying assessment signed by the Chief Test Pilot Experimental Flying Department, RAE, rated Artie as an above-average test pilot and pilot-navigator. By this time he had flown a wide range of aircraft on experimental duties.

He later wrote about some of his test pilot work:

On return from Australia I found I had inherited the prototype
Canberra. This aircraft I flew first of all investigating an auto-pilot.
Among other things, I was asked to take the aircraft on auto-pilot
through rough air. The air I found a bit too turbulent and among
other damage to the aircraft was the loss of an almost complete
circuit of the fuselage of rivets. As a consequence almost all
subsequent Canberras were fitted with strengthening plates on
both sides of the fuselage.

Also from this Canberra, I fired some of the early ejection seats.
During this series of tests, one of the flying doctors from the School
of Aviation Medicine told me that, if anything went wrong, I was
to ignore jettisoning the canopy, pull the blind and go straight
through it. I didn't take much notice with everything else going on
until I saw a film taken from the chase Meteor, which showed the
ejected seat passing just over the port tail plane and alongside the
fin and rudder!

Low level high speed night photography in a Meteor was one of
my most difficult tasks as there was no accurate method of reasoning the height above the ground and the boffins wanted high and
low building, with chimneys and fire escapes as well as flat land.

In his memoir he said that while in Australia he sent food parcels to a
friend and his wife at Farnborough. 'On return I discovered that he had
died from altitude wasting sickness while we were away. Roughly a year
later I married his widow, Kathleen (Kay) Baker, and we have stayed more
or less unhappily married ever since!'

At the end of December 1951 Artie was posted to the headquarters of
No. 1 Group, Bomber Command. On 5 January 1952, he was awarded the
Air Force Cross in the Birthday Honours List for his work at Farnborough.
He received many congratulatory messages from friends and relatives upon
his award of the AFC; one was from the officer commanding, No. 1 Group,
Air Vice-Marshal Brown, CB, CBE, DFC.

Artie's tour at Farnborough finished at the end of 1951 and he went
north to Bawtry in Yorkshire, where he became a staff officer at the headquarters of No. 1 Group under AVM Brown. He commented that 'even

if I say so, I am a better than average pen pusher'.

His stay at Bawtry ended in July 1953 when, after a short course at the Canberra Operational Training Unit, he took command of No. 139 (Jamaica) Squadron based at Hemswell. His memorable service with No. 139 Squadron is the subject of the next chapter.

PART 9:
RAF SERVICE, 1953–67

RECORD OF SERVICE

UNIT.	DATES. FROM	DATES. TO	UNIT.	DATES. FROM	DATES. TO
School of L.A.W.-Air Defence	5 Dec 1952	19 Dec 1952			
B.C.B.S., Lindholme	9 Jun 1953	13 Jun 1953			
Nº 231 O.C.U., Bassingbourn	15 Jun 1953	4 Jul 1953			
Nº 139 Sqdn., Hemswell	6 Jul 1953	23 Oct 1955			
Air Ministry (D.D.Ops.(B)).	24 Oct 1955	31 Dec 1955			
R.A.F.F.C., Manby	6 Jan 1956	15 Jun 1956			
H.Q. 2nd. A.T.A.F. Geilenkirchen	26 Jul 1956	7 Aug 1956			
Nº 59 Sqdn. Gutersloh	15 Nov 1957	12 May 1958			
'B' Squadron	8 Aug 1956	15 Nov 1957			
A.&A.E.E., Boscombe Down	15 May 1958	3 Apr 1961			
Air Ministry (D.F.S.)	4 Apr 1961	6 Jul 1964			
R.A.F. Laarbruch	7 Jul 1964				

Chapter 29

No. 139 (Jamaica) Squadron

Artie took command of No. 139 (Jamaica) Squadron on 6 July 1953. His time with the squadron saw him serve with distinction and be awarded his second Air Force Cross. He remained with No. 139 until October 1955.

The squadron had an interesting history. It was first formed in 1918 and saw service in Italy during the First World War, at the end of which it was disbanded. It was re-formed in 1936 as a bomber squadron as part of the RAF expansion programme at that time. At the outbreak of war in 1939, it was equipped with Blenheims and had the distinction of being the first RAF unit to go into action against the enemy within an hour of the declaration of war.

In 1940 the late Alec Gordon of Jamaica heard Winston Churchill making one of his wartime speeches: 'Is not this the appointed time for all to make the utmost exertions in the war? If the battle is to be won we must provide our men with ever-increasing quantities of the weapons and ammunition they need. We must have and quickly, more aeroplanes, more tanks, more shells, more guns.'

This speech inspired Mr Gordon to start the Jamaica Bombing Plane Fund. With the assistance of the Jamaican *Daily Gleaner* newspaper, £20,000 was collected within ten days. A number of firms donated one bomber each and soon Jamaica's contribution was sufficient to provide a squadron of twelve Bristol Blenheims. Churchill was so impressed with this achievement by the Jamaican people that in April 1941 he instructed that the squadron be renamed No. 139 (Jamaica) Squadron.

The squadron served with distinction during the war. It later became part of No. 8 Pathfinder Group flying Mosquitoes, whose role was as 'markers' for the main force Pathfinder bombers.

When Artie took command the unit was equipped with Canberra B2s: 'Later we were given training aircraft, a T4, and towards the end of my Tour, we were given B6s. The job here was low-level target marking at night, aiming bombs in a steep dive. All the checks of pilot's instruction in bombing techniques and instrument rating were done on aircraft with no dual controls. Although I had officers on the Squadron for that task, I took over the duties of instrument rating examiner and check pilot for my own squadron (and for the next). Consequently, I probably knew the flying ability of my pilots as well, if not better, than most Squadron Commanders.'

In August 1955 the squadron made a goodwill visit to Jamaica for the first time. It took part in the 'Jamaica 300', celebrating 300 years of membership of the British family of nations. The squadron flew via Iceland, Goose Bay (Labrador), St Hubert (Montreal), and then by way of Miami to Jamaica.

Some 129 officers and men took part in the operation. The ground crews were flown in five Hastings aircraft of Transport Command. Much of the 290,000 gallons of fuel and the supplies of oxygen for the high-flying Canberras was pre-delivered in the West Indies prior to the squadron arrival. Four days were spent in Jamaica, followed by visits and flying demonstrations in then British Guiana, Trinidad, Barbados, the Bahamas and Bermuda. The Canberras also flew over islands where they could not land – Antigua, Granada and St Kitts.

On leaving the West Indies, the squadron gave a display in Miami and spent two weeks exercising with units of the Royal Canadian Air Force at Goose Bay and St Hubert. They also participated in the flying at the Canadian national exhibition at Trenton, Ontario. It was reported that Squadron Leader Ashworth and Flight Lieutenant Peebles performed spectacular climbs, banks and high-speed runs over the airfield at Trenton. Artie said he took over the high-speed and aerobatic part himself.

The mission was reported to have been a huge success, the squadron being well received wherever it visited. It also gained much publicity. It was for his work in No. 139 Squadron that Artie was awarded his second AFC.

Peter Cole of England flew in No. 139 Squadron during Artie's time as commanding officer. He said he much enjoyed his eighteen months in the squadron under Artie's command: 'It was clear that he was a caring and gentle commander. Both he and his wife were regular visitors to the mess in the evening. I recall Artie's habit of clutching his tankard between his elbow and waist and asking for "just a half" which meant half a quart when accepting a refill.' Peter said the period he spent under Artie's command gave him valuable experience and much happiness.

In 1954 the man who had been largely responsible for the squadron name, Alec Gordon, visited Hemswell where he was afforded a great reception.

Artie left No. 139 Squadron in October 1955 on being posted to the Air Ministry in London. Before he left he received a letter of appreciation for his service to the squadron, from the governor of Jamaica.

Chapter 30

RAF Service, 1955–67

On 24 October 1955 Artie was posted to the Air Ministry in London as Deputy Director of Operations. He recalled that his stay at the Air Ministry didn't last very long, as someone who had been selected for a course at the Flying College at Manly had dropped out and they needed a replacement. Since Artie met the qualifications necessary for this course and there was (apparently) no one else available, he was, as he said, 'selected'. So after a period of only two months he went north again, this time to Manly in Lincolnshire, where he reported on 6 January 1956.

The Flying College had been formed in 1945 by the nucleus staff of the Empire Central Flying School. 'Here we were taught how to fight wars with Aeroplanes and what weapons to use, as well as some of the theory and practice of directions. I found myself much at home,' said Artie. A massive understatement for a man with 110 wartime operations and a DSO and two DFCs to his credit. 'As well as classroom work there was practical flying to test some of the theory. The students were more or less a cross-section of the Air Force and, as far as I can remember, this was the first time I had met this phenomena.'

The stay at Manly ended on 15 June 1956, following which Artie was posted to Gütersloh in Germany to form a Canberra squadron from the remnants of four Bomber Command squadrons. This became No. 59 Squadron, RAF. Before he took command of the squadron he was promoted to the rank of wing commander.

Gütersloh was a pre-war Luftwaffe station. Artie recalled it was a rather gloomy place. At first the squadron was equipped with Canberra B2s, which he said weren't really up to the job, which was low-level night interdiction.

Later, they were equipped with B(1)8s, which could at least carry 4 mm cannons and could have proved pretty effective against lightly defended soft targets. They were also fitted later with the LABS (Low Altitude Bombing System) but these weapons did not become available until he had left the squadron in May 1958. In the latter stages of 1957, the squadron moved to a NATO base at Geilenkirchen, near the Belgian border. During his time at Geilenkirchen, the squadron was paid an official visit by His Royal Highness the Duke of Edinburgh. Artie was among the local dignitaries and senior commanders who were introduced to the Duke. On the anniversary of the ending of the war, Artie commanded the squadron in a ceremonial parade.

Peter Masterman of England served in No. 139 Squadron under Artie's command. Peter was asked why Artie was held in such high esteem: 'It was because he projected an air of reliability, steadiness, sound judgement and discipline, which is just what is needed by new, young aircrew. He expected high standards from his crews, and I would not have liked to have been at the end of his tongue had I let the side down!'

Peter was grounded for three years due to a serious back injury. When he returned to No. 59 Squadron at Geilenkirchen he said it was a time when the Cold War was really serious and he spent many nights and days living beside a Canberra loaded with nuclear weapons.

Peter recalled that when he joined the squadron he was barely twenty years old. He had lived a very sheltered life, having attended a small boys' boarding school in Lincolnshire:

Alcohol had barely passed my lips having been trained as a navigator in Winnipeg, Canada, where it was illegal to drink alcohol under the age of 21. Also, I had only just discovered that girls were different. I was not one of the boys so to speak. It was therefore daunting on arrival to first meet Artie with my pilot in the cellar bar at Gütersloh. There Artie invited me to drink a chamber pot full of strong German beer as part of an initiation ceremony.

I remember him as a man who was sparing in his words, but his words were wisdom. To be honest, I was a bit frightened of him. It was difficult to discern his demeanour behind that moustache – I never knew if he was smiling or not when he talked to me.

I remember taking part in an international navigation and bombing competition. We were a little worried when Artie decided to lead our team because as CO he did not have the opportunity to practise. However, we need not have worried – he achieved impressive results: a measure of his experience and innate ability as a pilot.

When I think of Artie just one word comes to mind: respect. Respect for his experience, his judgement and his example.

Flight Lieutenant, RAF (Rtd), Tony Smythe served in No. 59 Squadron under Artie's command for just over a year in 1956–57. Tony recorded his memories of Artie: 'I think it is fair to say that from the word go, Artie was brimming with confidence and carried everyone along with him. You definitely knew that what he said you went along with, no nonsense, but somehow you were always happy to agree. I don't ever remember him losing his cool. He just carried people along with him. I also remember a chest full of 'gongs',[138] which you also took note of. … One thing I remember very clearly was that great moustache, a real Jimmy Edwards' style handlebar![139] This seemed to add even more to his tremendous cheerfulness.'

Tony served in No. 104 Squadron before being posted to No. 59. He said that flying in No. 59 immediately became more exciting: 'We were often down low, first at 1,000 feet and then at 500 feet day and night. We had a radar altimeter but couldn't detect high masts etc. So it was really 500 feet at night compared to whatever you wanted to make it during the day knowing as we did that any complaints from the unfortunate German population were unlikely to be taken seriously.'

Tony said that his tour with No. 59 Squadron ended in September 1957 and Artie did two generous things for him: 'In his own handwriting he assessed me as "above average" as a Night Ground Attack Pilot, and the same for Shallow Dive Bombing, as well as "above average" in Instrument Flying. … Then he influenced my next posting in a way I would not have believed possible. I told him my biggest ambition was to be posted to Fighter Command, notwithstanding that nobody thought it possible to move from Bombers to Fighters. However, Artie said he was due to visit

the Air Ministry soon and he would see what he could do for me. To my
great delight I was eventually posted to train to fly the delta winged Javelin
night-fighter. I was there for two very exciting years of my eight in the RAF.'

According to his 'record of service', Artie relinquished command of
No. 59 Squadron on 12 May 1957. The unofficial history of the squadron
recorded that the air officer commanding's inspection and parade took
place the following day and in the evening the squadron entertained
Wing Commander Ashworth and Mrs Ashworth to mark the highly
eventful time through which he led No. 59, and the considerable suc-
cesses the squadron had achieved under his command.

Artie later wrote that there he was tending his own squadron, properly equipped with men and with comfortable quarters, when he had a
call from a nabob in the Air Ministry. He said they were at a loss to find
a properly qualified incumbent for the 'B' Squadron at the Aeroplane
and Armament Experimental Establishment at Boscombe Down. So Artie
said: 'I was of course "elected" to go. So off we went back to England for
my last flying appointment. B Squadron was mostly concerned with the
V Bombers, although we also had a scattering of other types. One interesting thing I did was to fire the first two inch rocket pods from the Canberra
B(1)8 and I gave some demonstrations of their effectiveness. Of interest
also perhaps was the last aircraft I flew in the RAF. This was the Anson
– the same make as the first twin engine aircraft I had flown.'

Artie was the commanding officer of 'B' Squadron. The British V Bomber
Force was equipped with the Vickers Valiant, the Avro Vulcan and the
Handley Page Victor. This force formed Britain's independent nuclear
deterrent during the height of the Cold War in the late 1950s and 1960s.
The cost of maintaining the V Bomber Force was huge and with chang-
ing requirements, coupled with financial constraints, the RAF invested
its resources into fighter-bombers such as the Jaguar, and into developing the vertical-take-off Harrier jump jet. Thus the V Force was abandoned in the early 1970s.

Air Vice-Marshal Russ Law, RAAF (Rtd), of Australia – a new graduate
of the Empire Test Pilots' School – was posted on exchange duties in January 1958 to 'B' Squadron, which he said was responsible for the testing
of 'heavy' aircraft being introduced into the RAF. He returned to Australia

and the RAAF in early 1960. Russ admitted that he was in awe of Artie's medals: 'I only knew that "the Boss" was highly decorated in Bomber Command during World War II. He never talked about his past deeds at all. I found him a very decent, modest chap who did not fly a great deal but kept in touch with the work and flying in his squadron and of the ground crews, pilots, and other aircrew. He personally vetted every report we ever produced.'

From Boscombe Down Artie was posted in early April 1961 to the Air Ministry and the Directorate of Flight Safety, a job for which he thought he was a 'natural'. He later became the deputy director there. He recalled that he liked his job at the Air Ministry, the only real snag being the three hours and twenty minutes each day in a commuter train getting to and from work.

While he was at the Air Ministry his wife gave birth to their only child. 'His name, of course, is Corran,' said Artie. The name of his close friend and late fighter pilot brother. Artie was a proud and loving father to his only son.

Artie was deeply disappointed that he did not receive the promotion to group captain he expected and felt he deserved. I recall him writing to my mother expressing that disappointment and indicating that as a consequence he would be retiring earlier than he expected. In the end, however, it was ill health that forced his retirement.

'For my last posting [7 July 1964] I was sent to the huge NATO base at Laarbruch in Germany, where I was the Wing Commander in charge of administration. This was a job of which I was more than capable and we were comfortably housed on a base with a multitude of leisure facilities. The only difficulty was that I was never given sufficient men or money to do the task shovelled on to my shoulders.'

As mentioned previously, Artie had contracted recurrent malaria during his time in the Middle East. It would finally result in him having to retire from the RAF. He said that while at the Air Ministry an attack of malaria left him with damaged ends to the optic nerves in his left eye. Gradually this developed into cataracts in both eyes with the consequent loss of vision. These cataracts were removed just before he left the service. Subsequent malarial attacks resulted in tinnitus in both ears and, later still, a loss of hearing and a slow failure of both kidneys. 'A bit of a handicap,' he was to record.

In October 1966 increasing ill health resulted in him quitting the NATO base. 'I had to leave Laarbruch owing to increasing blindness, to go the RAF hospital at Halton, from where, in May 1967, I became a civilian.'

So ended the remarkable air force career of a distinguished officer, a truly 'great bloke' from a small, remote rural town in New Zealand. There is little doubt that he was reluctant to retire. The RAF was his life and his great love. It would be twenty-seven years before the 'final touchdown'.

PART 10:
THE RELUCTANT RETIREMENT

1991, Artie and Maria's mother and Corran and Maria.

Chapter 31

The Civilian, 1967–94

Following his admission to the RAF hospital at Halton, Artie's air force career came to an end. After twenty-eight years of service, Wing Commander Ashworth returned to civilian life.

This chapter is a brief outline of Artie's retirement years from 1967 until the last 'touchdown' in 1994: draughtsman, hotelier, holiday flats owner, Air Crew Association, Hotel Association, Conservative Club treasurer, school governor and, according to son Corran, 'all round terrible golfer'.[140]

Corran said it was sad that Artie never wanted to talk about his RAF career. To him that was the past. For the twenty-eight years after the family moved back to England from Germany, he would only refer to the present and plans for the future. When he attended RAF functions, funerals for comrades, Air Crew Association reunions, or flight displays, it was clearly understood that he went on his own with his old mates.[141]

Corran related that it was while stationed at Laarbruch that the cataracts in his eyes got steadily worse. 'He finished up wearing very heavy, oversized lenses which looked something like a couple of milk bottles in a frame on his face.' Although suffering from tunnel vision for the rest of his life, his eyesight strangely got better as the years went by. Apparently, the same nerves also affect the hearing and sadly this badly deteriorated over the next twenty years. 'If he didn't want to hear what was being said, somehow magically, the batteries in his hearing-aids would pack up.' Sometimes referred to as matrimonial deafness.

After leaving the RAF Artie first took up a job as a draughtsman in Harrogate, Yorkshire. He had been a draughtsman before he joined the air force in 1939. However, working an eight-hour day and not seeing much of his wife and son did not make him a happy man. Artie was a former RAF officer who didn't really know what to do in civilian life.

At the age of forty-seven he and Kay decided he should change his occupation. His eyesight wasn't perfect, his hearing was already starting to go, but most of all he had little money. His RAF pension would help, and they would make a small profit from the sale of the bungalow they had bought in Yorkshire.

Despite these constraints they eventually bought a twelve-bedroom private hotel about half a mile from Bournemouth centre in the south of England. It was a ten-minute walk to the beach. 'Within a year the Sunnyside Hotel was renamed the Silver Fern, reflecting no doubt Artie's New Zealand roots.'

In those days a small hotelier relied essentially for business on people knocking on the door every Saturday. Artie realised that some of his old air force buddies simply couldn't afford a holiday with their family at the usual south coast resorts. Moreover, they weren't allowed to bring their dogs, and all such residences were prevented by law from providing a beer after 10.30 p.m. So Artie set about offering something more accommodating, as well as less expensive.

New Zealand House[142] proved helpful with securing business. Artie also made a point of contacting old and new colleagues, most of whom had been in the same position with either no money or no skills relevant to peacetime occupations. Perhaps he was fortunate in not having loads of children to support but he also had that lucky built-in self-survival that we all aspire to but few achieve. Cheaper holidays meant more recommendations, and so more business. He got involved in the local Conservative Party Association and the Bournemouth Hotel and Restaurant Association. He would also write chance letters to any famous football or cricket club visiting the area and so on. In this way business steadily increased. However, both he and Kay found running a small private hotel a very demanding occupation.

After three years of twenty-four hours a day, seven days a week, Wing Commander Ashworth had had enough. The hotel was sold and a block of eight holiday flats about half a mile away were purchased. Corran said this meant solid work for five hours every Saturday morning, the rest of the week being purely maintenance and all for about the same income.

The real change in Artie's life was that he now had time on his hands. He also had a twelve-year-old boy to look after who kept beating him at golf. So within two years he was the treasurer of the local Conservative Association and on the board of the Holiday Flats Association. His ties with the RAF diminished quite rapidly from the mid-seventies. He was very involved with the Air Crew Association but, apart from reunions, the marriages of former colleagues' children and the increasing number of old RAF comrades' funerals, he knew he had long moved on.

Corran related how in November each year, as Remembrance Day approached, he would stand outside the most disreputable pub in the neighbourhood from 9a.m. until around 9p.m. selling poppies for the British Legion. 'Even the nastiest thugs would take one look at a quite short, bald old man in a smart trench coat wearing the most medals they had ever seen in the movies, and would hand over some cash.' This was the caring, patriotic Artie Ashworth who remembered those comrades who flew into hell and never returned.

For the last ten years of having the holiday apartments, they just opened for the six months of the summer. The income was satisfactory and pension and insurance policies were now maturing. Corran told the story of how on a whim Artie agreed to let a fellow over the road, whom he knew, stay for three months in a unit on the first floor. This burly Irishman was roughly 6 foot 5 inches and 16 stones. Apparently after a couple of weeks, one night the 'guest' came home blind drunk and started smashing the place up. Corran was the first to hear the commotion and ran to get his dad out of bed. 'Within a few minutes with very little conversation, a giant Irishman was thrown down the stairs with a terrified 17 year old standing behind him with the man's suitcase. We never saw him again.'

In 1987 Artie and Kay sold the holiday apartments and retired to a house just off the clifftop in Southport, Bournemouth. In 1991 Corran married his long-time girlfriend, Maria, in Gibraltar. Maria's parents and Artie[143] attended. Corran's great friend and best man Paul, together with Artie, stayed in the bar at their hotel late on their first night until Paul had to go to bed. Corran related how one drunk had collapsed on the stairway. Artie then tripped over him at around 2a.m. Somehow Artie got him breathing and banged enough doors to get an ambulance. The next morning Artie was a bit surprised to find his three-night stay was being paid for by the hotel. He couldn't remember a thing about it.

In 1971, along with my family, I was returning to New Zealand from a prolonged assignment in Afghanistan via the United Kingdom. All six of us stayed at the Silver Fern. It had been twenty-two years since I last saw Artie and he made us very welcome. He seemed to greatly enjoy my four children. I suspect one of his regrets was that he and Kay only ever had one child.

Later, during my residence in Washington DC (1976–87), my work with the World Bank entailed frequent travel to countries in central Asia, especially Afghanistan, the Middle East and eastern Europe. These journeys invariably required a stopover in London, either outward or homeward bound. If time permitted, I would try to spend at least one night with Artie and Kay in Bournemouth. It was always a pleasure. But we never ever talked about his air force career, one of my everlasting regrets.

The first signs of serious illness emerged during his trip to Gibraltar. Artie later admitted that it had been ongoing and he had been sick several times on the plane. Within six months terminal kidney failure was confirmed. He was decreed too far advanced for a transplant. Home dialysis started immediately and hospital visits became more regular during the next three years.

Corran related that in 1993 they played their last nine holes of golf at the course where Artie had taught him to play twenty-two years before. Even with a colostomy bag and an inhaler, and not having played for two years, Corran said they still ended up level. 'By then, as he was only allowed half a litre of liquid a day, our normal after match beer was out of the question and he had given up his pipe years ago. This was the time he let me into a little secret. … When he stayed overnight at Portsmouth Hospital his late night cup of tea was actually hot whisky with a tea bag. There he was charming the nurses till the end. Even towards the end and although most of his comrades had joined the station-in-the-sky, he was as actively involved as possible with the ACA and the RAF Benevolent Fund. He took immense pleasure in me driving him to the Bournemouth Air Show in 1993 and complained for days afterwards that he hadn't warned me how loud the Vulcan and Harrier were. The noise didn't worry him since he just turned his hearing aids off.'

Artie made the last touchdown in 1994 at Portsmouth. He was cremated in Bournemouth. One of his former comrades from No. 75 Squadron, Terry Kearns a fellow New Zealander, arranged the funeral details. Artie had been the best man at Terry's wedding in 1946. Over 200 former comrades and friends attended. Corran said it was quite surreal in many ways as he didn't have that many personal friends left. It was a reflection, however, of the enormous respect all had for Artie Ashworth.

I was privileged to attend his funeral. For me, it was a deeply emotive experience. Kay, Corran and myself followed his casket into the service. I recall passing between two, what seemed very long, lines of very bemedalled veterans. Artie's casket was clothed in the New Zealand flag, with his cap and medals placed on top.

Many of his former comrades introduced themselves and it is to my everlasting regret that I did not take the opportunity to get their contact details. With very few exceptions, they have all gone now. It had never occurred to me that one day I would have the privilege of writing the biography of this likeable, remarkable man.

Chapter 32

Memories of Artie Ashworth

'While not being physically impressive, Artie was always a strong and determined man. He had a great quiet yet loving disposition. He was a much loved father.' *(Corran Ashworth)*

Artie had a great sense of humour and the most mischievous smile. He was much loved by all those close to him.

He was an undistinguished golfer. While Artie loved to play the game, his eyesight prevented him from ever being really accomplished. Corran was a very good player, being a scratch golfer at one stage. Corran was also a talented artist as a caricature of him and Artie attests.

Artie's daughter-in-law, Maria Ashworth, shares her memories of the man:

Artie Ashworth was a wonderful person. I am privileged to have known him. I first met him in Bournemouth around 1981 when I was dating his son Corran, whom I later married. He was a lovely, kind-hearted soul, a real gentleman. He still had his rugged New Zealand ways about him, but was settled into the English way of life, having lived in the UK for longer than in New Zealand.

His wry sense of humour was understated in company but let loose with those he held close. He loved a good laugh and a joke but was careful to be very diplomatic where any risqué remarks might offend the more delicate ear. As a gentleman, he would be careful to keep the manly jokes for men only, well away from the ears of the ladies.

He had a steely determination. If there was a way to do something he would seek it out. He never liked to be beaten by anything if he could see a way to fix it. I remember once the kitchen sink in our house had blocked and being young novices we had no idea how to unblock it. So Artie duly turned up with a can of some ancient drain powder and dumped it in the sink. We had two or three cups of tea over a chat whilst waiting for something to happen with the still water. All of a sudden the water bubbled and then it cleared down the plug hole. Artie said with a lovely smile, 'Just call me when you need me.' And that's how he was, always there to help.

Sunday mornings were a treat that both Artie and Corran always looked forward to. On most Sundays they would meet up early for 18 holes of golf, usually at Meyrick Park Golf Course in Bournemouth. On some occasions one of Corran's good friends Mark Howe would join them. The end of the game always finished with a well earned pint and a good yarn at the 19th.

Simon Clarke, a friend of Corran Ashworth, recalled playing golf with Artie and son: 'Artie had an uncanny knack of selective sight: whenever he hit a good shot he could see it perfectly but if it was a bad-un he would ask "Where did that one go?"' Simon said he was one of the most interesting men he had ever met and was always in great humour.

Maria said Artie was one for adventure. 'When Corran and I told him we were going to Gibraltar to get married he was thrilled. As delighted as he was to hear of our betrothal, that twinkle in his eye glistened at the thought of visiting Gibraltar again. This was a place Artie knew well and had spent time there during the war. At one stage he was the officer responsible for teaching the other pilots short take-offs and landings on the all too short runway. He loved seeing the "rock" again. The runway had been lengthened since the war and he was keen to learn how things had changed. It was a great adventure for him.'

To remember fallen colleagues and friends and help where he could was dear to Artie's heart. Every year he would collect money for the Poppy Appeal in November, a benevolent fund to assist surviving families. Even in cold, wet, winter weather, Artie would proudly sport his medals, collect donations and give out memorial poppies. My mother would always make a point of only buying her poppy each year from Artie.

He never liked to talk about his wartime activities. For him it was not a subject to cherish. The wars he fought remained with him; it was documented well enough so he left it at that. For all that, he did have many cherished memories of former comrades and the wonderful people he had met along the way.

In latter years his eyesight deteriorated and he had to wear ever thicker lenses. When Artie cracked a smile from ear to ear with those 'big' eyes staring at one, everyone smiled with him. One could guarantee there would be mischief behind the smile.

Although in subsequent years his health ailed, he still had such pride that he fought his illness to the end. He passed away at the age of seventy-three in 1994. We all miss him dearly but will never ever forget him. Sadly, Corran passed away in 2007 after a long illness. I am sure the two of them, father and son, are somewhere enjoying a wonderful game of golf and sharing a joke or two along the way. He will never be forgotten.

Chapter 33

Artie Ashworth, the Legend

Artie Ashworth's career speaks for itself. Twenty-eight years in the Royal Air Force, during which time, according to his official RAF record of service, he recorded 110 wartime operations against enemy targets, 78 of them mostly flying through hell in attacks on heavily defended targets in Germany. During his career he logged a total of 3,904 flying hours, of which 3,828 were as captain of aircraft. He flew some 94 different types of aircraft. During this time he was awarded four decorations for bravery: DSO, DFC twice and MID, and two for distinguished RAF service, the AFC. His flying assessments were invariably rated 'above average' or 'exceptional'. He was a bomber pilot, fighter pilot, Pathfinder, test pilot, glider pilot, squadron commanding officer, Director of Flight Safety (Air Ministry), and squadron commander, administration.

But Artie Ashworth was not just a distinguished pilot. He was without any doubt a born leader who inspired confidence in all who worked with or under him. He was also a great character, liked and admired by all. Forever cheerful, and always that mischievous smile and twinkle in the eye behind the trademark moustache. Professionally, he was highly respected, known for his attention to detail, and as one who did not accept second best from his crew members or from those who served under his command.

As Val Crankshaw, widow of former rear gunner and Artie's crew member, Ken Crankshaw, said: 'Who could forget him? He was someone who seemed larger than life.'

In his book *Night After Night*, author Max Lambert referred to the 'legendary' and the 'redoubtable' Artie Ashworth. When asked what it was that led him to make these statements, Max said it was his reputation as a skilled pilot and his courage, coupled with his popularity with all who knew him. 'Few people in Bomber Command earned that title but Artie Ashworth was without doubt one of those few.'

When discussing Artie's wartime exploits, a former No. 75 Squadron aircrew member said he was a 'madman' but quickly added that he was very highly respected. Another who flew with him in No. 17F Squadron, RNZAF, in the Pacific said he was not one to stand on ceremony or rank. He preferred for all ranks to just call him Artie. This despite being a squadron leader with a DSO and DFC to his name at that time. Artie was popular with all ranks, he recalled.

One thing that consistently emerges about Artie: he was highly respected by all who knew and served with him. 'A real character', 'A truly great bloke', 'Bigger than life', 'Undoubted courage and skill as Captain of aircraft and devotion to duty', 'At all times displaying the perseverance, coolness and courage necessary to successfully execute bombing operations', 'It is impossible to speak too highly of this officer's courage, his determination, his utter fearlessness and his great enthusiasm', 'Ashworth's fine fighting spirit and devotion to duty have set an inspiring example to all', 'An exceptional pilot'.

'He was a caring and gentle commander. The time I spent under his command provided me with valuable experience and much happiness,' said Peter Cole, former No. 139 Squadron pilot.

Former No. 59 Squadron pilot, Tony Smythe, remarked that Artie was brimming with confidence and carried everyone along with him. 'And that great "Jimmy Edwards"-style moustache seemed to add even more to his tremendous cheerfulness. Artie was respected and held in high esteem because he projected an air of reliability, steadiness, sound judgement and discipline. Just what was needed by young aircrew. When I think of Artie just one word comes to mind: respect. Respect for his experience and his example. He was fun to be with but his professionalism was always obvious.'

Peter Masterman, former No. 59 Squadron aircrew recalled, 'In uniform, one could not help but be impressed by the array of decorations and campaign medal ribbons on his chest, with the Pathfinder badge above his left breast pocket being a distinctive item. His moustache was an eye-catching feature and he seemed to often smooth either end through his fingers when in conversation. I remember his wide smile and the twinkling in his eyes. We were young aircrew and Artie was perhaps a little distant in the early stages until we got to know him. I'm sure we were in awe of him.'

Air Vice-Marshal Don Atlee, RAF (Rtd), joined No. 59 Squadron as a flight commander at Gütersloh, flying Canberra B(1)8s: 'I was delighted to find Artie as the Squadron Commander. My first flight with the Squadron was a check flight with Artie. We disappeared into cloud at about 1,500 feet and then flew around above the clouds, while Artie had me carry out various exercises to check that I knew how the Canberra operated. Then he said "Where is the airfield?" I hadn't any idea so he gave me a heading to steer and told me to let down below the cloud. I was astonished to find the airfield in front of the aircraft when we broke the cloud. The memory of that flight and Artie's instinctive knowledge of exactly where he was, has struck me ever since. He taught me a lot. He was a great chap to work with.'

'To be invited into the Empire Test Pilots' School, one had to be an exceptional pilot. Make no mistake, Artie Ashworth was an exceptional pilot', according to Don Briggs, former test pilot instructor and No. 635 Pathfinder Squadron aircrew.

'I consider it was a privilege to have flown as a member of his crew. He was a credit to New Zealand,' said Ken Calton, No. 635 Pathfinder Squadron flight engineer.

These are just some of the comments describing Artie Ashworth.

And to his family and to his many New Zealand friends he was our hero.

From reading the literature and the exploits of many in Bomber Command, I now believe he never received the recognition for his skill and bravery in flying a damaged Wellington home single-handedly in 1943. Recognition he richly deserved. Many acts of bravery above and beyond the call of duty go unrecognised in wartime. This was certainly one of them. As a minimum he should have been awarded a Bar to his DSO. Perhaps, as was presented to at least one other who accomplished the same feat, it should have been, as many believed, a Victoria Cross.

When I set out to write this story I knew Artie had served with distinction throughout his career. But I did not fully appreciate just how distinguished and just how much this man from a small, rural New Zealand town packed into a comparatively short life. I pondered about the title and wondered if perhaps it was simply some romantic thought of someone who had always considered him a great man. I asked myself, is this just hero worship? Now, however, having researched his career, and having written the story, I am in no doubt that Artie Ashworth was a brave, skilled and honourable man, who served his country with distinction. But he was more than that. He was also a loving father and a kind and caring man. He was a humble, very special person.

He was indeed a legend in his time.

Notes

Chapter 1

1   John Faithful, a nephew of Tex Faithful, confirmed the fire incident.

2   Including baby Donald, the family consisted of eight children. Six, including Archie, went to the Falklands, while Margaret and Phyllis stayed at Queenstown with Aunt Maria Davies. Stanley John had died in 1916 after contracting pneumonia.

Chapter 2

3   My grandfather, John Ashworth, died in 1884, so my father never knew his own father.

4   Tors, as they are called, are a unique feature of the landscape of central Otago. They consist of upright schist rocks that have become exposed as a result of millions of years of natural erosion.

5   Playing tennis or any other sport on the Sabbath was strictly prohibited in those days.

6   Recreation ground in the centre of the town.

7   These were pools left behind from the gold-dredging days. They were close to the River Clutha. In some cases they were very deep and since the level of water was affected by the river, it was invariably cold. The river has its source in the southern lakes, which in turn are fed by waters from glaciers in the southern alps.

8   Colin Hanson, *By Such Deeds*, p. 439.

9   My father died intestate, which according to the law at that time, meant his estate was handled by the Public Trustee. After consultation with my uncle, Archie Ashworth, it was decided that the small savings would be held in trust for the six children under the age of twenty-one at the time of death. The funds were to be distributed when the youngest child, Vincent, reached the age of twenty-one. In 1952 I received the sum of 100 pounds (NZ \$5,500 in 2011). My mother received Corran's share.

Chapter 4

10   Blenheim bombers suffered heavy losses in the early part of the war.

11   Rex Daniell, RAF, DFC, AFC, FC (Neth.), in *What Did You Do in the War, Poppa Rekka*? p. 2.

12   Op. cit, p. 3.

13   Since the USA was not at war at this time, and the Panama Canal Zone was under American control, Allied servicemen were not permitted to wear military uniforms.

14   Later Flight Lieutenant, DFC.

15   Adapted from the diary of Frank Chunn.

Chapter 5

16   Spurdle, p. 21.

17   Errol Martyn, *For Your Tomorrow*, vol. 3, p. 589.

18   Martyn, vol. 1, p. 90.

19   Martyn, vol. 1, p. 131.

20   Martyn, vol. 1, p. 111.

21   Citations kindly provided by Errol Martyn. Personal communication, 12 June 2010.

22   Martyn, vol. 1, p. 130; vol. 3, p. 454.

23   Martyn, vol. 1, p. 96.

24   Martyn, vol. 2, p. 96.

25   Martyn, vol. 1, p. 99 and personal communication with Gary Cave of Morrinsville.

26   Martyn, vol. 1, p. 94.

27   Martyn, vol. 3, p. 311.

28   Squadron Leader Gasquoine survived.

29   Hanson, *By Such Deeds*, p. 452.

30   Rex Daniell, personal communication, 3 June 2010.

31   There were a number of other private operators but their services were essentially regionally focused, whereas SPANZ operated all over the country.

32   Overview of his career provided by Rex Daniell. Full details are contained in Daniell, *Poppa Rekka*.

33   Hanson, *By Such Deeds*, p. 153.

Chapter 6

34   Denis Richards, *The Hardest Victory*.

35   Max Lambert, *Night After Night*, pp. 63–64.

36   Martin Middlebrook, *The Battle of Hamburg*, pp. 34, 36.

37   A legendary story is told of some senior British officers in Cairo complaining to the New Zealand commander, General Freyberg, that his troops were not saluting them. Freyberg suggested they try waving instead and they would find the New Zealand soldiers would probably wave back.

38   David Bensusan-Butt, a civil servant in the War Cabinet secretariat, was given the task of assessing 633 target photos and comparing them with crews' claims. The results, first circulated in August 1941, were a shock to many, though not necessarily to those within the RAF, who were already largely aware of the failure of crews to navigate to, identify and bomb targets.

39   Arthur Harris, *Bomber Offensive*, p. 267.

40   Like many others he could not accept that a special medal was struck for those who served in the 8th Army, while those who served in Bomber Command were denied the distinction.

Chapter 7

41   Mel Rolfe, *Looking into Hell – Experiences of the Bomber Command War*.

42   Second lieutenant.

43   'Going over the top', involved the infantry leaving their deep trenches to go over the top to attack the enemy. In too many First World War battles in France and Belgium they were simply mowed down by well-entrenched enemy machine guns and the losses were catastrophic.

44   Lambert, *Night After Night*, p. 26.

Chapter 8

45   Unless otherwise acknowledged, these stories have been sourced from http://www.rafbombercommand.com/personals_1_earlydays.html

46   Bomber Command frequently employed 'diversions', which were designed to divert the German defences, especially the night fighters, away from the real target and the main bombing force. They were genuine targets but were subject to a smaller attacking force.

47   The Chandler story, taken from Rolfe, *Looking into Hell*.

48   Adapted from Mel Rolfe, *To Hell and Back – True Life Experiences of Bomber Command at War*.

49   Information on John Needham was kindly provided by his son Rod Needham of Morrinsville, New Zealand.

Chapter 9

50   Artie was the second pilot to Ron Simich on this operation.
51   Ted's younger brother Brian served in the RNZAF in the Pacific. He now lives in Christchurch.
52   Term used to describe being caught in the searchlights. Being coned was not a pleasant experience as the anti-aircraft guns were then able to see the bomber and know its altitude, which enabled them to focus on the unfortunate plane.
53   GEE was an improved navigation technique. See Appendix 1 for a description of the navigation techniques used by the RAF.
54   Harris: *Bomber Offensive.*

Chapter 10

55   Adapted from *Return at Dawn* by Hilary A. St George Saunders.

Chapter 11

56   The motto of No. 75 Squadron, meaning 'Forever Strong'.
57   No. 75 Squadron, Royal Flying Corps, was officially formed in October 1916. It was disbanded in 1919 and re-formed in 1937. In 1939 No. 75 became the pool for No. 3 Group Bomber Command. It essentially became the Operational Training Unit. When war broke out the then flight became a separate unit within the RAF.
58   'Popeye' Lucas was one of these pilots.
59   The Stirling, designed prior to the Lancaster and Halifax, was an enormous aircraft, with four engines and a crew of seven. Throughout its service its design limitations (chiefly its wings being too short for the large size of the aircraft) resulted in comparatively poor performance and a high loss rate.
60   Source: RAF Feltwell personnel stories: www.feltwell.net/raffeltwell/articles

Chapter 12

61   Later a squadron leader, winning a DFC, Johnnie and my fighter pilot brother Corran, who was killed in Normandy in August 1944, were close friends.
62   Gladiators were the obsolescent RAF torpedo-carrying biplanes, which were based in Malta at the outbreak of war.
63   Later Air Chief Marshal, RAF, GCB, KBE, MC and Bar, DFC, DCL.
64   The sections on Sir Keith Park and his role in Malta have been adapted from Allan W. Mitchell, *New Zealanders in the Air War.*
65   The George Cross is the civilian equivalent of the Victoria Cross.

Chapter 13

66   Robert Holford was posted back to England in early 1942. He subsequently went to Canada for further training and gained his pilot's badge in late 1943. He returned to New Zealand in October 1944. He was killed in an aircraft accident in early 1945 while serving in the RNZAF.
67   H.L. Thompson, *New Zealanders with the Royal Air Force.*
68   Artie commented that these evacuation sorties were classed as 'operational' but for some unknown reason he did not record them as such in his logbook.

Chapter 14

69   Navigational aid. See Appendix 1 for details of RAF navigational aids.
70   Martin Middlebrook and Chris Everitt, *Bomber Command War Diaries*, p. 286.
71   British Overseas Airways Corporation, later renamed British Airways.
72   Middlebrook, *Battle of Hamburg*, p. 84.

Chapter 15

73   An 'immediate award' carried the significance of being made for a specific act of bravery.

Chapter 16

74   Adapted from Wing Commander Ken Rees, *Lie in the Dark and Listen*.
75   Altogether Ken flew twelve times as a member of Artie's crew. The other flights were all aircraft testing.
76   Lysanders were used in the Second World War as Army-cooperation aircraft. They had the huge advantage of only needing a very short runway. They were used to land and bring back agents in enemy-occupied countries, especially France.
77   Information on Frank Chunn's career adapted from Hanson, *By Such Deeds*.
78   Lambert, *Night After Night*, p. 172.
79   Hanson, *By Such Deeds*.

Chapter 17

80   As far as is known, this is the only time he ever admitted to being frightened.
81   Author's comment.
82   Identification Friend or Foe. An electronic radio-based identification system.
83   Artie's personal memoir of his RAF career did not appear to have a title. I subsequently learned that it was actually entitled *I Never Saw Him Again*. It reflects how deeply he felt his brother's death.
84   See Vincent A. Ashworth, *For Our Tomorrow He Gave His Today – A Fighter Pilot's Story*.
85   He did not land at his base and he was not actually posted to No. 156 Squadron. The operation described was flown under the command of No. 156 Squadron. As Artie related, the Wellington he flew was borrowed from No. 156. It was the only sortie he flew for that squadron.
86   Later Air Vice-Marshal, CB, CBE, DSO.

Chapter 18

87   This may have been the first trip of the *Dominion Monarch* after refitting from a troop to a passenger liner.
88   New Zealand regarded itself as being a very loyal member of the British Empire, which at that time was still a pre-eminent power in the world.
89   In addition to Artie, my brothers Flying Officer Corran Ashworth and Warrant Officer Archie (Tex) Ashworth, were serving overseas at that period. Corran was a fighter pilot and Archie was training in Canada.

Chapter 19

90   This is the figure recorded by Artie.
91   Trevor Pearce, *Air Force Memories*, chapter 12, p. 3. Trevor's memory is not entirely correct in regard to his claim that Artie was known in the squadron as 'Auntie'. Others who either flew with him or knew him in the Pacific, always referred to him as Artie, by which name he was universally known.
92   At that time he not only had the DFC but the higher honour of the DSO.

Chapter 20

93   Adapted from Richards, *The Hardest Victory*, p. 193.
94   Extracted from Leo McKinstry, *Lancaster – The Second World War's Greatest Bomber*.
95   Five squadrons made up the initial group: No. 7 – Stirlings; No. 35 – Halifaxes; No. 83 – Lancasters; No. 156 – Wellingtons; and No. 109 – Wellingtons. No. 635 Squadron was not formed until March 1944.
96   See Appendix 1 for a detailed outline of the navigation systems, including OBOE.

97   Notes from Gordon Musgrove, *Pathfinder Force – A History of 8 Group.*
98   Michael Philip Wadsworth, *They Led the Way – the Story of 156 Pathfinder Squadron.*
99   Air Chief Marshal Sir Ralph Cochrane, RAF, OBE, KCB, AFC, MID was sent to New Zealand in
      1936 to assist with the establishment of the Royal New Zealand Air Force. In 1937 he was appointed
      Chief of the Air Staff, RNZAF.
100   In his book *Pathfinder* Don Bennett claimed that he used this name since it was the home town of
      one of his staff officers, Squadron Leader Ashworth. Artie stated in his autobiography that this
      was not correct. The nearest he had ever been to Wanganui was the RNZAF base at Ohakea, some
      40 kilometres distance from Wanganui.

Chapter 21

101   Adapted from Musgrove, *Pathfinder Force.*
102   The rockets were Hitler's 'secret' weapon, which he believed would bring about a German
      victory. The German rocket research and development was considerably more advanced than
      that of the Allies. Due to their effect on public morale and the damage being caused in Britain,
      the destruction of the production and launching facilities was a high priority for the British
      government. The V1 and V2 rockets were the forerunners of the advanced rockets used in the
      space programmes.
103   The C87 was the transport derivative of the B24 Liberator bomber.
104   Solomon Islands.
105   I assume he was referring here to the fact that the crew had not previously flown together.
      According to the flight engineer, Ken Calton, individually the members were actually very
      experienced.
106   These were dummy TIs laid in an attempt to lead the Germans away from the real target.
107   Christopher Coverdale, *Pathfinders 635 Squadron: Definitive History – March 1944–September
      1945*, p. 415.
108   'Tubby' Baker, squadron commander.
109   Term used by aircrews to describe the operation.
110   RAF jargon for being lost on operations.
111   'Window' consisted of aluminium strips dropped to confuse the German radar system.
112   Later doctor, OBE.
113   Peter Wheeler, *Kiwis Do Fly – New Zealanders in RAF Bomber Command*, p. 124.
114   Adapted from McKinstry, *Lancaster.*

Chapter 22

115   Adapted from Coverdale, *Pathfinders 635 Squadron.*
116   Although that is the figure entered in his logbook, Artie had actually completed more than this.
      The operations in the Western Desert in 1942 were classed as operational but for some reason he
      did not record all of these as such in his logbook. His official RAF record of service states that he
      completed 110 operational sorties. This number would include his fighter sorties in the Pacific.

Chapter 23

117   The name 'Manna' was taken from the second Book of Exodus in the Bible. Moses received a
      message from God during the long journey of the people of Israel through the desert: 'I will
      rain down bread from heaven for you. Each day the people shall go out and gather a day's
      supply.' The Israelites called the food Manna.
118   On this day Hitler committed suicide in his Berlin bunker.
119   Adapted from McKinstry, *Lancaster.*
120   Hans Onderwater, *Operation Manna/Chowhound – The Allied Food Droppings, April/May 1945.*

Chapter 24

121   That view would not be shared by those who had to live in the Nissen huts. They were reportedly
      continually damp and very cold in the winter.

122   Women's Auxiliary Air Force.
123   P.W. Dascombe, *We Lead. Others Follow – Personal Recollections of Air and Ground Crews, 635 Pathfinder Squadron, RAF Downham Market.*
124   Ninety-five aircraft were lost on this raid.
125   Adapted from Dascombe, *We Lead. Others Follow.*
126   John Hilling, *Strike Hard – A Bomber Airfield at War.*
127   Hilling, *Strike Hard*, p. 85.
128   McKinstry, *Lancaster.*
129   Adapted from McKinstry, *Lancaster.*
130   Coverdale, *Pathfinders 635 Squadron.*

Chapter 25

131   Coffee laced with rum was served to all operational crews on their return.
132   A larger town near Downham Market, which was too far for aircrew to walk or cycle.
133   By this time Frank had been posted to No. 217 Squadron at Graveley.
134   Personnel Dispatch Reception Centre.

Chapter 26

135   Interestingly, his name remained on the PWD establishment list until 1949!
136   Wing Commander F.J. Lucas, RNZAF, DFC and Bar. He and Artie served in No. 75 Squadron together.

Chapter 27

137   At that time deer were a serious pest in the bush-covered mountains of New Zealand. The government employed professional 'deer cullers' whose job was to shoot as many deer as possible. They lived rough in remote areas, sometimes spending many weeks in isolation, the only contact being the supply drops of food and ammunition, in this case by 'Popeye's' aircraft.

Chapter 30

138   The air force jargon for medals.
139   After the war Jimmy Edwards was the star in a very popular BBC radio programme *Take it from Here.*

Chapter 31

140   This chapter has been adapted from a draft prepared by Artie's son, the late Corran Anthony Ashworth.
141   One can only speculate on the reasons for not wanting to talk about his war career. With very few exceptions, it is a characteristic of most veterans I have met. One reason could be that those who have not experienced the horrors of war find it hard to believe the reality of the life of a wartime RAF bomber aircrew and Artie would have been conscious of this. He was a modest person not given to boasting about his achievements or his many skills. Exhibiting one's pride was just not done.
142   The New Zealand High Commission in London.
143   Corran's mother, Kay, was unable to attend.

RAF Navigational Aids

From the first tentative raids during 1939–41 using sextants and 'dead reckoning', Bomber Command had gradually evolved – with the help of complex navigation aids and radio countermeasures – into a high-tech striking force of devastating power and effectiveness. A brief outline of the improved navigation techniques used follows.

GEE. The first major development in navigational technology was GEE, a system perfected in early 1942. An onboard set received synchronised radio signals transmitted from ground stations in different locations in England. Two signals gave the navigator a 'fix' so he could work out his aircraft's position on the route to the target at any time.

When flying near the ground stations over a home territory, accuracy was good; at increasing distances, though, particularly into Germany, accuracy was reduced. However, within a range of about 300 miles, GEE at least ensured that each bomber crew entered enemy territory with a reasonable confidence as to their position. After a time the Germans worked out a way to jam the system (i.e. interrupt the radio signals from England). British scientists were forced to develop advanced GEE systems, new frequencies and jamming systems of their own.

OBOE. Ready for operations in December 1942, OBOE proved to be a particularly accurate device, at least for the shorter-range targets. Two OBOE ground stations in England sent out radio signals that the bomber carrying the OBOE equipment received and transmitted back. The two stations monitored the aircraft's progress. One station guided the aircraft along a predetermined track, the pilot receiving signals when he deviated to port or starboard. The second station measured the aircraft ground speed and calculated the correct moment of bomb release. The range was limited to 300 miles and since only one aircraft could be controlled at that time, OBOE was used primarily by Pathfinder Force aircraft (usually the fast Mosquitoes) to drop coloured flares to visually mark the target for the main force of bombers following behind.

After D-Day in June 1944, the advance of the Allies into the continent meant the RAF could move mobile ground stations to France and thereby extend the range of OBOE deep into Nazi Germany.

H2S. H2S became available in January 1943 and was regarded as astonishingly advanced. Kept top secret for as long as possible, large bulges began appearing under the bellies of some heavy bombers. Inside was a rotating parabolic dish that mapped the ground underneath, even through cloud, on to a screen in the aircraft. The fairly blurred picture on the screen differentiated between dark areas for sea, bright areas for land and very bright for built-up regions. It worked best on coastal targets or those with a broad river or lake nearby. At first, the new H2S sets were installed only in Pathfinder aircraft, which flew ahead of the other bombers to accurately mark the target with coloured flares.

The disadvantage of both H2S and OBOE was that the Germans could identify the aircraft as enemy. Also, as was feared, it was not long before an aircraft carrying one of the top-secret sets crashed and the Germans could examine the H2S equipment. Within months German fighters had an airborne device for homing in on RAF bombers using H2S. Nevertheless, H2S had a spectacular effect on bombing accuracy.

Appendix 2

List of Aircraft Flown

Argus
Athena
Avro 626
Battle
Chipmunk
Corsair
Firefly
Gloster E1/44
Gordon
Hant
Harvard
Horn
Hornet Moth
Hunter IV
F. Junior
Kittyhawk
Lysander
Mentor
Moth Minor
Pioneer
Prentice
Proctor
J. Provost
Rearwin
Scant
Seafire
Sea Fury
Sea Hawk
Sikorsky 555
Spitfire
Storch
Swift
Tempest
Tiger Moth
Tutor
Vampire
Vega Gull
Vildebeest
Whitney-Straight
Youngman-Baynes
Anson

Beverley
Bombay
Britannia
Canberra 1
Canberra B(1)8
Canberra B(1)12
Canberra B2
Canberra B6 and B(1)6
Canberra B15
Canberra PR3
Canberra PR7
Canberra PR9
Canberra T4
Canberra T11
Canberra T13
Comet
Consul
Convair Liner
Dakota
DC6
Devon
DH 86
Dominie
Fortress B17
Hastings
Hornet
Hudson
Lancaster
Liberator
Lincoln

Lodestar
Meteor
Mosquito
Oxford
T. Pioneer
Prince
Shackleton
Sturgeon
Tudor 11
Valetta

Valiant
Varsity
Ventura

Victor
Victor 1
Victor 1A
Victor 2
Viking
Vulcan
Wayfarer
Wellington
Whitley
York

Airfields Used, 1939–61

Australia
Darwin
Essendon
Laverton
Mallala
Nhil
Parafield
Schofields
Woomera

Bahrain
Bahrain

Bermuda
Kindley

Canada
Dorval
Gander
Goose Bay
St Hubert
Trenton

Canton Island
Canton

Ceylon
Negombo

Cyprus
Lakatamia
Nicosia
Paphos

Denmark
Aalborg

Egypt
Abu Qir
Abu Sueir
ALG 09

ALG 10
ALG 60
Almaza
Bilbeis
Burg El Arab
Edku
Fayid
Fuka
Gebel Hamid
Geneifa
Heliopolis
Hurghada
Ismalia
Kabrit
Maaten Bagush
Qsaba
Shallufa
Wadi El Natrun

England
Abington
Alconbury Hill
Aston Down
Baginton
Bassingbourn
Beaulieu
Benson
Bicester
Biggleswade
Binbrook
Bircham Newton
Bircotes
Bitteswell
Booker
Boscombe Down
Bovington
Brough
Burtonwood
Castle Bromwich
Chalgrove
Chelverston

Collyweston
Cosford
Cranfield
Defford
Dettling
Digby
Dishforth
Downham
  Market
Duxford
Edgeford
Edgehill
Exeter
Fairoaks
Farborough
Feltwell
Filton
Finningley
Ford
Glatton
Gosport
Gransden Lodge
Graveley
Grimsby
Halton
Hampstead
  Norris
Hamswell
Harwell
Hemswell
Hendon
Henley
Henlow
Heston
Hibaldstow
High Ercall
Honiley
Honnington
Hornchurch
Hucknall
Hullavington

Kembel
Kirkbride
Kirmington
Lakenheath
Lasham
Leeming
Lee-on-the-
  Solent
Little Solent
London Airport
Luton
Lympne
Lyneham
Manby
Marham
Marshalls
Martlesham
  Heath
Mepal
Methwold
Middle
  Wallop
Mildenhall
Moreton-in-
  Marsh
Moreton Valence
Mount Farm
Newmarket
Newton
North
  Luffenham
Northolt
North Weald
Oakington
Pershore
Portsmouth
Redhill
Rochester
St Eval
St Mary's
Samlesbury

Scampton
Sculthorpe
Shawbury
Sherburn-in
  Elmet
Silloth
Speke
Squires Gate
Staverton
Stradishall
Strubby
Swinderby
Tangmere
Tarrant Rushton
Ternhill
Tibenham
Upper Heyford
Upwood
Walton
Warboys
Warmswell
Warton
Waterbeach
Wattisham
Wellesbourne
  Mountford
Westcott
West Malling
West Raynham
Wisley
Wolverhampton
Woodbridge
Woodford
Woolfox Lodge
Wyton
Yeovil Ham

Fiji
Nandi
Nausori

French Equatorial Africa
Fort Lamy

Germany
Ahlhorn
Bruggen
Bückeburg
Butzweilerhof
Eschborn
Geilenkirchen
Gütersloh
Laarbruch
Lubeck
Whan
Wildenrath
Wunstorf

Ghana
Takoradi

Gibraltar
North Front

Hawaii
Hickham

Holland
Woensdrecht

Iceland
Keflavik

Indonesia
Kema Joran

Iran
Abadan
Andimishk
Dezful
Kut Abdullah
Teheran

Iraq
Baghdad
Basra
Diwaniya
H3
H4
Habbaniya
Kirkuk
Mosul
Quyara
Shaibah

Israel
Aqir
Gaza
Haifa
Kolundia
Lydda
Ramat David

Italy
Bari
Ciampino
Pomigliano

Jamaica
Montego Bay
Palisados

Jordan
Aqaba
Amman
Ma'an
Mafraq

Lebanon
Beirut

Liberia
Marshall

Libya
Bu Amud
El Adem
El Gazala 2 and 3
El Gubbi
Maus
Timimi
Whittaker LG

Malaya
Changi

Malta
Luqa

Nassau
Oakes

New Caledonia
Tontouta

New Hebrides
Pallikulo

New Zealand
Alexandra
Ardmore
Ashburton

Bendigo
Frankton
Franz Joseph

Gisborne
Grassmere
Greymouth
Harewood
Hastings
Hawera
Lake Ellesmere
Makarora
Mangere
Milson
New Plymouth
Paraparaumu
Rongotai
Rukuhia
Taieri
Tauranga
Waiho
Wataroa
Whenuapai
Wigram
Woodbourne

Nigeria
Accra
Apapa
Fort Kano
Maiduguri

Norfolk Island
Norfolk

Northern Ireland
Aldergrove
Sydenham

Pakistan
Jiwani
Mauripur

Scotland
Kinloss
Leuchars
Prestwick
Renfrew
Ternhouse
West Freugh

Sierra Leone
Hastings

Solomon Islands
Carney
Green Island

Henderson
Kukum Field
Munda
Ondonga
Piva North
Piva South
Renard
Torokina

Sudan
El Fasher
Geneina
Port Sudan
Summit
Wadi Seidna

Switzerland
Zurich

Tonga
Tonga

Trinidad
Piarco

Trucial Oman
Sharjah

USA
Hamilton
Lindbergh
Love
Miami
International
Washington

Wales
Cardiff
Llandow
Pembrey
Penrhos
Porthcawl
St Athan

Source:
A. Ashworth as recorded post-retirement on a separate document at the back of his logbook. I have assumed that these are airfields that he used as a pilot or, in some cases, as a passenger. Some names will have changed.

About the Author

Vincent Ashworth was educated at Alexandra District High School (ADHS), Otago Boys' High School (OBHS), and Massey and Lincoln Universities. He graduated from Lincoln in 1955 with a diploma of Valuation and Farm Management, passing with credit.

In 1960, after a brief stint in the Lands Department and as farm adviser to a farm improvement club in Te Aroha, he established in Morrinsville what was to become the successful firm of Ashworth and Associates, Farm Management Consultants, the first of its kind in the country. During the early 1970s he participated in a number of international consulting assignments in places like Afghanistan, Yemen Arab Republic, Samoa, Tanzania and Somalia.

In 1976 he was invited to join the permanent staff of the World Bank as a senior agriculturalist and took his family to live in Washington DC. He spent ten years in Washington and two years in the bank's Nairobi-based East Africa office. During his time he took on assignments in eastern Europe (Romania, Yugoslavia), Middle East (Yemen, Saudi Arabia), central Asia (Afghanistan), and East Africa (Kenya, Ethiopia).

Upon taking early retirement in 1987, Vince went deer farming. He also continued his professional career with consulting assignments, mostly for the World Bank, in Yugoslavia, Macedonia, China, Ethiopia, Kenya, Uganda, Zambia, Zimbabwe, Lesotho, Tanzania, Australia and South Africa. He also did volunteer work for the Save the Children Fund (SCF) in Vanuatu and Papua New Guinea as well as chairing the SCF Overseas Project Committee for some years.

He is a fellow of the Institute of Agricultural Science and a fellow and life member of the New Zealand Institute of Primary Industry Management. In 1980 he was awarded the Lincoln University Bledisloe Medal for distinguished services to New Zealand agriculture. More recently he was made a Robert Harris fellow by Rotary International.

As a keen sportsman, Vince represented his schools and universities at cricket and rugby. He also represented Manawatu (1956–57) and Thames Valley (1958–59) provincial rugby. Now fully retired, he enjoys a game of golf, takes a keen interest in New Zealand and international affairs, along with wife May tends their large garden, and enjoys writing.

Bibliography

Ashworth, Wing Commander A., RAF, DSO, DFC and Bar, AFC and Bar, MID, *I Never Saw Him Again*, a personal memoir, mimeograph copy.

——, *Logbooks* (1939–67).

Ashworth, Vincent with Dhollande, Fabrice, *For Our Tomorrow He Gave His Today – A Fighter Pilot's Story* (2009).

Bennett, Donald, *Pathfinder* (1998).

Bishop, Patrick, *Bomber Boys – Fighting Back* 1940–1945 (2008).

Bowman, Martin W., *RAF Bomber Stories, Dramatic First Hand Accounts of British and Commonwealth Airmen during World War 2* (1998).

Bowyer, Chaz, *Pathfinders at War* (1977).

——*The Wellington Bomber* (1996).

Brookes, Andrew, *Fighter and Bomber Squadrons at War* (1983).

Chandler, Chan, *Tail Gunner – 98 Raids in World War II* (2002).

Charlwood, Don, *No Moon Tonight* (2000).

Chunn, Flight Lieutenant Frank, DFC, personal war diaries and logbook.

Clutton-Brook, Oliver, *Footprints on the Sands of Time – RAF Bomber Command Prisoners of War in Germany 1939–45* (2003).

Coverdale, Christopher, *Pathfinders 635 Squadron: Definitive History – March 1944–September 1945* (2010).

Currie, Jack, *Lancaster Target* (1981).

Dascombe, P.W., *We Lead. Others Follow – Personal Recollections of Air and Ground Crews, 635 Pathfinder Squadron, RAF Downham Market*.

Feast, Sean, *Master Bombers – The Experiences of a Pathfinder Squadron at War 1944–1945* (2008).

Franks, Norman, *Forever Strong – The Story of 75 Squadron RNZAF 1916–1990* (1991).

Garbett, Mike and Goulding, Brian, *The Lancaster at War* (1971).

Hancock, Kenneth, *New Zealand at War* (1946).

Harris, Sir Arthur, Marshal of the Royal Air Force, GCB, OBE, AFC, *Bomber Offensive* (1947).

Hastings, Max, *Bomber Command* (1979).

Hill, Larry R., *An Aviation Bibliography for New Zealand* (2009).

Hilling, John B., *Strike Hard – A Bomber Airfield at War* (1995).

HMSO, *Prisoners of War, Naval and Air Forces of Great Britain and the Empire 1939–45*.

Lambert, Max, *Night After Night – New Zealanders in Bomber Command* (2005).

Lawrence, W.J., *No. 5 Bomber Command Group RAF (1939–1945)* (1951).

Lucas, F.J., *Popeye Lucas, Queenstown* (1968).

Lucas, Laddie, *Voices in the Air – 1939–1945* (2003).

Lucas, Lorie, *Popeye's War* (1996).

Martyn, Errol, *For Your Tomorrow* (1999).

McGreal, Captain Maurice, *A Noble Chance* (1994).

McKinstry, Leo, *Lancaster – The Second World War's Greatest Bomber* (2010).

Middlebrook, Martin, *The Battle of Hamburg – The Firestorm Raid* (1980).

—— and Everitt, Chris, *Bomber Command War Diaries – Operational Reference Book 1939–1945* (1985).

Mitchell, Alan W., *New Zealanders in the Air War* (1945).

Musgrove, Gordon, *Pathfinder Force – A History of 8 Group* (1976).

Onderwater, Hans, *Operation Manna/Chowhound – The Allied Food Droppings, April/May 1945* (1991).

Pearce, Trevor, *Air Force Memories – An Autobiography* (2007).

Prebble, Frank, personal diaries.

Pugh, Wing Commander A.G.E., OBE, *A Fistful of Sparks* (1998).

Rees, Ken with Arrandale, Karen, *Lie in the Dark and Listen. The Remarkable Exploits of a WWII Bomber Pilot and Great Escaper* (2006).

Richards, Denis, *RAF Bomber Command in the Second World War – The Hardest Victory* (1995).

Rolfe, Mel, *Looking into Hell – Experiences of Bomber Command War* (1995).

——, *To Hell and Back* (1998).

Saunders, Hilary A. St George, *Return at Dawn – The Official Story of the New Zealand Squadron in Bomber Command of the RAF, June 1939–July 1942* (1942).

Smith, Ron, *Rear Gunner Pathfinders* (1987).

Smithies, Edward, *Aces, Erks & Backroom Boys* (2002).

Spurdle, R.L., *Blue Arena* (1986).

Thompson, Wing Commander H.L., *New Zealanders with the Royal Air Force – Vols 1 and 2* (1953).

Thorne, Alex, *Lancaster at War 4: Pathfinder Squadron* (1990).

Wadsworth, Michael Philip, *They Led the Way – the Story of 156 Pathfinder Squadron* (1992).

Wheeler, Peter J., *Kiwis Do Fly – New Zealanders in RAF Bomber Command* (2010).

Wilson, Kevin, *Men of the Air – The Doomed Youth of Bomber Command* (2007).

Yates, Harry, DFC, *Luck and a Lancaster* (1999).

Abbreviations

A/C	Aircraft
ADHS	Alexandra District High School
AFC	Air Force Cross
AOC	Air officer commanding
AVM	Air Vice-Marshal
CCS	Casualty Clearing Station
CO	Commanding officer
CMG	Most Distinguished Order of Saint Michael and Saint George
DCL	Doctor of Civil Law
DFC	Distinguished Flying Cross
DFM	Distinguished Flying Medal
DSO	Distinguished Service Order
ETPS	Empire Test Pilots' School
F/Lt	Flight Lieutenant
F/O	Flying Officer
F/Sgt	Flight Sergeant
HC	High-capacity bombs – usually 4,000 pounds
HMSO	His Majesty's Stationery Office
KIA	Killed in Action
MEF	Middle East forces
MFH	Military Field Hospital
MID	Mentioned in Despatches
Op	Operation
OR	Operations Record
OTU	Operational Training Unit
PDRC	Personnel Despatch and Recovery Centre
PFF	Pathfinder Force
PTNU	Pathfinder Training and Navigation Unit
RAAF	Royal Australian Air Force
RAF	Royal Air Force
RAFVR	Royal Air Force Volunteer Reserve
RCAF	Royal Canadian Air Force
RNZAF	Royal New Zealand Air Force
SBC	Small bomb container
SCF	Save the Children Fund
S/Ldr	Squadron Leader
SMV	Star of Military Valour (Canada)
TI	Target indicator
U/S	Unserviceable
VC	Victoria Cross
VHF	Very High Frequency
WAAF	Women's Auxiliary Air Force
W/Cdr	Wing Commander
W/O	Warrant Officer

Index